CUBA:
THE REVOLUTION OF 1933, THE 1952 COUP D'ÉTAT, AND THE REPRESSION OF COMMUNISM

MEMOIRS OF MAJOR GENERAL MARTÍN DÍAZ TAMAYO

CUBA Y SUS JUECES COLLECTION

EDICIONES UNIVERSAL, Miami, Florida, 2024

Antonio Rafael de la Cova

CUBA:
THE REVOLUTION OF 1933, THE 1952 COUP D'ÉTAT, AND THE REPRESSION OF COMMUNISM

MEMOIRS OF MAJOR GENERAL MARTÍN DÍAZ TAMAYO

Copyright © 2024 by legal successors of Martín Díaz Tamayo

First Edition in Spanish, 2017 (978-1-59388-288-4)
First Edition in English, 2024 (978-1-59388-351-5)

EDICIONES UNIVERSAL
P.O. Box 450353 (Shenandoah Station)
Miami, FL 33245-0353. USA
(Since 1965)

E-mail: ediciones@ediciones.com
http://www.ediciones.com

Library of Congress Catalog Card No.: 2024933081
I.S.B.N.: 978-1-59388-351-5

Composition of texts: María Cristina Zarraluqui

Cover design: Luis García Fresquet

On the cover portrait of Major General Martín Díaz Tamayo

All rights are reserved.
No part of this book may be reproduced or transmitted in any form or by any electronic or mechanical form, including photocopiers, recorders or computerized systems, without the written consent of the author, except for brief excerpts incorporated in book reviews or in magazines. For additional information contact Ediciones Universal

TABLE OF CONTENTS

DEDICATION 7

INTRODUCTION 9

PREFACE 33

CHAPTER I
SOLDIER OF THE REPUBLIC 35

CHAPTER II
THE REVOLUTION OF 1933 55

CHAPTER III
FULGENCIO BATISTA 85

CHAPTER IV
THE ARMED FORCES 1944-1952 113

CHAPTER V
THE DAWN OF MARCH 10, 1952 137

CHAPTER VI
THE ARMED FORCES 1952-1958 169

CHAPTER VII
THE CIA AND THE BRAC 193

CHAPTER VIII
THE DRUNKEN CONSPIRACY 227

PHOTOS 249

ONOMASTIC INDEX 265

DEDICATION

To fulfill the promise I made to my father on his deathbed, I decided to publish his memoirs he wrote during the long illness that ultimately took his life. My father wanted the truth about many events that occurred during his years in the army, to be known to everyone.

His obsession, after finishing his military career, was to bring to light the truth behind many facts that were distorted when they were published.

I will never forget the lessons he taught me during his life. He instructed me to be clear, communicative, honest, and to live life doing what is beneficial to humanity.

My admiration for my father was not only for his prestigious military command and his love for his homeland, but also for the example he showed i n our home. In addition, the love he always had for my mother, Rosaura, and the happy home that I enjoyed throughout my life.

I wouldn't be the person I am today if I hadn't had an exemplary father like him.

Roraima Díaz de Kanar

INTRODUCTION

After the fall of the regime of Fulgencio Batista, on January 1, 1959, the «War of Memories» began, blaming each other their anti-partisans, for Fidel Castro's triumph. Former Vice President Rafael Guas Inclán, dean of the Havana Bar Association and president of the Liberal Party, was among the first to criticize Batista saying that "his egomania blinded him and sinned at the last moment of being a bad ruler."[1]

The autobiography of Major General Martín Díaz Tamayo is the last volume of this controversy between Batista and his military. After Batista published *Respuesta* in 1960, he was vilified by Lieutenant General Francisco J. Tabernilla Dolz.[2] Other officials who insulted Batista in his memoirs were the Colonel-in-Chief of the Corps of Engineers Florentino E. Rosell Leyva (1960), the Colonel of the Army Pedro Barrera Pérez (1961), the police choir Esteban Ventura Novo (1961), the seditious Army Colonel Ramón M. Barquín López (1978) and Army General Francisco "Silito" Tabernilla Palmero (2009). Batista had unconditional support in the memoirs of the head of the Investigations Bureau, Colonel Orlando Piedra Negueruela (1994) and his brother-in-law General Roberto R. Fernández Miranda (1999). Lieutenant pilot Carlos Lazo Cuba in his autobiography *La guerra aérea en Cuba en 1958* (2017) coincides with Díaz Tamayo when he pointed out that Batista controlled all military operations, made strategic errors

---

[1] "Guas Inclán calls Batista 'Bad ruler' and 'egomaniac'," Diario de la Marina, March 13, 1959, 1.

[2] Francisco Tabernilla Dolz sent two insulting missives to Batista, on December 31, 1959, and August 24, 1960, where in the last one he told him that his recently published answer memoirs was a mammoth "that could well have been called 'GARBAGE'." The letters were reproduced in the book by José Suárez Núñez, El Gran Culpable (1963) and in the memoirs of his son Silito Tabernilla (2009).

against Castroist guerrillas and official promotions were based on political connections and nepotism bypassing the ranks.

Díaz Tamayo was an illiterate peasant, orphaned from Brazil, dedicated to the cutting cane and the sowing of tobacco and pineapple on the land of wealthy Spaniards in Pinar del Río. In 1926, at the age of 16 and without his mother's permission, he enlisted in the Army giving false birth date of 1904 in order to enter. He came from the same humble background as Batista and from thousands of peasants who enlisted in the Army to stabilize their economy and well-being.

These memoirs offer a brief history of the evolution of the Cuban army during the republic. It recounts the daily life of the soldiers and details the development and modernization of the main Columbia camp in Havana. It also describes the composition of the army and its participation in the formation of the Rural Schools and Civic-Military Institutes. Díaz Tamayo criticizes how the Army had a long history of being used as a political instrument by Presidents Tomás Estrada Palma, José Miguel Gómez, Mario García Menocal and Gerardo Machado. The Constitution allowed the president to dismiss or withdraw any officer or soldier without giving an explanation. This clause allowed President Ramón Grau San Martín to dismantle the military cadres established by Batista in 1944. The insecurity created among some soldiers, who were banned from participating in the elections, made these men to support the warlord who emerged from their ranks and who guaranteed their future.

Díaz Tamayo participated in the September 4 Revolution. Two days earlier, he was invited by Sergeant José Eleuterio Pedraza to a conspiracy meeting at the Grand Masonic Lodge but did not attend so as not to be absent without the permission of his detachment.

However, the night before the coup, he was with the troops at the Columbia Camp Enlistment Club assembly when he heard Sergeant Fulgencio Batista give them orders to take over the barracks. Díaz Tamayo participated in the uprising of his company that resulted in his immediate appointment as first sergeant. He regrets that, if he had participated in the conspiracy, he would have "meteorically promoted" to officer and describes the circumstances that allowed Batista to be the military leader of the revolution.

As first sergeant, Díaz Tamayo led the infantry company that on September 29, 1933, suppressed the communist demonstration that was going to bury the ashes of its leader Julio Antonio Mella in a cenotaph in the Fraternity Park. The confrontation left eight deaths, twenty-seven injured, the destruction of the monument and the disappearance of the ashes. Six weeks later, Díaz Tamayo fought against the uprising of military aviation and three garrisons in Havana, backed by the ABC organization. In December he was promoted to second lieutenant and in 1936 he began a three-year equestrian stage in which he participated in international competitions. He remembered with nostalgia the jockey competitions that took him to Chile, Mexico, the United States and Canada, before "the presence of beautiful women, from high Pan-American and European society." The tall, stout, blue-eyed lieutenant had many affairs and almost lost his career because of his relationship with the wife of a prominent man who insisted that he be expelled from the army. As punishment, Díaz Tamayo was sent to the province of Oriente for more than a year. On his return to Havana, he remarried on July 17, 1942. His memoirs do not mention that in 1938 he was blamed for loss of military effects and four years later for damage to other people's property and injury from an apparent accident.

Díaz Tamayo was a graduate of the School of Officers and the Higher School of War when he was retired from the army with the rank of captain by President Carlos Prío Socarrás in mid-February 1951. He tells us that it was for criticizing the government due to impunity for political assassinations. However, the historians Herminio Portell Vilá and José Duarte Oropesa pointed out that the withdrawal of Díaz Tamayo and other officers and soldiers was for opposing the sending of a Cuban battalion to fight in Korea under the flag of the UN. In October 1951, Díaz Tamayo was invited by Batista to participate in the conspiracy that carried out the coup d'état five months later.[3] Díaz Tamayo, whose economy

---

[3] In contrast, the biography by Edmund Chester, A Sergeant Named Batista, (1954) alleges on page 223 that the coup was prepared by young officers who invited Batista to join them in February 1952.

was precarious as a night clerk at the Omnibus Terminal, wanted to return you'll be in your infantry captain's seat. He accepted the proposal because Batista's initial agreements at his farm, Kuquine, in Arroyo Arenas "were very different from what was subsequently done. Batista would be at the head of the government only for a while, enough to get the country on track and call for new elections."

Batista told the conspirators that he would not immediately aspire to the presidency. Díaz Tamayo estimated that "Batista, with his magnetism, with his ascendancy over the troops, would remain as a possibility for the future, but not as an immediate aspirant in an election that, necessarily, would have to be fraudulent. But nothing was like this. Once in the chair, his mastery of the circumscriptions was too complete. Nothing limited him, and he could not resist the temptation to continue in the presidency."

Díaz Tamayo was one of the conspirators who, in the early hours of March 10, 1952, entered the Columbia Camp next to Batista in the back seat of the car that crossed the Posta 4. Their mission was to occupy the General Staff and telephone all the regiment leaders about what happened and ask them to join or, otherwise, to hand over the command to a subordinate. Díaz Tamayo does not regret the facts that violated the Constitution and granted him the rank of general, since "the conditions were more than created" by the looting of the treasury and electoral frauds. However, those same conditions continued under the Batista regime.

The general regrets that during his military career he was never in combat. This was since the fight against the guerrillas for two years was led by tactical officers to the degree of lieutenant colonel. Batista did not allow any general or colonel to be at the head of the troops campaigning in the mountains. Díaz Tamayo dedicated himself during his military career to roll call, inspections, guard, next maneuvers, studies, and grade climbing. He held the administrative positions of military controller of the Allied Omnibus Cooperative; Inspector General of the Army; founder and director of the Bureau for the Repression of Communist Activities (BRAC); head of the military districts of the Province of the Orient and the fortress of La Cabaña; Assistant General (G-3); director of the Savings and Insurance Fund of the Armed Forces (CASFA) until April 1957; president of the Military and Naval Circle of the 1953-1958; and traveled on diplomatic missions to Mexico, the United States and Venezuela. He also chaired the Cuban Polo Federation and the Equestrian Federation of Cuba. The general recalls how his "position required a fairly active social life. Official events, music, gala dances, receptions and cocktail parties were frequent, and I was expected to attend most of them."

Díaz Tamayo believes that the animosity of Lieutenant General Francisco Tabernilla Dolz, with whom he never had sane relations, hindered his military career. The origin of this controversy was mentioned during the preparations for the coup d'état when, at the request of Batista, Díaz Tamayo suggested that Colonel Eulogio Cantillo should be appointed head of the Army and recommended Tabernilla as Minister of Defense. Díaz Tamayo acknowledges that the Ministry of Defense was "a sinecure" without control of the armed forces. He claims that his recommendation won him the enmity of Tabernilla, who did not participate in the coup d'état, but entered La Cabaña after he surrendered. His support for Cantillo turned out to be erroneous since he describes him as a "man of the bureau, of the operating room, of maps," very "efficient, capable and magnificent planner," but lacking in the gift of command with the troops in operations, limited by "his excessive adherence to American military doctrine" and "without taking into account our idiosyncrasy."

Díaz Tamayo treated Batista for twenty-five years, from 1933 to 1958, and was very close to him for the last six years. They came from the same peasant origin with goals of improvement. He considers Batista more political than military and points out that the president did not touch a rifle after passing the school of recruits. He praised Batista for his ability to run the country during 1933-1944, achieving economic prosperity and the repeal of the Platt Amendment. Batista's alliance with communism during that time is attributed to his emulating the policy of US President Franklin Roosevelt. During the Cold War, Batista was guided by the American compass to persecute the Communists and establish the Bureau for the Repression of Communist Activities (BRAC).

In May 1955, the Central Intelligence Agency (CIA), through the US State Department, recommended to Batista that they wanted Díaz Tamayo to be the director of the BRAC. Díaz Tamayo, First Lieutenant José Castaño Quevedo and retired commander of the Secret Police, Enrique Fernández Parajón, were sent to the CIA for training. They arrived in Washington on May 17 and the next day the general was celebrated by Lieutenant General Carter B. Magruder[4]. The three officers were instructed at CIA headquarters in Langley, Virginia, for one month for ten hours a day, five days a week, on the history of international communism and its tactics, in preparation for organizing the BRAC. Díaz Tamayo points out that "the CIA's attention to the events in Cuba was intense, and its knowledge of our situation meticulous."

Díaz Tamayo points out that Batista was "extremely cunning" and felt very confident of his authority. In his desire to control everything and appear to be the victor, Batista went as far as to cheat in combination with others when he played canasta with his family and close friends to win. This indicates that Batista did not yield to anyone, but he was not resentful once his enemy did not represent any danger.

Circumstances influenced Batista, but no person, including his wife Martha, ever influenced him. In an initial version of the manuscript, which was later omitted from the final copy typed by his assistant, he says: "Batista wanted to juggle so much with Cuba, with Fidel and politics, that the trick went wrong. So bad, that he sank his friends, he sank himself and his name, and he sank one of the most beautiful and advanced republics in the world for a hundred years or more."

The general believes that Batista "being unable to reach power democratically, he used other means to do so." He subsidized the press, including $37,000 a month for his friend Sergio Carbó, the

---

[4] Carter Bowie Magruder (April 3, 1900-March 14, 1988) graduated from the West Point Military Academy as an artillery officer in 1923. During the Second World War he was a logistics officer in Europe. He commanded the 24th Infantry Division in the Korean War and in 1954 he was head of the 9th Army Corps. In 1959 he was promoted to four-star general in command of all American and United Nations forces in Korea until his retirement in 1961.

director of *Prensa Libre*. He says that Batista "did not decide for absolute democracy or total dictatorship, because to establish that total democracy he would have had to leave the presidency and, as for being an absolute dictator of body and soul, he lacked a vocation for it. For all this, his policy was erratic and indecisive. He was not bloody, but at no price was he willing to renounce what was so dear to him, and for this he had to kill." However, Díaz Tamayo points out that Batista personally prevented Fidel Castro from being eliminated after the attack on the Moncada barracks on July 26, 1953, and when the Granma expedition landed in 1956. This occurred days after the events, when the living forces of civil society appealed to Batista on behalf of the disbanded rebels.

Díaz Tamayo arrived at the Moncada barracks hours after the attack and the subsequent massacre of more than thirty captured rebels authorized by Colonel Alberto del Río Chaviano, head of Regiment No. 1. The corpses were scattered around the barracks to simulate that they died in combat. The general remained in Moncada for the next two days, visited the wounded in the military hospital, and attended the funeral of the nineteen soldiers and police officers who had died. During that time, more than a dozen fugitive rebels were captured in the camp and executed. Díaz Tamayo was aware of the events, but his autobiography offers us the official version, which contrasts with the facts.[5]

The general agrees with his nemesis Francisco Tabernilla Dolz when he said that "Batista did not allow his subordinates to adopt military decisions, it being he who ordered each and every one of the plans." Nor did he "allow the military to interfere in the country's politics. Moreover, he did not even let them address the issue in his presence." In the war against Castro's guerrillas during 1956- 1958, "at all times the strategy, and even many tactical aspects, were dictated from Havana" by Batista.

Díaz Tamayo was the head of Regiment No. 1 of the Moncada barracks on November 30, 1956, during the rebel uprising in San-

---

[5] The story of the events of the assault on the Moncada barracks is detailed in Antonio de la Cova, The Moncada Attack: Birth of the Cuban Revolution (2007).

tiago de Cuba and the disembarkation of Fidel Castro and 81 men in the Granma expedition two days later. The general ordered the troops to be grounded to prevent them from being targeted by snipers. Díaz Tamayo complains that Batista sent an airborne battalion that night, with 23 officers and 250 enlisted, to quell the revolt without first consulting him. The commander of the troops, Colonel Pedro Barrera Pérez, was appointed by Batista as the military commander of the city of Santiago de Cuba. Batista estimated that Díaz Tamayo did not respond properly to the attack led by Frank País, nor did he operate properly against Castro's bridgehead. Barrera appeased Santiago de Cuba in three days and returned to Havana two weeks later.

Colonel Barrera noted that: "General Tabernilla, upon learning of the disembarkation of the expeditionaries, instead of instructing Díaz Tamayo to act with the men of his command, co-leaders of those areas and request the necessary reinforcements, chose to appoint one of his assistants, Commander Juan González, as chief of Operations, with a battalion from the Artillery Regime of La Cabaña, to move to the Niquero region and assume the responsibility of capturing the invaders."[6] González fortified his troops at Niquero's barracks, instead of following the rebels, so he was replaced as head of operations by Colonel Ramón Cruz Vidal, who was second in command of Regiment No. 1. On December 5, 1956, the troops of Cruz Vidal surprised the expeditionaries at the La Alegría de Pío estate, causing them 60 casualties between dead and prisoners. The colonel was relieved, and the Rural Guard assigned to the persecution and capture of the dispersed survivors.

Díaz Tamayo points out that "the president had absolute power in his hands. He did not delegate that power to anyone." Batista led all military operations and no unit moved without his approval. He was a notorious military incompetent who "repeatedly disallowed the operations plans that the General Staff supplied him to impose his own ideas." Batista carried out military promotions without taking advantage of the ranks, subordinating the tactical to the political. The president was benevolent with the incompetent offi-

---

[6] Pedro A. Barrera Pérez, "Why the Army Didn't Defeat Castro," Bohemia Libre, August 13, 1961.

cials and military conspirators and the leniency of his sanctions encouraged others to do the same.

In January 1958, retired General Jorge García Tuñón, a participant in the March 10 coup, and Ricardo Artigas, Carlos Prío's seven[7] advisers, met in the State Department with William Arthur Wieland,[8] director of the Caribbean and Mexico Division and deliv-

---

[7] Ricardo Anacleto Artigas Rabelo (July 13, 1912-December 10, 1972) had been commander of the National Police, head of the Bureau of Investigations, founder of the Authentic Party, councilor of the Province of Havana, director of the radio program «Hora Programática Auténtica," and active in Prío's presidential campaign in 1948. As a result, Prío appointed him assistant director of the National Lottery and became a millionaire. In 1949, the Association of Lottery Sellers accused Artigas of corruption and demanded his replacement. He aspired to be a senator of the Province of Havana for the Authentic Party in the frustrated elections of 1952. On March 13, 1952, he received political asylum in Miami with his wife, Maria Soledad "Marisol" Alba Luque, whom he divorced in 1955. She and her second husband, Daniel "El Ñato" Vásquez Coeja, were later identified as Batista's spies. Artigas died in Tampa, Florida.

[8] William Arthur Wieland (November 17, 1907-September 23, 1987) was born in New York and when the family moved to Cuba in 1925, he began to be called Guillermo Arturo Montenegro, adopting the surname of his Venezuelan stepfather, the mechanical engineer Manuel Ralph Montenegro. Wieland returned to the United States in 1926 to attend Villanova University and served in the Army from September 13, 1927 to December 21, 1928. Upon returning to Havana, he resided with his parents and sister Dorothy at Calle Cuba No. 21-A and worked for the General Electric Company, the Cuban Electricity Company and Morro Castle Supply Co. His mother died in 1930 and his stepfather died the following year; both being buried in Colón Cemetery. In late 1932 he was a reporter for the Havana Post until 1937, when he was fired for giving an unauthorized person access to the Associated Press records. He worked for Associated Press from then until 1941. That year he enlisted in the 51st New York Guard Regiment for six months. His friendship with Benjamin Sumner Welles helped him on June 4, 1941, to obtain employment in the State Department as a special assistant to the American ambassador to Brazil until 1946. Appointed deputy consul and then consul in Bogotá 1947-1949, where he learned of Fidel Castro's participation in the Bogotazo; consul in San Salvador 1949-1951; consul in Rio de Janeiro 1951-1952; and consul in Quito 1952-1956. On February 10, 1957, he was appointed special assistant for public affairs in the Department of Inter-American Affairs. After three months he was promoted to director of the Office of Middle American Affairs and traveled to Cuba at the end of 1957. In March 1958, Wieland recommended the US arms embargo on the Batista government. On September 7, 1958, he held the position of Director of the Office of Caribbean and Mexican Affairs. From these positions he advised and recommended to senior officials the diplomatic policy

ered a paper pointing to Fidel Castro's communist ideology and suggesting replacing Batista with a military junta. When asked who would form the board, the former general said that he himself with Generals Martín Díaz Tamayo, Arístides V. Sosa de Quesada, and Eulogio Cantillo Porras, in addition to Colonel Ramón Barquín López. Wieland replied that he would report the information to his superiors.[9] As a result, months later the CIA began plotting to replace Batista with said board.

On March 22, 1958, C. Allan Stewart, assistant director of the Office of Middle American Affairs, received a letter from Dr. Carlos Piad, approved by Manuel Antonio de Varona, with a proposal authorized by Prío, to support a coup against the Baist and replace it with a civic-military junta. The members of the board would be Generals Eulogio Cantillo and Martín Díaz Tamayo; imprisoned colonels Ramón Barquín and Enrique Borbonet; Gustavo Cuervo Rubio, former vice-president of Batista during 1940-1944; José Miró Cardona, president of the Havana Bar Association; Dr. Raúl Velazco, director of the Medical Association of Havana; and former magistrate Manuel Urrutia Lleó. Wieland, who had just recommended the arms embargo to Batista, opposed the board's plan, pointing out that it was "a mechanism foreign to Cuban tradition," which would last a short time and would provoke the resumption of a period of revolution.[10]

---

towards Cuba, especially Roy R. Rubottom, Jr., Undersecretary of State for Inter-American Affairs. He was promoted to first class officer of the Foreign Service in early 1959. His loyalty was investigated by a Congressional security committee in 1961 and 1962. He was questioned about homosexual tendencies in the State Department, which he denied knowing. It was determined that Wie-land was an active apologist of Fidel Castro who did not inform his superiors during 1957-1958 of the intelligence reports that confirmed the communist nature of the Castro movement and its leadership. He died in Saint Marys, Maryland.

[9] United States Senate. Committee on the Judiciary. Communist Threat to the United States Though the Caribbean, Part 13. March 29, April 26, June 1, and July 27, 1961 (Washington: U.S. Government Printing Office, 1962), 858.

[10] United States Department of State, Foreign Relations of the United States, 1958- 1960, Volume VI, Cuba (Washington: United States Government Printing Office, 1991), 68-70.

In early 1958, Colonel Clark Lynn, head of the U.S. Army mission, offered Díaz Tamayo training in Fort Gulick, Panama, to at least two counterinsurgency companies to defeat the guerrillas. Batista rejected the proposal. The state of war was used for the president and Congress to justify and extend press censorship and the suspension of constitutional guarantees while the legislature approved large, extraordinary war credits for millions of pesos that mostly went into the pockets of Batista and corrupt politicians and military personnel.

Defense and internal security spending during the last six months of 1958 was $81 million, with just over half going to the War Department.

Díaz Tamayo estimates that Batista took the country "to the economic boom" but "did not give political exit. He dedicated himself, however, to clean up his private economy." His wealth was affected after the divorce of his first wife Elisa, his exile in Daytona Beach and the maintenance of a retinue of sycophants that continued throughout his life. Díaz Tamayo confirms that most of the accusations that General Tabernilla made against Batista in a public letter on August 24, 1960, are true. However, he says that Tabernilla could not complain of not having had any authority since Batista placed him in the highest military position so that he would not discuss his command. He points out that Tabernilla accusing Batista of being a "voracious thief," the accuser was no different. It was known that the Tabernillas took large quantities of electrical equipment that did not pay taxes at Customs from Miami in planes from Cuba Aeropostal to the military airport of Columbia. The Tabernillas' business, Casa Minerva, sold the refrigerators they bought at $320 at prices that had no competition.

Díaz Tamayo speculates that, in the presidential election of November 1958, Batista was going to hand over the command to his opponent Carlos Márquez-Sterling and Guiral but changed his mind at the last minute. He believes that perhaps Batista hoped to be the head of the Joint Chiefs of Staff when his candidate, Andrés Rivero Agüero, won. That way he would effectively remain in power as he did during 1934 to 1940 with other presidents. Díaz Tamayo concludes that Batista never trusted anyone with his true purposes. He believes that, if Márquez-Sterling won, most of the people "would have abandoned their attitude of struggle and left Castro alone with his small group of communists. I firmly believed that this was the plan, the already prepared ballot papers were sent in bags to the eastern provinces, with the gubernatorial candidate as the winner." The electoral trap was so obvious that the US government objected and helped foment a conspiracy to remove Batista from power.

Díaz Tamayo was part of a conspiracy to capture Batista with the help of members of the July 26 Movement and to promote a transitional government. The conspirators included his brother, First Lieutenant Clemente Díaz Tamayo,[11] General Arístides V. Sosa de Quesada[12] and about thirty chiefs and officers in the Columbia Camp. Brigadier Francisco "Silito" Tabernilla Palmero stated in his memoirs that "at the end of 1958, Major General Martin Díaz Tamayo was conspiring with the CIA to depose Batista. This conspiracy was fully proven, and Batista chose to withdraw it to avoid speculation on the subject."[13]

According to the rebel commander Julio Camacho Aguilera,[14] Sergeant José *El Chino* Fernández Wong, of the 17th Police Station, led a clandestine cell of the July 26 Movement that included eight Marianao police officers. *El Chino* had a friendship with Naranjito, a dry-cleaning worker, cousin of Díaz Tamayo. Through the help of Clemente, an employee in the General Staff, *El Chino* reached his brother in early October 1958 to coordinate the contact that Díaz Tamayo wanted with the 26 de Julio Move-

---

[11] Clemente Díaz Tamayo (November 23, 1910-November 3, 2005) married GeorginaTrinck. He arrived in exile in Miami on October 14, 1962.

[12] Arístides V. Sosa de Quesada (January 22, 1908-May 31, 2000) was born in Limonar, Matanzas, and enlisted in the Army on September 19, 1932. Jurist and distinguished author. Head of the Military Legal Service. Author of Motivaciones Escolares, the textbook of the Rural Civic Schools. Appointed brigadier general and general adviser to the Army in April 1952. He was promoted to major general and Director of Personnel G- 1 in 1957. He died in Miami.

[13] Gabriel E. Taborda, Palabras Esperadas: Memorias de Francisco H. Tabernilla Palmero (Miami: Ediciones Universal, 2009), 152.

[14] Georgina Leyva Pagán, Historia de una gesta liberadora 1952-1958 (2014).

ment. Camacho indicated that the approach was made because "Díaz Tamayo had had no involvement in crimes." This contradicts Fidel Castro's false accusation in *La Historia me Absolverá* where he points out that Díaz Tamayo was in a meeting with Batista, Tabernilla and other officials in Havana on July 26, 1953, where it was agreed "that ten prisoners should be killed for each soldier killed" after the assault on the Moncada barracks and that the general immediately took the instructions to Santiago de Cuba.

When Díaz Tamayo was notified by *El Chino*, he agreed to meet with Camacho that night at the La Carreta ranch on the Autopista del Mediodía at eight o'clock. However, he did not attend and sent his assistant, Captain Laureano Pino Cruz, accompanied by Clemente, with apologies for the limitations he had after "his demonstrations against the regime had undermined his confidence and at that time he was quite marginalized." Díaz Tamayo admits that Batista was "fed up" with his tensions with General Tabernilla. Camacho went to the appointment with Dr. Adolfo Rodríguez de la Vega and Mario Hernández.[15] Clemente told them that his brother was a supporter of a "coup d'état and of forming a government through a Civic Military Junta." Camacho opposed the coup d'état and suggested that Díaz Tamayo "could lead an army column with its commanders to join the Rebel Army in the Sierra Maestra, which would cause a devastating impact that would destabilize Batista's confidence in his own Armed Forces." Clemente agreed to pass the information on to his brother. The conspirators briefly met again in the famous Tropicana cabaret without the assistance of the general.

Díaz Tamayo later sent a request to Camacho for a meeting at the Military Circle. The rebel chief went with Dr. Ricardo de la Flor and received Clemente and Captain Pino in sportswear. They were walking while Clemente explained to Camacho that his brother said he was being watched for not sharing the turn the regime had taken and that there was very little he could do. The general communicated that it was not prudent for him to meet with Camacho

---

[15] Mario Hernández was the son of Colonel Blas Hernández, killed by a Batista officer after surrendering in the Castillo de Atares during the November 1933 insurrection.

and that they had better keep in touch through Clemente. Camacho then sent another military conspirator, Captain José Rodríguez San Pedro,[16] to speak with Díaz Tamayo "to preach important aspects related to the type of government that would be formed at the triumph of the revolution in Cuba, it would never be a Military Junta, but a civilian government." The general reiterated to the captain that his cooperation would be very little "because he was virtually relegated to his house for having discrepancies with the Government, which made it difficult for him to contact other commands."

Díaz Tamayo did not get a chance to see Camacho because the plot was disrupted by the SIM on November 26. The government nicknamed it the "drunken" conspiracy for having reunited in the Tropicana. Captain Pino and other officers were arrested. Captains Félix Gutiérrez Fernández and José Rodríguez San Pedro took refuge in Latin American embassies in the capital when the conspiracy was discovered.

The seditious Colonel Ramón Barquín points out in his work *Las Luchas Guerrilleras en Cuba*, Volume II (1975), that the conspirators José Viamonte Jardines and José E. Menéndez and the captains Félix Gutiérrez, Laureano Pino Cruz and José Rodríguez San Pedro provided him with the data of the conspiracy. Díaz Tamayo "had been active against the command of the head of the Joint Chiefs of Staff, General Francisco Tabernilla Dolz, acting first associated with other colleagues from the astonished barracks of 1952, then withleaders and finally, associated with leaders of the July 26 Movement through the Commander of the Militias Julio Camacho Aguilera."

Díaz Tamayo was arrested on Saturday, November 29, at 3:30 AM in his residence and escorted to the SIM offices, where he was interrogated by Colonel Irenaldo García Báez. The general denied all the accusations but assured his interrogator: "This is slowly

---

[16] Captain José Rodríguez San Pedro was unharmed and his wife Laura Leguina Martínez was wounded in an attack perpetrated by members of the Directory of Revocation (DR) in the Montmartre cabaret on August 28, 1956, being murdered Colonel Antonio Blanco Rico, head of the SIM, and wounded Colonel Marcelo Tabernilla Palmero and his wife Marta Poli.

collapsing. As I see it, there will soon be terrible events in Cuba" and the destruction of the "political-economic system." He was released after 17 hours by Batista's order and was discharged from the army on 3 December 1958. In his autobiography, Díaz Tamayo does not mention his or his brother's involvement in the conspiracy or the link with the CIA. He only recounts that after his retirement, he was visited at his residence by a priest friend, the young Spanish Friar Balbino, of the Discalced Carmelites, to deliver him "a letter from Fidel Castro, asking me to go and meet him in the Sierra." The general claims that he rejected the letter because he considered the rebel movement to be communist. He indicates that among some military leaders, "there were those who spoke with the enemy to buy his security" but does not mention that he also went to the same thing.

Six days after his retirement, on December 9, the special envoy of the US State Department, William D. Pawley,[17] a former CIA collaborator and friend of Díaz Tamayo, offered Batista that he could retire to his residence in Daytona Beach if he left power and that President Dwight Eisenhower would support an interim government composed of Díaz Tamayo and Ramón Barquín and Enrique Borbonet, and two towns, Pepín Bosch, owner of the Bacardi distillery and Raúl Chibás Rivas. Thus, Fidel Castro would have to leave the Sierra Maestra or admit that he fought against anyone to take power.

As Batista delayed his response, on December 17 the US ambassador Earl E. T. Smith visited him and told him that his government had withdrawn his support, that he would hand over power

---

[17] William Douglas Pawley (September 7, 1896-January 7, 1977) was born in Florence, South Carolina, and grew up in Havana and Santiago de Cuba, where his father had business. In 1928 he was president of Cuban National Aviation Curtiss which was sold to Pan American Airlines four years later. During World War II he organized the Flying Tigers in Asia and at the end of the conflict in 1945 he was appointed American ambassador to Peru. The following year he was ambassador to Brazil until 1948. He was president of Autobuses Modernos S.A. in Havana and the Miami Transit Company. He collaborated with the CIA to overthrow President Jacobo Arbenz of Guatemala in 1954 and was subsequently active in the anti-Castro struggle. He committed suicide in Miami Beach because of a chronic illness.

to a cabinet of National Unity, annul the November 3 elections that Washington did not recognize and that he would reside with his family in Spain. That night, Batista met with the chiefs of the General Staff, Generals Francisco Tabernilla Dolz and Pedro Rodríguez Ávila and Admiral José Rodríguez Calderón to inform them that the US government no longer supported them.

On December 20, Colonel José A. Estévez Maymir, a Cuban military attaché in the Dominican Republic, gave Batista a message from Generalissimo Rafael Trujillo offering to send 2,000 Dominican soldiers to fight the rebels in Las Villas and another 2,000 to the Sierra Maestra to defeat Fidel Castro. Batista rejected the proposal. Eight days later, General Tabernilla Dolz, accompanied by his son Brigadier Chief of Aviation Carlos "Winsy" Tabernilla Palmero, and his brother-in-law, Brigadier Alberto del Río Chaviano, Chief of Las Villas, discussed a coup d'état against Batista with Ambassador Smith, but they were rejected. Del Río, who had been conspiring with Colonel Florentino Rosell Leyva, immediately fled to the Dominican Republic. Batista, accompanied by the Tabernilla and a large entourage, left the country in two planes in the early hours of January 1, 1959.

Rebel forces soon began arresting and shooting hundreds of Batistans without trial. Around January 6, 1959, Díaz Tamayo, wearing a checked sports bag, was brought to Galley 14 of the fortress of La Cabaña. He sat on a columbine next to former Information Minister Ernesto de la Fe Pérez, who told him to get comfortable. De la Fa recounts in his memoirs[18] how the general responded with a modest smile: "No, in a while I'm leaving, because I was fortunate to stumble upon a sister of Fidel and his mother, and they are outraged to see that I am imprisoned... When I was Head of the Regiment of Santiago de Cuba, I attended them with all due consideration." De la Fe states that shortly afterwards they went to look for the general and let him go free. Díaz Tamayo does not mention these facts in his memoirs or say that he was imprisoned. He points out that while he was not at home in those days, some bearded men from the Second National Front of the Escambray

---

[18] Ernesto de la Fe, Prohibido Pensar (Miami: Editorial SIBI, 1991), 127-28.

appeared there, who on behalf of Commander Dr. Armando M. Fleites Díaz took his new 1959 Oldsmobile at gunpoint. His wife Rosaura Menéndez and a friend, with spare keys, recovered the vehicle when they located it in front of the Hotel Capri, the headquarters of the Second Front. This caused a dozen rebels to return home armed to expropriate the vehicle.

Díaz Tamayo was released after being excluded from Case No. 4 of 1959 against all those who participated in the Batista coup d'état.[19] He was also not prosecuted for Fidel Castro's false accusation in *La Historia Me Absolverá* that after the assault on the Moncada barracks he took a message from Batista to the regiment leader ordering that for each dead soldier ten prisoners should be executed. Lieutenant José Castaño Quevedo, head of BRAC Operations, was executed in his cell in La Cabaña by orders of Ernesto "Che" Guevara on March 6, 1959, for being "an agent of the CIA," according to what he told the journalist Andrew St. George. However, Díaz Tamayo, the founder and director of the BRAC linked to Castaño by the CIA, and a conspirator with the CIA to bring Batista down, was released from La Cabaña two months earlier.

The first *Bohemia* magazine published after the escape of Batista, on January 11, 1959, contains the article "March 10: Beginning of the Tragedy," with a photo of Díaz Tamayo with the generals Francisco Tabernilla Dolz, Eulogio Cantillo, and Luis Robaina, Batista's consul. The article identifies them as four of the coup leaders and mentions that Díaz Tamayo was "withdrawn shortly before January 1 for 'health reasons.'" On March, 8th of 1959, the article "March 10, 1952: a black date in history" appeared in *Bohemia*, with a "Traitor's Picture" that contains a list of the participants in the barracks, but omits Díaz Tamayo. However, they reproduce their photo again with the coup leaders. It is intriguing how Castro's propaganda did not mention Díaz Tamayo and excluded him from the "Gallery of Assassins" section, despite

---

[19] On 1 June 1959, 33 former officers of the armed forces, including former Brigadier Julio Sánchez Gómez and Brigadier Hernando Hernández Hernández, were sentenced to 5 to 25 years in prison for their complicity in the 1952 coup d'état.

Castro's accusation that he was the instrument of the massacre of the detained Moncadists.

In the first days of February, Díaz Tamayo obtained asylum at the Embassy of Ecuador before going into exile on March 16, 1959, shortly after eight o'clock in the morning. He departed on a Braniff plane to Guayaquil, Ecuador, with the asylum seekers Evelio Pentón, former Minister of Education and his daughter María, Evaristo Marina and Manuel Ampudia, former Director General of Health.[20] His memoirs conclude with his arrival in Miami on June 8, 1959. His wife, children and mother-in-law arrived in exile on the ferry from Havana to Key West ten days later.

On July 27, 1959, his mother-in-law Aurora Hernández de Tejada sent a letter from Miami to Faustino Pérez Hernández, Minister of Recovery of Embezzled Property, protesting that, at the beginning of January 1959, her safe deposit box was intervened in the Trust Company of Cuba with the jewels that were a gift from her husband and the furniture of her house, and asked for them to be returned. He affirms that the 1959 Oldsmobile and $54,200 in a box at the Agricultural and Industrial Bank that were intervened from the general, were not embezzled but were obtained "according to his life and the high salaries he received." The letter concludes by stating to the minister: "Apart from all this, you know my son-in-law very well, because I think you have had direct or indirect contact on some previous occasion, and you know very well the kind of person he is." This admission leaves undoubtedly the previous contact of the general with leaders of the July 26 Movement. Aurora returned to Cuba briefly two years later and was only able to recover part of her jewelry.

On September 25, 1959, the CIA agent in Miami, Patrick I. Karnley, sent a report to his chief of the Division of Western Hemisphere, Colonel Joseph Caldwell King,[21] indicating that he

---

[20] «Twenty-three more Cubans went into political exile yesterday», Diario de la Marina, March 17, 1959, 9-B.

[21] Joseph Caldwell King (October 5, 1900-January 27, 1977) was head of the Western Hemisphere Division of the CIA in the 1950s and 1960s. His pseudonym for operations was Oliver G. Galbond.

had told Pawley that his agency had an interest in Díaz Tamayo and that King asked him to help the general get a job. Pawley said he knew Díaz Tamayo, that he had already talked to King about him, and that he would soon help him in whatever way he could. The CIA was beginning to organize Operation 40 to overthrow Fidel Castro's communist regime. Díaz Tamayo went to the Pentagon for support.[22]

Pawley met with former General José Eleuterio Pedraza from December 3 to 5, 1959, and showed him a list with the name of Díaz Tamayo and six others[23] to see if he could work with them. Pedraza responded favorably. Four days later, Pawley met Diaz Tamayo and eight representatives of opposition groups in his Miami office.[24] Díaz Tamayo said he would immediately start working with Pedraza to organize some 750 military exiles in the United States. The organization created was the Cuban Anticommunist Board, chaired by General Manuel Benítez Valdés. Díaz Tamayo was assigned key number C3-2 in the Junta and belonged to the military section, headed by Pedraza, with Lieutenant Colonel Francisco Ángel Sánchez Mosquera and Deputy Admiral José Rodríguez Hernández. The general was assigned to organize the occupation army called the National Guard and created an organization chart for seven regiments. Due to internal struggles in the grouping, Díaz Tamayo submitted his written resignation to Benitez on February 23, 1960. Upon separation he signed a receipt for $2,400 that Pawley gave him.

On March 10, 1960, Díaz Tamayo telephoned Bernard E. Reichhardt[25] in Washington to inform him of confidential news that

---

[22] United States Department of State, Foreign Relations of the United States, 1958- 1960, Volume VI, Cuba, 675.

[23] The other names on the list were Dr. Jorge Mañach, Colonel Ramón Barquín, Colonel Enrique Borbonet, José M. Bosch, Antonio de Varona and Melchor Gastón.

[24] Raúl Menocal, Jorge García Montes, Alberto Sosa, Manuel Blanco Cañizares, José Regalado Santana, Francisco Rodríguez Couzeiro, Fabio Freyre and Colonel José Raúl Corzo Izaguirre.

[25] Bernard E. Reichhardt (February 22, 1914-November 3, 2005) was born in Washing- ton, DC, and was a paratrooper in the U.S. Army during World War II. In October 1963 he was acting head of the CIA's Western Hemisphere Opera-

between April 17 and May 1, 1960, three boats full of weapons that the Cuban government had bought three months earlier would arrive in Cuba from Europe. The general had previously reported to Justin F. Gleichauf, a CIA agent who was monitoring Cuba from Miami, but Reichhardt agreed that Diaz Tamayo would only be in contact with him from that point on.

On January 15, 1961, former Vice President Guillermo Alonso Pujol invited Díaz Tamayo to a luncheon to discuss how to achieve the unity of the exiled groups. Both agreed that Manuel Antonio de Varona was discordant and opposed to Manuel Ray Rivero and his People's Revolutionary Movement (MRP), whom the general considered fidelism without Fidel. According to E. Howard Hunt, CIA agent who participated in the overthrow of President Jacobo Arbenz in Guatemala and helped organize the Bay of Pigs invasion by the 2506 Brigade, the new President John F. Kennedy and his liberal administration-imposed Ray in the leadership of the coalition of exiles and omitted the Batistans.

After the failure of the invasion, Díaz Tamayo traveled to Managua, Nicaragua, where the CIA had established a base for operations against Cuba and returned to Miami on November 8, 1961. The general was a military coordinator of the organization Fuerzas Armadas de Cuba en el Exilio (FACE)[26]. In April 1962, Díaz Tamayo and former General Jorge García Tuñón participated in a discussion of the formation of a government in exile headed by former Supreme Court Justice Dr. Julio Garcerán de Vall y Souza. Three months later, Díaz Tamayo declared that the US government would entrust FACE with the maintenance of public order when Cuba was liberated. The plans were unraveled at the end of

---

tions Section and in 1969 he was head of the CIA station in Asunción, Paraguay. He retired after 25 years with the CIA.

[26] The leaders of FACE included coordinator Dr. Rubén de León García, former Minister of Defense of the government of Carlos Prío; military coordinator Martín Díaz Tamayo; commander Jorge Gutiérrez, delegate in Washington, D.C.; sergeant José R. Pérez, representative in Tampa; general Jorge García Tuñón; colonels Daniel G. Martínez Mora; and José D. Ferrer Guerra; commanders Juan M. Batista Tamayo, José M. Castillo and Tulio Figarola Infante; captain Nicolás Cartaya Gómez; colonel Joaquín Varela Canosa of the Navy of Guerra; and captain Luis Morales Patino.

1962 when President Kennedy concluded the Missile Crisis with a secret understanding with the Soviet Union. In exchange for the Russians removing 42 nuclear rockets from the island, Kennedy agreed to remove 104 nuclear rockets from England, Italy and Turkey; never invade Cuba again; prohibit attacks by Cubans exiled from the United States; and allowed the indefinite permanence of a Soviet combat brigade in Cuba, in violation of the Monroe Doctrine.

Díaz Tamayo got a job as a car salesman and resided in Hialeah with his family. The general was naturalized as an American citizen on August 1, 1978 and the following month he traveled to Madrid for a week. In 1979, he was appointed representative of Councilor Andy Mejides on the Community Relations Board of the City of Hialeah. He was active as a leader of the grouping of the Professional Armed Forces of Cuba in Exile.

In the early 1980s, he began writing his memoirs chronologically shortly before becoming ill with amyotrophic lateral sclerosis, sometimes called Lou Gehrig's disease, which postponed the project. This progressive neurological disease attacks the nerve cells that control the voluntary muscles and is invariably fatal. In 1990, while Díaz Tamayo was confined to his bed, he began to dictate his memoirs to former commander Claudio Medel Fuentes, who appears in the typed manuscript as co-author. Medel transcribed 134 pages of 8½ x 11 inches, single-spaced. Some sheets are written on the front and back, others on one side only. Thirteen sheets are on letterhead from Sheehan Buick in Miami and seven from Vic Potamkin Chevrolet in Miami Beach, where Díaz Tamayo was employed in both companies as a salesman. Fourteen pages have the company logo of Military & Commercial Aircrafts, Engines & Accessories, Inc. Fifty-three pages were written on the back of sheets of the so-called Cuban National Guard, which was to serve as the Occupation Army. The dictation process caused frequent digressions, added by Medel, especially about his knowledge of the Napoleonic wars of the nineteenth century. With the approval of his daughter Roraima Díaz Menéndez de Kanar, I excluded these references from the book. Although the title of the manuscript initially included "My Family" and was later crossed out, mention of his two marriages and two children were excluded.

Two sheets of the manuscript, listed on both sides from 67 to 70, have disappeared. The sequence of the years coincides with the time of the divorce of his first wife and his second marriage on July 17, 1942 with Rosaura Menéndez Hernández de Tejada. Rosaura is mentioned only once, pointing out that she helped him hide documents during the coup plot.

The major general had five brothers: Luis, Salvador, Ramón, Julio, and Clemente, and three sisters, Elena, Isabel, and Marcela. The memoirs only briefly mention Salvador, who remained in Cuba, and his older brother Luis, who taught him to read and write. It does not say that Clemente was captain of the National Police in command of the Seventeenth and Eighth Stations in Havana before the coup d'état and that they then conspired together against Batista. Nor does it mention that his son Martín Díaz Menéndez was born in 1943, and only mentions that his daughter Roraima before she was born in 1953, Martha Batista organized a baby shower for Rosaura.

In addition to the manuscript typed by Medel, there are twenty-four pages in his handwriting that were the beginning of this work that he titled "My Memories My Family Military Life." There are five other segments of less than a dozen pages each, handwritten by the general, that recount the most important events of the autobiography and were excluded by Medel. I have incorporated all parts of this text that redundant into the book in *italics*. I have added the footnotes to the pages to identify some of the characters he mentions, in addition to specifying some exact dates and facts he does not remember. The manuscript contains some lapses of dates, errors and omissions, some intentional and others due to memory failure after many decades. For example, he points out that his math teacher, Lieutenant Colonel Ángel Custodio Bisset Coll, was shot by Castroists, which is wrong. The revolutionary government gave him an annual retirement of $3,000. He indicates that Medel and his family left Cuba in early 1959 with the help from Major General Ralph Truman, brother of President Harry Truman. This is also not true, since Medel immediately joined the Rebel Army with the rank of captain. He was arrested in August 1959 for participating in the conspiracy of Trinidad and sentenced to prison. It appears that Medel made the omissions and changes to the typed manuscript.

I met Roraima Díaz de Kanar through Facebook in 2012. She indicated that she possessed her father's memories, which aroused my interest in rescuing this unknown history of Cuba. During a trip to Miami with my wife Carlina, we were greeted by Roraima and her family. I was able to examine the general's manuscript, photos, and documents while his daughter assured me that her father's wish was for the book to be published. After several years and my persistence in obtaining a copy of the manuscript, Roraima sent me the original for publication. I sent a copy to Werner Korte in San José, Costa Rica, who transcribed it in a digital form. The photos, documents, and manuscript that I received on loan were added to a webpage dedicated to Díaz Tamayo at http://www.latinamericanstudies.org/diaz-tamayo.htm. The result has been reflected in this work, which is the latest addition to the military history of republican Cuba.

Antonio Rafael de la Cova
West, Columbia, SC, 2017

PREFACE

My Memories ~~My Family~~ Military Life

I decided to write this book with the effective cooperation of my friendCommander C. M.²⁷ because of what someone said that every man must have a son, plant a tree and write a book.

I know myself well enough to understand that almost all the readers of this work, who know me, know that I am not a scholar, nor a university student, nor even irresponsible who wants to say what he knows just by saying it. There are three things here: great traits of life, historical truths, and rectification from behind.

I am not a controversial man, nor do I want to invent arguments fabricated by my mind. I want that yes, to say unpublished things, to rectify other sayings by men who had a lot of responsibility and others who emptied their thoughts turned into gall, not only about me, but also about others who did not agree with the bad things done. This issue about things being badly done is nothing new, it's already history. The only ones who do not know it are those who put first the favors received and then the things of the homeland.

I think I am a controversial man if to debate is to go against everything and against all those who oppose the good of the homeland, of the Armed Forces and, without departing from what is in the interests of our people democratically. I suffered great anguish in my military career for not agreeing on how some of our leaders in the army proceeded. I believe that my military conduct and as a citizen itself, accredits that position of intransigent in whatever was against logic, honesty and justice, in a general sense.

---

[27] Claudio Manuel Medel Fuentes (December 18, 1920-September 10, 2003).

My controversies without publicity, but certain, brought me many inconveniences that almost no one knew about. It is true that I am controversial, but without publicity. I am not a lover of notoriety in the bad or in the good. Perhaps that is why certain injusteces were committed with me that I have wanted to make public, because some of the guilty are already dead and others are enjoying the product of those injustices. I'm sure when you read this book, you'll remember them.

Major General Martín Díaz Tamayo

CHAPTER I

SOLDIER OF THE REPUBLIC

Cuba is a long and narrow island, in the form of an arc stretched northward. Its length is about 1700 kilometers long. Its apex is the Bay of Havana. From this point it descends towards the southeast, along five of its provinces. The shorter western branch falls to the southwest and will die in the Cabo de San Antonio: this is my small homeland. It is the province of Pinar del Río.

A mountainous ridge, the Cordillera de los Órganos, also called de Guaniguanico, runs through this region almost from one end to the other. It is thus subdivided into two slopes, one North and one South, but they are very uneven slopes. Very nestled in the mountains to the North Coast, the terrain here is narrow and broken. The southern plain, on the other hand, is flat, wide and very fertile.

The main products of the Province are sugar, especially in the Northern Slopes, because the breadth of its bays makes it easy to ship. The mountains give very good wood, although the exploitation has been merciless, and there are few left. Pine tobacco is considered the best in the world, and also cattle and horses abound in the southern basin. Naturally, minor fruits are seen everywhere, as well as some citrus and pineapple. On this pineapple I must advance something: it is magnificent and in recent years plants have been established to can it, but its collection is difficult and even painful. My work as a pineapple picker turned out, in the end, to be an important factor in my determination, at the age of 16, to emigrate to Havana and join the Army.

When I was born, on November 11, 1904[28], my province was in full recovery. The Republic, under the best auspices, had been

---

[28] Díaz Tamayo then admits that when he joined the army in 1926 he was 17 years old and that he falsified the year of birth from 1908 to 1904 so that he

inaugurated in 1902, but already the political struggles had provoked a second American intervention, and Mr. Charles E. Magoon[29] governed the Island.

I came into the world in the neighborhood of La Leña, in Consolación del Sur. My father's name was Nicolás Díaz and my mother was Paulina Tamayo, "offspring," respectively, from Asturias and the Canary Islands.

My whole family was made up of country people. Humble, poor, hardworking. We had never known anything else. There, in that region of Pinar del Río, almost all the relatives I still have continue, except for an uncle who emigrated to the eastern part of the Republic, and we never heard from him again.

Dad used to raise cattle on a farm he had rented. Mom was dedicated to the house and to the care of the offspring, which was numerous. We became nine brothers, three females and six males. However, I did not know my father. I hadn't been born for a year when she died, when my mother was pregnant with her ninth child.

The circumstances of my father's death are not familiar to me. It happened in 1909, in the *Barrio La Leña, Consolación del Sur*, and I was always told it was an accident. On the other hand, Mom was always reluctant to talk about it. However, I have always suspected that it was because of some difference in interest.

For some time, our status didn't change. A guy who lived near us took care of the business my father left, but either because he was unlucky or because of maladministration, the money evaporated,

---

could enlist without his mother's permission and that it was then the official date.

[29] Charles E. Magoon (December 5, 1861-January 14, 1920) was a Washington War Department attorney in 1899. Appointed Governor of the Panama Canal Zone in 1905. He was appointed governor of Cuba on October 13, 1906 during the military intervention due to the resignation of President Tomás Estrada Palma. Under his mandate, 200 kilometers of highway were built, and the Rural Guard became a regular Army. Nationalist Cubans accused him of government corruption, but President William Taft officially congratulated him at the end of his term on January 29, 1909. Magoon retired to Washington, where he later died.

and in the long run we were reduced to the greatest misery. There was no other remedy for Mom than to "place herself," as they used to say in Cuba. She worked as a cook at the home of the luckiest people.

She kept her little house and kept as many children as she could near her, but the others, as was common at the time, she divided among various families.

The latter is somewhat reminiscent of the Middle Ages. The custom, which came to us from the colony, is still a reminder of it. The child was given to the teacher of some trade to learn it. The apprentice received house, food and knowledge, and in return, he rendered all kinds of services at his masters' house. And since I was the son of peasants and destined to be, what other trade was I to master?

The family entrusted to me was also named Diaz. They did not treat me badly, and I recognize that the owner of the house, Mrs. Clara Sánchez de Díaz, did everything in her power to make me a good Christian. Night after night, before going to bed, she made me stand in front of her and recite my prayers. I can't say the same about the master's children. I was often mistreated, though, to tell the truth, I was pretty damned, too.

The routine was carried out day by day: the day began at dawn and, after a meager breakfast, worked in the fields until nightfall and, finally, returned exhausted, to eat, sleep and gather strength for the next day.

From a very early age, I learned to plate, to dry oxen, to plow, to drive a wagon, to sow, to crush, and something that was very valuable to me in the Army: to ride a horse. This situation continued, if I remember correctly, from 1914, the year World War I began, until 1919. Mom would see me whenever she could, I mean, when her job allowed her to. He then spent his day off visiting his children, one by one. This happened every two or three months. He then traveled great distances on foot, which no other vehicle had at his disposal, and he was with each of us for a while.

Other memories come to mind, from this stage of my life. One of them is that Mr. Andrés Díaz (we had the same surname, although no kinship) and his family, unlike most of our peasants, were extremely clean. They had running water, and the bathroom was frequent. I will also say that we were thirteen people in the house. I was the only child, so that, little thing that was lost, you can already imagine who took it. One thing I've always kept in mind, though, is that they never bothered to send me to school. This was a very widespread attitude in the countryside of Cuba.

Our peasants at the beginning of the century were generally ignorant. Sending their children to school simply meant depriving themselves of two hands to help in the field. Keeping a mouth that produced nothing was beyond his comprehension. I believe that in all those years I attended a total of 29 days of school. My first letters I learned later, when I returned to my mother's side, I guess asking here and there.

By 1919, the year I returned home, our situation had improved somewhat. One factor was that being all men and women (I was only eleven years old, but I was too gleaned for my age.

Moreover, almost all the boys of the country work as men, and I was no exception) we were able to close ranks around our mother; this allowed her to emancipate herself from servitude and consecrate herself again to the home. The other factor was Mr. Alfredo Mason. This gentleman was married to a sister of my father. He, his wife and children were one big family. They were also field and work people, like the Diaz, and with the same relief situation. They had a farm called *San Jorge*, in the Bacunagua area, where they grew tobacco, cane, potatoes, bananas and other minor fruits.

Mr. Mason provided us with a newly built house. I remember it well: very ramshackle dirt floor, wooden walls and guano roof. We were provided with the house and facility to carry out our own crops in exchange for our work. And the work was as exhausting there as it was everywhere. In tobacco growing season we would get up at one o'clock in the morning, and work would continue uninterrupted until the evening. Not less than fifteen or sixteen hours a day. But old Mason was the first. By staying hunched over for so many years to veneer along the grooves, his back had acquired a permanent hump. That is, he walked with an inclination of almost 90 degrees from the waist up.

When the tobacco season was over, the latter's dead time came, as after the sugarcane harvest came the cane's dead time. From 1921, my brother Salvador and I began to go to an estate called *El Pañolón*, belonging to a Spaniard named Severo Jorge. *El Pañolón* was located near Santa Cruz de los Pinos, also on the southern slope of Pinar del Río. Here, and in how many parts I was introduced, Salvador and I worked in the cane cutting, in various kinds of sowing, in the pineapple harvest in the plantation of a man named Belén, and again in the work. It's been that way, year after year. For a while I managed to get into Central Andorra, near Artemisa. There I was a painter, and I even got a promotion working, first in the centrifuge and then as an assistant in the tacks.

When I was about 16, my brother Salvador (now in Cuba) and I leased a farm to grow tobacco. This was special tobacco only for layering or covering. We worked as two strays that year. You had to work from 1:00 AM until dark, except on Sundays. All this for a year: from the preparation of the land to the sale of the harvest. Value of the sale $5,000.00. The result of all this, so as not to make him tired; the profits of my good brother and I were $1.40 in Cuban money for both of us. The owners were two or three very wealthy and very chivalrous Spaniards, who swallowed it all.

When this happened in Cuba, in most cases, to the poor peasant, there was no communism. Communism came later, when all this abuse of the poor worker had already changed a lot; when the worker earned much more; there was the right to strike; the worker had the right to confront the employer and the employer could defend his industry and his money; there were unions for the defense of the worker and associations of employers to avoid the abuses of either party. Cuba already had extraordinary laws in favor of labor and capital (both make the life of a nation).

Wages at the time were derisory, although it is also true that things were cheap. My salary in all that time fluctuated, from twenty cents a day in the cane cut, to a peso when I worked in Central Andorra[30]. With all this I had to cover my expenses and help our mother. Something that greatly relieved my situation when I

---

[30] Central Andorra, four kilometers from Artemis, was founded in 1917.

walked around Artemisa was that we were staying at the home of a cousin named Anita.

Over the years, the Cuban guajiro received more protection, but at the beginning of the Republic, and practically until 1933, it lacked any defense. For example, most of the sugar mills did not pay with money, but with vouchers and tokens valid only for the establishments of said sugar mill, which they sold with the consequent surcharge. By 1912, that is, during the time of President José Miguel Gómez, this practice was abolished by the so-called "Arteaga Law" although, we repeat, until 1933, it did not completely disappear. There were also no social laws to protect it, no retirement, no minimum wages, no compensation for accidents at work, no hospitals. Only the field doctor, that old doctor who traveled on horseback miles and miles to care for a sick person, and whom very few could afford, was almost our only hope. Also, those guajiros who did not own their land (the vast majority) could be evicted from the place where they lived, either because they could not pay the rent, or because their lot was needed for another type of cultivation. Simply, the court arrived, and they put him and the family with their poor articles in the middle of the Royal Road.

I was not lacking during that time the diversions, quite innocent, by the way. During my stay in our house in San José, my cousins, the children of my uncle Flores Díaz, two of my brothers and I formed a sort of orchestra. It consisted of an accordion, a tre, a guitar, a bongó, a güiro and claves. I played the guitar You can imagine what all that would sound like. But we were invited to guateques, and we had our audience. Nor will I say that I knew hunger. In the field, if you work, there is no lack of the most essential things on the table. This time in San José was when, on my own, I finally learned, with the help of my older brother, Luis, to read and write.

My poor brother kept scratching the ground for a living. Soon after, I went to Havana and hoping to be older to join the Army in search of other things, without feeling hatred against anyone. I always felt like being a soldier, not knowing why.

But in 1926, finding myself in the pineapple harvest at Finca *El Pañolón*, I made an even more transcendental decision. One day, I don't know exactly why it was that day, I stopped in the middle of work. I looked at my swollen hands full of infected cuts and sores, caused by the thorns, and thought that, if I continued as before, there would be no future for me. A pawn, a poor guajiro, and nothing else. I had a guataca in my hand, and with it I hit a palm. The handle broke and I kept some of it in my hand. I threw it away too and exclaimed: — The field is over for me! I'm going to Havana. I'm joining the Army!

It should not be thought that my decision to join the Army was a kind of divine revelation, much less. That was an idea that had been haunting me for some time. The generations of Cubans before the arrival of communism in Cuba will remember the famous couples of the Rural Guard, who patrolled the fields of our homeland. There was no worker who did not lift his head from the groove, or guajirita who did not look at the door of his bohío to see them pass. Khaki yellow uniform, stiff wide-brimmed hat, saber and rifle in the bow of the chair. They seemed to us, as Victor Hugo sings, "gigantic men on colossal horses." We saw them as something majestic, inaccessible, as far away as the stars. The Rural Guard filled us with admiration, not without fear.

There was a fellow countryman of ours, *a childhood friend*, who also belonged to the Army. His name was Clemente Perez, and as I learned later, he was a member of Infantry Battalion 2, based in [camp] Columbia. Clemente was cheerful, decisive, in love. When he came to use his license, he would join us in the guateques and, like us, sing tenths. He was about twelve years older than me, but he always cared for me kindly. It was he who made me notice how tall I was for my age (16 years) and that made me appear older. On more than one occasion he told me that if I ever wanted to enlist, I would go to Columbia, on the outskirts of Havana, and ask for him.

However, taking the resolution forward was not easy. First, he didn't have a penny in his pocket, not even for the relatively short trip Artemisa to Havana. The only thing that occurred to me was to get to work in a circus, one of those famous circuses of "ripiera" that went from town to town, but that were so welcomed among the people of the countryside, where entertainment was not abundant. The characters were always the same: the black, the Galician, the mulatto. Sometimes they had a monkey, or a trained bear. My circus, however, had no animals, but a group of dancing girls, although it was not a bad performance.

Coincidence led me to meet its owner, Mr. Regal Sánchez. He was trying to convince an uncle of mine from his father to rent him a truck of the "three kicks" type that he had. My uncle wasn't very inclined to make the deal. I had approached the two of them and I threshed in the conversation, and I offered to handle it if my uncle rented it to him. Maybe for helping me, or maybe because he trusted me and in this way the business seemed acceptable to him, the truth is that my uncle agreed. I barely knew how to drive. He was also unlicensed, but since all travel would be on local roads, it was unlikely that there would be a bad time. It should also be added that, in those times of low traffic, even the main roads were poorly patrolled. My mission was to take the circus from one town to another. Being the small truck, each move involved several trips: first the tent; then the chairs; then the artists, the props, etc. One night I got stuck near a village called Quiebra-Hacha (mentioned by Cirilo Villaverde in *Cecilia Valdés*) and I had to stay there, eaten by mosquitoes, until the next day they took me out with a yoke of oxen.

After about two months it seemed to me that I already had enough means to undertake the adventure and I returned the truck to my uncle. I must admit, however, a mental reserve that I had at the time. Prior to the day when I broke the handle of the guataca, I had already told Mom about the possibilities of becoming a soldier. Our mother always treated us with gentleness, but also with firmness. And such was the concept that existed at that time about parental authority, that its judgments were definitive for us. Neither I nor my already married brothers would have dared to discuss them. In this case, he flatly refused to let me be a military man. If I were not far from her, in Artemis, I would not have dared to disobey her. Still, I didn't have the courage to send him to say it.
. .

But finally, the day came, and taking one of those decrepit buses of the time, with wide seats, one behind the other, and exit on both sides, tumbling down the road, which was very far from what was later the "Central," I moved away towards my destination. And the towns followed: Guanajay, Caimito del Guayabal, Bauta, Punta Brava, Arroyo Arenas, La Lisa and, finally, Marianao and the Columbia Camp. In front of this historic camp, I found myself walking away from the bus in September 1926. He left me in front of Post 4, precisely where, 26 years later, in the early morning of March 10, 1952, I would enter with General Batista. And there, in that post, I had the first glimpse of what military life was: the metallic snap of the rifle as the sentry presented weapons in the path of the officers. The greetings, the rigidity of the attitudes, and everything so different from what I had known until then, as if it were another planet.

Needless to say, the poster soldier barred my passage, squaring up before me and carrying the gun. He shouted then: Corporal Guard! when I manifested my intentions to pass. The corporal came with the same severity in the gesture, but everything changed when I expressed my intentions to enlist. And at that time, I was unaware that, almost from the beginning of the Republic, our armed forces suffered from a chronic lack of soldiers. Partly because of the country's small population, and partly because of prosperity, few men came to swell their ranks.

There was a phone by the gate, and the corporal immediately called the Guard Corps. I had inquired about the soldier Clemente López, of Battalion 2; therefore, the Guard Corps called Battalion 2. The Command of Battalion 2 called in turn the First Company, to which Clemente belonged (of all this I found out later. At the time, I was too impressed to realize what was happening.)

Being about ten o'clock in the morning, the Regiment was in the midst of exercises and tasks, and Clemente was in the field, with his company, but the first sergeant of the same, José López, married in turn to a woman from Pinar, and perhaps for this reason, took a special interest in me and requested the Guard Corps to let me pass. Then the Guard Corporal, and I think two more soldiers, showed me the way to go: straight ahead until I stumbled over the Polygon, and then to the right, almost to the end of the camp, where the 2nd Infantry Battalion was located.

Over the years I did this tour hundreds of times, but that first day was indelibly etched in my mind, and there was no scene that was not new to me... Everything is so different from what I knew...!

As I entered that citadel, moving platoons crossed paths with me. Officers on horseback everywhere. Horn blasts in the distance. Then, later, the regimental music that I rehearsed and, when I stumbled across the Polygon, I saw everywhere units deployed in battle, in everything that included that huge field. Then, mastering everything, emerging from here and there, the voices of command, those virile expressions that season the spirit of our profession. What impact wouldn't all this have on this poor 16-year-old guajirito?

And there are those who claim that there is no poetry in the Army! I say that, after the woman, nothing has inspired as many poets as military glory. No other subject so inflamed Victor Hugo's pen. Not in vain are there so many statues raised to the great victorious captains, because who would think to raise a statue to a seller of furniture in comfortable payments?

I finally made it to Battalion 2 headquarters. From there, I was directed to the Company and Sergeant Lopez immediately began to prepare my file. But suddenly, upon consulting the payroll, it appeared that there was no vacancy in the Battalion, although there was in the Cavalry.

Immediately a captain emerged. I do not forget his name: Colin Herrera, who jumped on me like a tiger on his prey. I'd go with him for the Tactical Third. I would be a man on horseback, just like those Rural Guards I admired so much. Captain Herrera prepared everything pertinent, and I was about to stamp my signature, when Battalion 2 reacted. Who said there were no places in the Battalion? Also, a soldier from Battalion 2 had recruited me, and it wasn't fair for Third to snatch me away.

Then came my friend the soldier Clemente Pérez with the news that there was a vacancy and that I was expected. And now it occurs to me to go ahead: Who would say that, over the years, I would be Captain Assistant to the Third Tactician? But for the time being, and as a matter of ethics, Captain Herrera gave me a choice. Either I went to the infantry, or I stayed with the people on horseback. I'd decide. Truly, I would have stayed in the cavalry, but considering my friendship with Clemente Perez and the requests of Sergeant Lopez, I opted for the troop on foot, and there I returned.

Anyone who knew the thoroughness with which a soldier's file was filled in in Cuba, and the number of documents that were necessary, will not fail to be surprised by the ease with which they were overlooked in my case. The fact that I was a minor didn't seem to bother anyone. Nor that I did not present a criminal record or birth registration, because, as I mentioned earlier, the shortage of recruits was such that, shortly afterwards, I could see the music bands of the regiments, accompanied by recruiting sergeants, scouring the towns with the aim of getting enlisted ("hooking up" is the appropriate military term). In Cuba, the shortage of staff was a constant cause for concern.

MY FIRST STEPS

And finally, on September 19, 1926, I became a soldier of the Republic. *I joined the 2nd Infantry Battalion 2 Company as a recruit. I was then 17 21 years old.* I just remember the outer aspects of what would become my career of a lifetime. A career that I loved passionately while it lasted, and whose memory I venerate as much as that of my own homeland.

In the army there was not much to gain, there was a lot of discipline and you always had to scurry around quickly, but it was always a School of men. There were rare exceptions, as everywhere and at all times, but that was a real forge of citizens. I will never forget any time lived in the Army, nor do I regret what it was for me. I don't regret what I did or didn't do either. Because every act done in my military life has a reason and in my opinion a reason, a perfect agreement with my conscience.

At that time, the Presidio Modelo (Model Prison), another of President Machado's great works, was being built on Isla de Pinos, in southern Cuba. This garrison consisted of five circular- shaped buildings, known as "circulares." Seen from the air, they look like the number 5 on a die. The central one contained the kitchens, canteens and services, while the other four were intended for inmates. Each circular had fifty-two cells per floor. Each cell has two beds, sanitary facilities and a washbasin. The idea was to concentrate all the common prisoners of the island there, for their rehabilitation through work. As time went on, many political prisoners were sent there. It is said that on one occasion they asked President Machado why such a large penal institution, with such a small population in Cuba. Machado replied, "Some madman will come after me to fill it." It was prophetic: under [Fidel] Castro, each cell had up to six tenants, without counting that the sheds that are directly under the roof were enabled to receive prisoners.

Well, for the custody of the prison staff working on the construction of the prison, and of the works in general, Battalion 1 was sent to the Isla de Pinos. This was at the beginning of October 1926. In Columbia, all newly enlisted soldiers went through the School of Recruits. Two of the empty barracks of Battalion 1 were used for its accommodation.

While everything was like honey on flakes until the moment I stamped my signature, everything changed immediately. The treatment of the soldiers was not inhuman, but it was rigorous. At the Recruitment School, the target was 5:00 a.m. Then, the instruction, the work and the exercises followed each other without any interruption other than a brief break for lunch until 11 o'clock at night, when we fell exhausted on our beds. All this at a pace that I will not hesitate to describe as violent. Also, the punishments followed the punishments, and I can't say that it happened every day, but on several occasions, I saw instructing officers hitting with the plane of the saber or with the whip the defaulting soldiers.

But none of this surprised me or seemed out of place, not even difficult. The Spanish proverb tells us: "Take the good soldier out of the plow." For, indeed, what was it for me, or for so many others like me, to jump out of bed at five in the morning, when it was customary for me to do so at one in the morning? Nor the exercises in the Polygon: to advance, stretch, march hours and hours in the sun, form in closed order or deploy in guerrilla, with being so tiring, could rival the hours and hours veneering in the groove, or cutting cane. Much more painful for me was the "dry" inspection on Saturdays.

The cleaning of equipment at the end of each day was obsessive and, on Saturday morning, before leaving the pass, a thorough inspection of all the soldier's belongings took place. This inspection began almost at the touch of a target and lasted until noon. The grand finale was the dry inspection: uniform, rifle, and bayonet in the middle of the Polygon, in full sun. During all the days of the week, the weapons were greased at dusk, after the exercises. On Saturdays, on the contrary, they had to be presented completely clean, and without the slightest trace of oil. Once the School was formed, when the ranks were opened, the inspector checked, man by man, if there was any remnant of grease in the chamber, rust in the soul, in the bolt, or in the elevator mechanism of ammunition. This means that, from Friday afternoon, after the toilet ceremony, the work of cleaning and preparing for the next day's inspection began.

These works lasted until after the touch of silence. Back in the middle of the night, the sergeant instructors were conducting a pre-investigation, checking that everything was ready for the next day. Only then were we allowed a few short hours of sleep.

As I said before, none of this bothered me much. To tell the truth, I have always liked cleanliness and, when I became an officer, I was quite demanding in that regard. Only, after those quiet hours in the midday sun, the test was to be feared.

Man for man the inspector officer took his rifle and asked the number. He then examined it very carefully. Then the buttons of the uniform, the shine of shoes and leggings. When he reached the last soldier, he bordered the flank of the formation and made the reverse route, now inspecting the bayonets. Those reported lost their pass or were sent to the kitchens. All this could last more than an hour per platoon, and we were several platoons. This exposure to the midday sun, in the immobility of the attention position, sometimes produced fades. I'm ashamed to confess it, but one day it was my turn. As my companions told me, I fell to the ground face to face, stiff as a stake.

This school of recruits had a sudden interruption. One of the most violent hurricanes that ever-hit Cuba, the "Cyclone of '26"[31], passed over Havana and the camp. As in its greatest fury, the wind blew from the east, the barracks of battalions one and two fell one after the other. If I remember correctly, seven fell in total. The trees bordering the Polygon were uprooted. From that day, and for several weeks, the staff of Battalion 2 and the recruits had to camp in tents. Every day, and once the exercises were over, we would go on to help the rest of the regiment rebuild everything, replant the trees, etc.

The school lasted three months and, finally, in January 1927, Battalion 2 passed to Isla de Pinos and relieved the 1st. There we also camped under tent, but after the Recruit School, the line service seemed child's play to me. On the Island, apart from the usual work in a camp, we were in charge of the custody of the prisoners who worked in the construction of the Presidio Modelo. This was a routine stage until, in April, relieved by Battalion 3, we returned to Columbia.

In this world it cannot be said that there are isolated events. Everything comes in chains, and each step leads to the next in each person's life. Thus, perhaps it was because of the cleaning habits acquired during my years with the Díaz family, or because of contagion with the army, the truth is that I always tried to dress as best as possible. At the Guard Relay Ceremony, the best dressed soldier with the most polished weapons was chosen as the "Chief of Staff Ordinance." The ordinance did not put the rifle on his shoulder, but remained in the Guard Corps, carried messages and carried out minor work. During the night, and unless something special came up, I slept on my feet. I was fortunate enough to be appointed on several occasions by the Chief of Service Ordinance. This led me to be chosen as a "Distinguished Soldier of Unity." Later I became a "Distinguished Battalion Soldier," after the Regiment, until I competed for that same position as a "Distinguished National Soldier." But so far, fortune has not accompanied me,

---

[31] The hurricane passed through Havana on October 20, 1926, with winds of 150 miles per hour, and left twenty inches of water in the city. About 150 houses were destroyed, as was a quarter of the Columbia camp.

and this last one I could not achieve. These things seem insignificant compared to the positions I came to occupy later, but for a soldier, the small distinctions this brought were a source of pride and joy.

My salary for that time was $19.20 a month and considering what I had to send my mother from there, what would be left can be calculated. But you could always read, and reading costs little, especially having each unit a small library. So, I devoted myself to reading and learning for myself as much as I could.

The captain of the company was José Córdoba Gómez. A little influenced perhaps by Sergeant First López, or perhaps observing that I almost did not leave the barracks, and that I spent many free hours reading and writing, he had my file brought and, on a good day, he called me to his office. Once there he suggested the idea of me applying to the School of Classes. So, I did, and in the month of April, 1927, I was *accepted to aspire to the most exciting rank of an enlisted man: that of Corporal*.

This School lasted four months, from September to December 1927. It was an even more rigorous version, if possible, of that of Recruits, since it now included higher studies and, in addition, riding and cavalry classes.

Why an infantry school received combat instruction mounted and disassembled shows the extent to which the equestrian spirit dominated our army. Cavalry was always a weapon of shock and boarding: its great advantages lay in the speed of its movements, and its psychological effect on the hostile infantry. It was also incomparable as a reconnaissance force. His great disadvantage was that, in the face of a standing force in position and determined to defend itself, the horse was impotent.

It is well known that almost all Cuban peasants learned to ride horses from childhood. I was no exception, but by taking riding lessons, I learned to do it with elegance. And this was invaluable to me years later. This School of Classes ended in December 1927. I was approved and returned to my company as an "interim corporal." I immediately began to act as such. *He was already squadron leader and with future aspirations*. The regulation stipulated that if, after two years, I did not become the owner, my diploma would expire, and I would have to revalidate it through a new course.

One thing I always observed in the Army was that, when a man showed intentions of overcoming himself, he received help from his superiors and many comrades. In November 1928 he vacated a square in another company, and Captain Córdoba facilitated the transfer to it of a corporal from the 2nd, in order for me to fill the vacancy. My salary went up to $21.25. Also, in 1928 there was another movement in my company that, as time went on, was going to have consequences for me. This was Sergeant López's promotion to battalion sergeant major, and his replacement as first sergeant by Sergeant [José] Eleuterio Pedraza[32].

Now came a period of tranquility. Until 1933, it was my routine life of guard duty, exercises, checkpoints, and duty francs. But as I continued to suffer from a lack of money, I chose to continue studying. I finished my first education "for free" and enrolled, also "for free," the baccalaureate at the Institute of Pinar del Río.

I will be asked why I enrolled in Pinar del Río, so far away, and not in Havana, which was right there. Simplicimus! In Pinar del Río I was in my land, I knew many people and, without hesitation, more than one teacher would shake my hand. Another thing, and this was the advice of my bosses, the soldiers were not well seen by the students whom, in those days, the communists were already

---

[32] José Eleuterio Pedraza Cabrera (April 18, 1903-July 17, 1989) born in Esperanza, Las Villas. He enlisted in the Army in 1919 and was sergeant first when he participated in the September 4, 1933, Revolution. The following month he was promoted to lieutenant colonel and appointed chief of the Havana Police in April 1934. Two years later he was chief of the National Police and in 1940 he was appointed chief of the Army. Batista dismissed him the following year for planning a coup and went to reside in Mexico. He returned to Cuba clandestinely with an arms cache in mid-March 1945 following the assassination of Dr. Eugenio Llanillo by the head of the Bureau of Investigations. He was arrested two days later in Batabanó with some 30 former Army and National Police officers and civilians in a conspiracy meeting against President Grau's government and sentenced to one year in prison. Batista returned him to the Army on December 26, 1958, as major general and chief of operations at Las Villas. Six days later, he accompanied Batista into exile in the Dominican Republic. He died in Miami and was buried in Woodlawn Cemetery.

starting to whip up and use. More than once some comrade changed his guard with me so that I could attend an exam. More than once the first sergeant, or the head of the company, granted me a few hours of leave. . . How can you forget those things? Also, in our Army, there were officers and classes that offered private classes, and I would address them when I couldn't learn things for myself.

All this hustle and bustle of studies attracted the attention of the new first sergeant [José] Eleuterio Pedraza. In every army, this position is the thorniest. First sergeants are the nerve center of the companies. They transmit orders from the chiefs, establish services for all staff, keep their files up to date.

Pedraza was a very serious man; he never smiled and spoke very little. I'm also a man of few words, and maybe that's why we understood each other. He began to call me from time to time to lend a hand in his work, and this continued, whenever he was rushed into the service, until 1933. And despite his dryness, he later proved that he had not forgotten me.

In 1928, by order of the president, it was ordered that all the military had to present their papers in order. For me this was a terrible blow, as I felt that no documentation was as critical as mine. The criminal record would be easy for me to obtain, and on that side, I felt no fear at all. But remember that I had enlisted at the age of 17, although my file said that I had done it at the age of 21, so that my mother's authorization was not required. If all this were found out, I thought, I would be guilty of the crime of 'fraudulent enlistment'. My alarm was wrong.

Like me, there were many other soldiers. In reality, the coup was directed against certain rogue elements who, as in the French Foreign Legion, had sought refuge in their ranks.

Battalion 4, for example, which they called "the redskins," had a large number of criminals. The Government preferred to get rid of them, as their conduct was causing countless problems. But I was so scared that, at the first opportunity, I ran to Pinar del Río. In the Court I was Mayor of Diario, one of those Diaz in whose house spent part of my childhood. Thanks to him, an inscription was prepared for me where I was born four years before, and so it has remained until today!

Another thing I couldn't stop doing was visiting my mother. For more than two years, and fearful of a scolding, I delayed day by day going to see her. The money that I sent her, and the letters that I wrote to her, appeared dated in Artemisa, where she supposed that I continued as a worker. Finally, I decided, and taking advantage of one of my study trips to Pinar del Río, I went to see her. She didn't recognize me, I had changed so much and looked so different in my uniform. One of my brothers said, "Mom, look who's here!" She stared at me. I took off the rigid wide-brimmed hat worn by the army, and it was then that she exclaimed: — Finally you did what you wanted!

She broke into tears, but that was it, and never afterwards did she address a single reproach to me.

Something else I want to write about this stage of my life. Sports, especially handball and baseball, were practiced by several Columbia officers. Handball was played with two couples. Lieutenant Colonel Erasmo Delgado, Havana's Chief Military Officer, Captain Marín and Lieutenant González were big fans. They often lacked a player to integrate the two pairs, and I do not remember who suggested that I could replace that fourth player. It seems a contradiction to what I have said about the distance between officers and enlisted, but this did not prevent them from calling me one day, and then continuing to call me.

A first lieutenant, Rufino Blanco, was the one who had organized the ball team (baseball). Sometimes Lieutenant Arteaga del Tercio, Lieutenant Enrique Meléndez of the Military Intelligence, and Lieutenant Manuel Benítez Valdés, currently[33] residing in Miami

---

[33] Manuel Nilo Benítez Valdés (September 26, 1910-January 6, 2003), born in Pinar del Río, was Director General of Immigration in 1939 and head of the National Police in 1940-1944. He was dismissed by Batista on June 13, 1944, and deported to Miami for five months when he tried to give a quartering to prevent the inauguration of President-elect Ramón Grau San Martín. In 1948 he was elected representative of the Liberal Party. He held his seat in Congress until 1958. He went into exile in Miami, where he naturalized as a U.S. citizen on January 13, 1984, to aspire in the mayoral election the following year promis-

as a retired general, played, albeit outside the team. I, for one, had also practiced some sort of manigua baseball when I was on Mr. Mason's estate. Already accepted by the officers in the handball, the day arrived when I was also proposed to play the ball. Even today I am aware of the honor that was done to me, allowing me to compete on a level playing field. More than half a century has passed since then; almost none belongs to the world of the living, but gratitude has remained alive in me. When in 1933 circumstances confronted soldiers and officers, I was infinitely glad that my unit did not take part in the fight at the Hotel Nacional. It would have been painful to fight with my former superiors. At all times they were strict with me, but just, and more than once, kind.

OUR WEAPONRY

After World War I (1914-1918), the war surplus of the United States Army allowed Cuba to endow its army with the famous Springfield. The United States had sent its expeditionary forces to Europe without light artillery. It was easier for them to acquire it in France, whose 75 mm cannon was superior to any other at that time. After the war, a light battery and two 75 mm mountain batteries arrived in Cuba. Schneider, and, later, 60 mm trench mortars.

As for Browning 30.06 heavy machine guns with tape feed and water cooling, they were typically American, and excellent, by the way. So was the Colt caliber revolver.45 and the *Collins* machete, our famous "Paraguayan." The sabers of our officers were in some cases German *Solingen*, but mostly came from Toledo. No country has been able to surpass the Motherland in the quality of its steel.

CLOUDS ON THE HORIZON

Life in the barracks was going on as usual, but the political situation was worsening around us. At the end of his first presidential term, President Machado was re-elected and, what is more, ex-

---

ing "law and order." After his electoral defeat, he established a radio program. He died in that city.

tended his powers through a referendum. That is, in his second term he would remain in power no longer four years, but six. Reelection was always disastrous in Cuba, and Machado's was no exception. Apart from that, the 1929 depression had repercussions on the island. The discontent was evident, and if we add to this the entry into dispute of masters of disturbance such as the Communists, we will have an idea of what was brewing. Until we reached a point, the soldiers earned little, but our basic needs were met, and we were paid on time. Now we begin to stop perceiving our possessions. There were times when we were owed up to three months. However, the discipline was so rigid that everything went on as usual, and if someone murmured, it was in a very low voice.

CHAPTER II

THE REVOLUTION OF 1933

In the absence of a political solution in Cuba, the struggle between the government and the opposition had festered. Failing the opposition on the battlefield, he plunged into hiding. Bombs and bombings started. The government responded with equally rigorous methods. By 1933 the situation was so dramatic that the United States government felt compelled to mediate on the matter.

At that time, Democratic candidate Franklin Delano Roosevelt came to power in the United States. This president sent to Havana, as ambassador, a career diplomat, Mr. Sumner Welles[34]. Let us not forget, in dealing with this issue, that the Platt Amendment authorized the United States to intervene in the affairs of Cuba whenever the order and security of one or the other were threatened. It is logical to think that, with the coming of Welles to Cuba, Machado's destiny was sealed.

Reading [Orestes] Ferrara, one realizes that Machado agreed to resign, but did not find the right formula. Welles met with both regime and opposition officials. *Mr. Welles used his means without having prompt results, because some agreed and others did not, to make an arrangement without President Machado. The University of Havana opposed it.* To further aggravate the situa-

---

[34] Benjamin Sumner Welles (October 14, 1892-September 14, 1961), a member of an aristocratic family in New York, entered the State Department after graduating from Harvard University, and specialized in Latin American affairs. He arrived in Havana in May 1933 as a special envoy of President Franklin Roosevelt and architect of Good Neighbor politics. He tried to negotiate an agreement between Machado and the opposition to prevent American intervention under the Platt Amendment. Roosevelt appointed him undersecretary of state in 1937 but had to resign six years later after a scandal when he solicited homosexual relations from two black goalkeepers during a railroad trip from Alabama to Washington. Wells retired prematurely and wrote several books.

tion, there was a general strike. *When Mr. Wells realized that he had no chance of agreement, and a strike was declared by [Rubén] Martínez Villena[35], Mr. Welles decided to contact senior Army officers and announced the intervention if Pres. Machado did not resign.* The ambassador's pressure became stronger and stronger, but unexpectedly, it was for the academic officer of the Army that the outcome came.

The senior officers who were consulted by Mr. Welles tried to control and direct the situation, but the influence of the students and some tolerance had in Columbia to the sergeants, made that change of resource, becoming strong sergeants P. Rodriguez and F. Batista. The high officials who had intervened, to remind me today, among others, were Colonel Sanguily, Erasmo Delgado, who was head of the Plaza de La Habana, Lt. Cor. Perdomo and Capt. [Mario] Torres Menier. The Cor. Cruz Bustillo, head of the Cabaña Fortress, was also involved or tried to interfere in a conspiracy against the Pres. Machado.

In my opinion, the real cause of the resentment of the official was in the stagnation of the ladder. Machado followed from the beginning the practice of filling the upper cadres with men he trusted, usually veterans, many of them taken out of retirement. This was, as usual, to the detriment of the aspirations of the subordinates. Years went by and there was no promotion. In fact, it was a two-generation clash, that of 1995, which had enjoyed power since 1902, and the younger, which was now struggling to achieve it.

And as the oath to defend the Magna Carta mediated, a group of *academy officials* began to deliberate to restore it, end the wave of repression and channel the country through democratic channels. In other words, part of the officialdom began to conspire.

As can be seen, conspiracy had become a customary, almost a sport, among academy officers. And it is logical, therefore, that Machado distrusted this academic officialdom.

---

[35] Rubén Martínez Villena (December 20, 1899-June 16, 1934) was a native of Alquízar, Havana, a lawyer and leader of the Communist Party of Cuba. He worked in the Latin American Section of the KOMINTERN in Moscow during 1930-1932. He died of tuberculosis at La Esperanza sanatorium in Havana.

In every politician there are always edges of demagoguery. Effective blows are necessary for him to, in due course, win votes. The president was first and foremost a politician, and then a liberal. The Army constituted its only effective base of support. It is logical that, when cracks appear in that base, it acted accordingly. Machado was a clever peasant and not a soldier. His rank as major general had earned him in the sleeve, fighting and beating the academic officer of the Spanish army. His status as a soldier had been circumstantial and, therefore, the Army and all its traditions had no regard for him. To the disaffection of the academic officer, he responded relying even more on his former companions, the veterans, and the sergeants, because if something did not escape his observation, it was that the effective command of the army had these. The officers offered technical knowledge, superior direction and, when the time came, even inspiration, but that in the acts of daily life their origin and their lifestyle kept them away from the troops. And of course, he responded to the officers' challenge by appealing to those sergeants, and those soldiers, mostly peasants, like him.

The visible head of that maneuver consisted of a banquet, a local lunch, which the sergeants and the troop class offered him at Columbia Camp. Lunch took place at the Polygon, outdoors. I attended him, like all the soldiers and, like all, I received a very nice wallet with a note of weight inside, and with an inscription in golden letters that said "Gift of General Gerardo Machado y Morales. October 10, 1930." The officers, even their most intimate members of the General Staff, were totally excluded. Upon his arrival in Columbia, he was greeted by a commission of sergeants, and cheered by soldiers. In response to the welcoming speech, the president emphasized the fact that "he had appointed more officers from the troop class than all the other previous presidents combined."

Machado's maneuver was of little use. As his position weakened under the pressure of the American ambassador, and noting the crisis of authority, the academic officers ended up toppling him. With that banquet, with the propaganda carried out in the barracks, the seed was sown. Through a kind of tacit agreement between the sergeants and Machado's former comrades, still in the Army, the famous September 4, 1933, coup took place, and this academic officer was dismissed en masse. The seed had borne fruit. For better or for worse, Cuba was entering a new era. With the help of the texts I have at hand, the memories of some comrades who are still alive here in exile, and with my own, I will try to make a very brief account of the event.

Let's get into the early days of August. The ambassador of the United States comes and goes, meets with him, holds a round table with the main opposition groups. Agreements are reached, and the main one, of course, is that Machado must resign. The opposition, seeing its victory assured, redoubled the attacks. Communists, masters of agitation, direct or influence violent action, in the campaign of rumors. A general strike is declared. Public life is paralyzed, the main people of the government, frightened by what they see coming, are on the defensive. Machado, increasingly tied his hands by the ambassador's actions, acts with what he has left. One night, on August 7, the "experts" of the Secret Police machine-gunned the crowd who, at the rumor of their departure, threw themselves into the street. All this restlessness is pressed in the Army. The officers talk to each other in a low voice. The lion doesn't hit anymore! The lion is impotent! The president knows that the academic officer is hostile to him. He trusts only the troops of the 6th Military District, that is, Columbia, headed by Colonel Rafael del Castillo Márquez, a veteran of the War of Independence and his personal friend. Thus, Machado orders to collect the machine guns from the military units and take them to Columbia, starting with Artillery Battalion 1.

It should be remembered that the General Staff was at that time in the Castillo de la Fuerza. Next to it, on the grounds of the castle, and with one of its corners inside the moat, there was a building built in the times of Menocal. This building, where the Havana Audience was later, was finally demolished in 1958, when the Castillo de La Fuerza was destined for the Army Museum. But in 1933 he stationed in it the 1st Artillery Battalion, as protection of the General Staff. And for this battalion, upon receiving the order to surrender the machine guns, the rebellion of the officers began. Lieutenant Colonel Erasmo Delgado, Second District Chief, had just been transferred to Cienfuegos, but while still in Havana, he appeared in the battalion and assumed command. His first directive, very intelligent, by the way, was the occupation of the neighboring General Staff. Of course, the authority of the government was already crumbling in plain sight, and the conditions for rebellion were obvious, but possibly the occupation of the General Staff was decisive. One of its first effects was the presentation at the Castillo of Colonel Julio Sanguily Echarte[36]. Because he was of higher rank, Lieutenant Colonel Delgado gave him the command. Now Sanguily acted: he ordered all the commands, except Columbia (he knew that Colonel Castillo would not support him) and invited them to revolt. Possibly it was to prevent the call of the General Staff, who all answered in the affirmative.

Upon learning these facts, Machado chose to take refuge in Columbia. Colonel Castillo didn't let him down. He waited for him and gave him shelter. But the news had permeated inside the Camp. Let's leave it to Dr. Ricardo Adam Silva in his book *Cuba: Raíces del Desastre*:

> Colonel Rafael del Castillo, chief of the Sixth Military District (Columbia), remained faithful to the president to the last. After the troops had been formed in anticipation of the arrival of General Machado, who had come there to resist, the uprising began when Lieutenant Abelardo Concepción wanted to shoot him and his men with machine guns from the 3rd Infantry Battalion, which were located in front of the Officers' Club. The author of these lines was the head of that unit for several years. The swift and timely mediation of other officers, and in particular that of the Assistant District Captain, Andrés Angulo, avoided the clash, but the rest of the troops joined the revolt that had just broken out, with the demand that Machado renounce the point. It was then that

---

[36] Julio Sanguily Echarte (1879-December 25, 1935), son of Major General Julio Sanguily Garrite, was colonel of the Liberation Army in the War of 1895. He was Colonel-in-Chief of the Army Aviation Corps on August 12, 1933, when he announced on the Army radio the military uprising that overthrew President. Machado. The interim president Carlos Manuel de Céspedes named him major general and chief of the Army General Staff. He was dismissed by the September 4 Revolution and replaced by Fulgencio Batista. The general and his two sons were arrested at the Hotel Nacional after the fighting of October 8, 1933, and imprisoned in the fortress of La Cabaña. He died when he was hit by a tram in Havana.

> Colonel Castillo informed the Executive that he could not count on his forces.

After this, General Machado had no choice but to resign and leave, and he did. He then took a plane and disappeared from the scene. As successor, he left the Secretary of War and Navy, General Alberto Herrera as successor. To that end, he appointed him Secretary of State. To that end, and to give him his final instructions, he summoned him to Columbia.

I did not witness any of these events. On the morning of August 12, I was ordered to occupy the Pote Bridge, with four men from my squadron. This bridge, almost at the mouth of the ancient river Casiguaya, today, Almendares, united the aristocratic neighborhood of El Vedado with the no less aristocratic Miramar. My instructions were to let no one, absolutely no one, cross from El Vedado (Havana) to Miramar (Marianao). I placed two men at each head of the bridge and proceeded to divert traffic which, by the way, was not much.

At mid-afternoon, General Herrera, accompanied by two assistants, and of course the driver, appeared from Havana. I respectfully gave you the order. The general then asked me to allow his assistant to cross the bridge, to make a phone call from a cafe that was at the entrance of the Reparto de Miramar, where later the Kasalta restaurant was. I authorized the passage of the assistant, and little by little he called me to put me in the apparatus. It was the Assistant Captain of Columbia, who said to me, "Captain Diaz, let General Herrera pass."

Then I gave way to the general, whom I greeted as he passed by. But the general stopped the car, called me and said, "Corporal, congratulations." You have done your duty.

This was a relief for me, because with bosses, you never know. . . A pickup picked us up at dusk, and we drove back to Camp. Everything had already passed, but the staff's expectation was evident. As always, the soldiers were the least aware of everything, including what had happened before their eyes. All the whispers revolved around, "What is going on here?" and I too, with that question in mind, went to bed...

THE NEXT DAY

A few years ago, in the United States, Vice President [Spiro Agnew] and later President [Richard Nixon] himself, were forced to resign under a heap of accusations, without the slightest disturbance, not a single citizen stopped coming to work. But in our latitudes, where in a pendular movement, chaos makes dictatorship imperative, dictatorship, after fulfilling its mission, is spent. Because dictatorships are order and progress in exchange for repression of the individual. As time goes on, this dictatorship becomes odious, it must continue to be maintained by violence, and when circumstances bring it down, it is like uncovering the Pandora's Box. That was Machado's fall. The crowds took to the streets to loot and kill. Many "experts" and policemen were shot, beaten and stoned to death. Many close to the president, foreseeing such a situation, had hidden or left the country in advance. Their houses were abandoned, and the rabble was thrown upon them.

Reading Ferrara, I found a passage that reminded me of something very true, and that I had the opportunity to observe, at least on two occasions: in many of these looting, members (usually women) of prominent families, and even close to the assaulted, were at the head. His slogan was: "before someone else takes it, I'll take it." And phrases like this: "There, there, in the drawer of the center! That's where she keeps the tablecloths!"

To contain these disturbances as much as possible, troops were sent to Havana to supply the police, who had disappeared. The mobs did not look at us with ojeriza, and even cheered us, but little could be done if the weapons were not used, and the order was rather to appease and not to win the antipathy of the populace. Contact with it led to fraternization, and this is always demoralizing for the troop. There is a photograph, very widespread in his time, in which you see a soldier elevated on footpaths around him. The soldier had joined the mobs in this witch hunt, and had killed, with a certain bullet, a chief of the former secret police. I ignored this little soldier, very zealous for having killed an old comrade who, in the revolutions, the heroes of today are taken to the guillotine the next day by the same ones who cheered them yesterday. As for me, I was highlighted with eleven men in the Buenavista

Department, not far from the Camp. We are stationed in the residence of Colonel Espinoza, former director of the Institute of Havana. The portal of his house was running, all around the ground floor. We were staying overnight there. From there we started patrolling the streets of the distribution. We could have done something to contain the excesses, but not much. Thus, the days passed until September 4.

The plan of the American ambassador had been to depose Machado, replacing him with General Herrera, who had been appointed Secretary of State for that purpose. The officers' blow surprised and irritated him, but the fact was consummated. To complicate matters further, the officers refused to accept General Herrera, whom they considered too close to Machado. After bitter discussions between Sumner Welles and Colonel Sanguily, Dr. Carlos Manuel de Céspedes y Quesada[37], son of the Father of the Homeland, was appointed in his place.

Some academic officials then began to speak of cleansing, but this word has always had ominous resonances. It means that a group of individuals constitutes a "Purification Board" and determines who is "pure" and who is not. The procedures of these purification boards, and we have had a few of them, are necessarily irregular

---

[37] Carlos Manuel de Céspedes y Quesada (August 12, 1871-March 28, 1939) son of the Father of the Homeland, was born in New York where his mother was exiled. In 1879, he resided in Paris, with his mother and sister. He studied. at the Charlier Institute in New York, Germany, France and Law at the University of Havana. He spoke six languages. He was a farmer in Venezuela during 1892-1895. Expeditionary of the "Laurada," he landed in Oriente on October 28, 1895. Civil Governor of Oriente during the Armed Republic, delegate to the Constituent Assembly of the Yaya, and Colonel-in-Chief of the General Staff of the General Inspectorate of the Liberation Army. Elected Representative to the House for Oriente in 1901 and 1904. Minister Plenipotentiary in Italy and Argentina (1909-1913) and Washington (1914-1922). He married the divorced Italian Countess Laura Bertini Alessandri (July 30, 1880-February 21, 1956) in the mayor's office of New York on February 25,1915, at a civil ceremony held by the mayor. Secretary of State for Finance and War (1922-1926). Minister Plenipotentiary in Paris and London (1927-August 1932) and Ambassador to Mexico until May 1933. Appointed president by agreement of oppositionists and mediators on August 12, 1933, he was removed from office by the September 4 revolution. He died in Havana after along illness.

and incomplete. Limited in their time and imbued with the passions of the moment, interests, antipathy or friendship prevail in them, even in the best intentions, but their final result is always the same. That is to say, many men, guilty or not, lose their profession, their way of life, and once we start on the path of purification, we never know which heads to roll, nor who will be considered "stained." The real cleansing was directed against the top cadres of the Army, against most of the non-academic officers, and against what was left of the veterans.

Perhaps all this could have taken place, but fate played tricks on the officers. His boss, now General Sanguily, was operated on by a perforated ulcer just three days after Machado fell. This left the movement of the officers unabated, because to replace it a prestigious general was appointed in his place, but already retired and oblivious to what was happening, General [Armando] Montes. The latter, who apparently lived in the best of worlds, instead of assuming command with an iron hand, and with an iron hand restoring order in the country, left in union with the president to visit an affected area in Camagüey. By statutory substitution — oh, my God, what an irony! — the temporary command passed into the hands of a non-academic officer, and future "clean," Lieutenant Colonel [Héctor de] Quesada[38].

From the Middle Ages, the King and the Plain State, with the distance between them, understood each other in front of the common enemy, which was the feudal nobility. In 1933, the General Staff and the sergeants understood each other beautifully in the face of the imminent cleansing posed by certain academy officers.

Tacit or express agreement? The co-author of this book [Claudio Medel] was the lodge brother of then Sergeant Pablo Rodríguez[39]. From 1944 until their death this year [1987] they were friends,

---

[38] Lieutenant Colonel Héctor de Quesada is described as "a consummate clerk who never sent troops and lacked character." Ricardo Adam Silva, *La Gran Mentira: 4 Septiembre 1933 y sus Importantes Consecuencias* (Santo Domingo: Editora Corripio, 1986), 81.

[39] Pablo Rodríguez Silverio (June 22, 1897-October 15, 1987), a native of Jovellanos, was the headquarters of the third company, Infantry Battalion 2. He sought asylum in the United States in 1968.

apart from their Masonic bond. Many times, this issue was addressed in the secretariat of the "Americas" Lodge. Paul always affirmed that he, who led the conspiracy of the sergeants, which followed that of the officers, received encouragement from the General Staff at all times, being the Lieutenant Colonel [Joseph] I forgive the bond between the two. Says Dr. Adam Silva (pp. 32-33, op. cit.):

> By Pablo Rodríguez, president of the Enlistment Club, I managed to see Perdomo without difficulty, and although it was a crime of sedition to make collective requests, I send him a list of improvements: a spa for the troops, two more buttons in the uniform, amplitude in the permits and salary increase. Perdomo agreed to everything then.

It should be noted that, although many officers had conspired against Machado since 1930, there were also sergeants who saw as far as they did, and with or without him, tried to secure their future situation. Pablo Rodriguez was one. Perhaps his Masonic ties alerted him to that. In secret, Pablo joined ABC, one of the most powerful clandestine organizations. As for Sergeant Batista, he did not miss the opportunity to establish contact with many opposition individuals. His performance as a sergeant stenographer in the war councils held for political prisoners facilitated these contacts. Batista managed to meet many of them and even provide them with small services, such as taking messages to their relatives or making phone calls on their behalf. As we shall see, all this had its consequences later.

I don't remember if on September 1st or 2nd, I received the message from Sergeant Pedraza to appear at a certain time, I think in the Grand Masonic Lodge located in Belascoaín and Carlos III[40]. This wish of Pedraza I could not fulfill remember that I was in the house of Colonel Espinoza. No one could relieve me, and I did not dare to leave without the Colonel's permission. I later learned that the meeting was about the assembly of classes and soldiers to be held on the 4th of that same month. If Pedraza was upset that I wasn't there, I never knew, because he never told me anything

---

[40] The first of the conspiracy meetings at the lodge was on August 21, 1933.

about it. He didn't take it into account either, because he kept treating me like he always did. But sometimes I wonder what my fate would have been if I had attended. Perhaps it would have been at the core of events and would have risen meteorically, and not step by step, over the years. But I don't complain; I think it was better that way, and I can't complain about how life has treated me.

Another thing that comes to mind is that in those days Sergeants Pablo Rodríguez, Batista and Pedraza had lunch together, either in one company or in another, but there were also other meetings in Sergeant Rodríguez's office, although they were in no way hidden. It is clear, however, that the final touches of the act of 4 September were being made.

From August 12 to September 4 (23 days) Cuba was ruled by many presidents, but almost without a government. The Armed Forces were the ones that actually sustained that chaotic situation from the same August 12 and until later.

Immediately after the military coup started by officers of the National Army, I realized how it escaped from the hands of those experienced officers something that so gently slipped or escaped the control of the constituted government, to go through so many stages and come to fall gently at the feet of the classes and soldiers.

The 4th of September brought a marked destiny. President Machado's behavior provoked him, the students desired it, a group of National Army officers caressed him and the enlisted enjoyed it. And it was so, because they were the ones who knew how to hold it and direct it against everything and everyone. If it hadn't been so, we would have witnessed a long-running chaos.

And it arrived on September 4, 1933. The sergeants, many chiefs and delegate soldiers of all the military units of the Republic, formed an assembly at the Columbia Enlisted Club. It began at noon and developed on the basis of asking for improvements for the troop class. It was followed by speeches, some with exaltation. It goes without saying that most of the officers did not care little or much about all that, and that almost all remained in their usual occupations or absent from their homes. In my unit, Second Company of Battalion 2, none of them showed up all day. Of the neighboring companies, I remember only the Seventh Lieutenant,

O'Bourke, and Lieutenant Máximo Gómez, also in their routine work. A small group did worry me. Several of them did not stop hanging around the Enlistment Club, and even made an appearance in it. One of them, Lieutenant Rabelo[41], tried to reach Pablo Rodríguez and Batista armed. He was arrested, disarmed and ordered to leave.

Captain [Mario] Torres Menier also attended the meeting. From his sickbed, General Sanguily had commissioned him to find out what was going on at the Enlistment Club. I understand the captain told the sergeants that this was a sedition and invited them to dissolve. Pablo Rodríguez said to Batista: —You answer him! I venture to say that, in fact, it was at that moment that the leadership passed into the hands of the latter.

Here is a point that, for years, has intrigued many scholars of this process. Why, being Pablo Rodríguez the main organizer of the movement, was he eliminated from it in such a sudden and definitive way, by his comrade and friend Fulgencio Batista?

How could Batista have taken over the situation so completely? If you know both characters intimately, the truth is not difficult to establish. Both the co-author of this book and I had a long relationship with both. Naturally, [Claudio] Medel, by reason of his degree, had less access to President Batista than I did.

Instead, I only remember Pablo Rodríguez in his days as Sergeant Barracks-Master, but when changing impressions and memories, we both agreed: Pablo was an organizer, but a complete introvert. In intimate circles it was pleasant and pleasant, but in unexpected situations he reacted like all introverts. That is, he stuttered and ended up silent. Batista, on the other hand, was decisive and spectacular. He felt at ease in front of people who heard him. That his oratory was not one of the most brilliant is irrelevant. At that famous assembly, when Paul asked Batista to answer Captain Torres Menier, Paul placed himself in the position that was most comfortable for him.

---

[41] Captain Demetrio Ravelo was the Camp Day Officer who spoke to Batista. Ravelo was later wounded during the fight at the Hotel Nacional. Adam Silva, *La Gran Mentira*, 108-109, 167.

Batista, taking charge of the situation, and even with his primitive oratory of those days, entangled Torres Menier, also a man of few words. It also helped Batista the attitude of the assembly which, like him, sniffed the danger, and with gestures and attitudes backed the sergeant. Seeing himself alone before that semi-hostile crowd, the captain withdrew slowly, worthily, like the great lords, and returned no more. From here, all the eyes of the assembly turned to Batista, who without hesitation continued to give orders and dispositions, while Paul remained silent.

According to Dr. Adam Silva, who says he witnessed the scene, Sergeant Batista responded demagogically, albeit not without courtesy, to Torres Menier, because also the then Captain Adam Silva, accompanied by another captain, Evelio Dina, had appeared in the Enlistment Club. After this incident, he went immediately to see the Chief of the Regiment, to inform him and urge him to authorize him to dissolve the meeting by force.

Lieutenant Colonel Perdomo had been transferred to Camagüey that same morning, and relieved by the chief of the Third, Commander Antonio Pineda. But that did not change the state of affairs. This commander was, like the colonel of the Márquez Castillo, Machado's friend. I have the affirmation of an eyewitness, who I regret does not authorize me to pronounce his name, that on August 12, knowing already in Columbia the capture of the Castillo de la Fuerza by the 1st Artillery Battalion, he appeared before the president, who was already in the Camp, and asked for authorization to march on Havana with the Third and recover the General Staff. Machado appreciated the initiative but did not authorize it. As can be seen, Pineda was another "purified" future, and in no way did he ignore it.

As innocuous as the presence of the aforementioned officers at the sergeants' meeting was, however, he had the virtue of disturbing them. At mid-afternoon there was a break for deliberation, followed by a second meeting at eight o'clock in the evening.

My detachment had returned to Columbia, though I don't remember exactly the day. I did not attend the midday session, as I had been working in the first sergeant's office. But on the second, shortly before eight o'clock at night, I was summoned to the club. I arrived in time to hear how Sergeant Batista, after expressing himself with great respect to the inferior officers, arranged for all the attendants to return to their units, arm the personnel and assume command.

It is undeniable that there was ferment in the troop. As disciplined as we were, three weeks ago we lived among looting, disorder and fraternization with the populace. Part of the press, influenced by the Communists, urged the soldiers to join students and workers, and to carry forward "the true revolution." Throughout that 4 September, we had remained in our barracks, [awaiting] the agreements that would emerge from the Assembly. When shortly after eight o'clock in the evening we returned to the barracks with the order to arm ourselves, the anxiety of those who waited burst into action. In my company, the soldiers ran to the gunsmiths and took their rifles, but there were many unarmed men, because the assistants and all the administrative staff were quartered.

The spare weaponry was locked up at the company's headquarters. Sergeant Quartermaster, surnamed Lastres, was my companion. Like Sergeant Pedraza, I sometimes helped Weights in the preparation of the payroll, and apart from having baptized him a daughter, he had a certain friendship with me, but that day he did not appear anywhere, and only he had the keys of the enclosure where the weapons and ammunition were in reserve.

Knowing all this, the sergeant of the third torrent asked me: — Do you have the keys of the headquarters-master? because Lastres does not appear. I replied, "I don't have the key, but if you authorize me, I can break the lock." "Break it!" Sergeant Torriente told me. And I shrugged and broke the door. Those who were unarmed rushed from the compound, took rifles and opened the boxes of ammunition. Shortly thereafter, a new order came from the sergeants, now constituted as a board: "In the future, the soldiers will only obey orders from the new General Staff." And furthermore: "Treat the officers with courtesy and respect but warn them to stay out of this movement until further notice and, if they wish, return to their homes." This is how it ended on September 4.

Two aspects of this' coup 'I would like to help clarify. One is the dismissal of officers by sergeants. This has been described by some historians as unprecedented, but these abound. I think I have dealt with the other aspect quite clearly. I refer to the replacement of Sergeant Pablo Rodríguez by Batista. However, I have at hand a good antecedent that History has collected. The outbreak of the Ten Years' War was the result of a long conspiracy. If we are to attribute any credit to the memories of the son of Don Francisco Vicente Aguilera, oriental landowner, and one of the richest men in Spanish Cuba, it was Aguilera who, in a patient effort of years, prepared the uprising that culminated on October 10, 1868. Using Freemasonry as a vehicle for the propagation of his ideas and giving the peasants of the area the fruit of his innumerable estates, he managed to articulate a movement, with such accuracy and secrecy, that when the arrest warrant arrived for those engaged to [Carlos Manuel de] Céspedes, neither Aguilera nor any of his were included. Following closely these memoirs, published by the Cuban Academy of History, we see that someone proposed to Aguilera, about six months before the Shout of Yara, the initiation of Céspedes in the conspiracy. Aguilera objected, among other things, on the grounds that Céspedes was too exalted and indiscreet. The pressure of the friends made him give in, with the result that, entering the secret of the conspiracy, Céspedes, with his conduct, alarmed the Spanish authorities, who ordered his arrest. Knowing of his next arrest, the future Father of the Homeland revolted on his own and withdrew the direction of the movement from Aguilera. Can this be justified? History only accepts realities and not subjectivisms. Time proved Lawns right. "Phantom" and everything as Máximo Gómez calls it in his diary, Céspedes increased the revolution and took it forward where Aguilera, with his mild and complacent temperament, could have failed.

Pablo Rodríguez's mistake was not to be content with the role of second that circumstances pointed out to him. For the time being, Batista made him commander. As a friend and a man of his trust, he could have aspired to anything, except that first position that Batista did not give to anyone. Perhaps ill-advised, Pablo Rodríguez reacted a posteriori. Named head of the military house of the interim president, Dr. Ramón Grau San Martín, they both tried to eliminate Batista, who eliminated them both. Although when I run from the pen, I will speak of President Batista without sparing him criticism, just to say that he was not at all resentful. For him, an enemy ceased to be an enemy when it did not represent a danger. Paul was retired with his rank of commander and received, in addition, a bureaucratic position that allowed him to live decently. The orderly and modest life he led afterwards, until his death, is the best exponent of his true personality.

THE NEXT DAY

Pablo Rodríguez and Batista had strong civil ties. It is even credible that they were advised by some of these civilians in the days leading up to September 4. Thus, as soon as they became aware of the success of the coup, all these gentlemen seized, with the approval of the sergeants, the civil power. President Céspedes and General Montes vanished from the political-military stage. But who were these civilians? Not ABC, by the way. The ABC was conservative and included in the ousted government, but there were other organizations that were not considered by the U.S. ambassador in the formation of the Lawns government. Among these are the communists and their more or less conscious instruments, the students. In his History of Cuba, Dr. Márquez-Sterling calls "amalgam" this whole set of dissimilar personalities, but concurrent to the same end. In this case, the end was power, but since there were so many appetites to satisfy, a collegial government of five members was chosen, the famous "Pentarchy," which represented them all. Two of the members of this pentarchy, Dr. Grau San Martín and Mr. Sergio Carbó[42],

---

[42] Sergio Carbó Morera (July 29, 1891-April 18, 1971), born in Havana, was a public teacher and began writing the theatrical chronicle in *El Fígaro* and *La Prensa*. He joined the editorial staff of *El Día* before taking over in 1915. In 1921 he founded the newspaper *La Libertad*, supporting President Alfredo Zayas, and his position in the newspaper provoked on August 17, 1922, a duel where he was wounded by Senator Rosendo Collazo. In 1926 he was nominated for House Representative for the National Conservative Party but was not elected. Founder and director of the satirical weekly La Semana (1926-1933) for which he was imprisoned and exiled several times during the machadato. In 1927 he travelled to the Soviet Union to celebrate the tenth anniversary of the October Revolution and published a eulogy of the communist system in his book *Un Viaje a la Rusia Roja*

subsequently played a role; the other three disappeared shortly after public life[43].

Turning to the sergeants, the success of his coup had been so absolute that they were probably the first to be surprised. For the time being, his aspirations were limited to being appointed officers and, of course, to obtaining guarantees for his future. Outside of turning the tables to the purifiers, purifying them in turn, at no time did they think to do without the Officers' Corps, because most of these officers had not conspired against Machado, nor were these men poorly seen by the troops, but for a matter of ethics, almost none accepted the reality of finding the sergeants in charge and left for their homes.

Sergeant Batista and his immediate collaborators legitimately worried about the exodus of the officers, and it is true that they tried to get them to return to their posts . . . and they began to elaborate formulas and more formulas that would satisfy both parties, and that would make this return possible[44].

But no formula appeared. The conversations were shaken, and more or less conciliatory efforts were made. As usual, the officers wanted command without hindrance, without limitations, such as corresponded to their hierarchy, but the sergeants had effective

---

(1928). He joined Gibara's failed armed expedition in 1931 and returned to exile until the fall of Machado. As Minister of the Interior, War and Navy of the Pentarquia, he appointed Batista colonel and head of the Armed Forces. When he put three stars on his shoulders, he said: "You are Petrus (stone) and on your shoulders I will build the new Cuban State." Founder and director of "Radiario Nacional" (1937-1941) and the newspaper *Prensa Libre*. In September 1933 he created the National Revolutionary Party (Realista) which supported Batista's presidential candidacy in 1940. He was a professor at the Manuel Márquez-Sterling Professional School of Journalism. *Prensa Libre* gave coverage to both the opposition and the Batista government. On May 16, 1960, the Castro militia seized *Prensa Libre*, the last independent newspaper left on the island. Carbó immediately sought asylum in Miami where he later died.

[43] The other three with members of the Pentarquia were: Guillermo Portela Möller, Porfirio Franca Álvarez de la Campa and José Miguel Irisarri Gamio.

[44] Almost 20 percent of the junior officers, some 112 lieutenants and captains, joined the sergeants' movement.

command and feared that, if that command returned to the officers, they would be treated as seditious.

The last administration took place in the Presidential Palace on September 7. Although the commission appointed to represent the officers consisted of only four persons, more and more of them continued to arrive during the day, reaching about 200. For the government there were three civilians, or rather, four, if we include Mr. Carbó, and Sergeant Batista. Carbó, a journalist by profession and a former Gibara expeditionary, held the position of War and Navy Commissioner (Minister) at the time.

Carbó realized perfectly well that Batista, military after all, felt scruples towards his former bosses, and that he was willing to compromise on many things. After hours and hours of discussion, the negotiation was not progressing. There was then a scene that I will narrate later, but of which I cannot attest, because those who witnessed it did not authorize me in Cuba, nor now in exile, to quote their names. In the former Presidential Palace, built in Menocal times, there is a corridor on the first floor that connects the President's office with the Council of Ministers' hall. According to my informants, Carbó called Sergeant Batista into this hallway and said, more or less: "You're eating garbage! If those people take over again, they'll execute you. There's no man here but you! Get out in that room right now and send them to hell!"

He then signed a decree appointing Batista as colonel and Chief of Staff of the Army.

SERGIO CARBÓ: A few words about this character. Carbó ran a political-satirical weekly called *La Semana*. His cartoons against Machado spoiled him with this one, and he finally had to go into exile. He returned in 1931 on Gibara's expedition and was the only expeditionary who managed to escape into the encirclement of the Army.

When Machado fell and the government of Céspedes was formed, it seems that the US ambassador did not deserve enough credit, because he did not take it into consideration to be part of it. Therefore, Carbó went to the opposition and published article after article of fiery revolutionary prose. On September 4, his background as a former expeditionary and journalist of some renown earned him membership in the Pentarquia. From his position he realized that the Army was the only real power in Cuba, and that this Army had to be in friendly hands, under pain that the hesitant scaffolding that was the de facto government would collapse. That at that time he signed the decree naming Batista colonel without counting on the rest of the Pentarchía perhaps was not a legitimate act, but the truth is that the rest of the so-called government complied . . . and also the troop. Events did the rest.

Batista thanked Carbó all his life for that initial impulse. The newspaper *Prensa Libre*, which Carbó later founded, received a large confidential subsidy from the government. I can testify that the monthly sums the newspaper received in the 1950s sometimes exceeded $37,000. Despite the semblance of opposition that Carbó made to Batista during his last period, deep down they were always friends. Batista even forgave Carbó some mischief, such as publishing a portrait of the First Lady alongside another of Havana's high society to whom the vulgar attributed loves with the president.

On September 10, the Pentarquia was abolished and Dr. Grau San Martín was appointed as sole head of the provisional government. The students enthusiastically supported him. Grau San Martín repealed the 1901 Constitution that had re-established Céspedes, approving new statutes and declaring this to be a "real revolution."

Returning to the night of September 7, the now ex-officers, angry, left the Palace. Also, like Pablo Rodríguez, they had a late reaction. A large number of them went to the Hotel Nacional and ended up getting strong in it. It so happens that the US ambassador was staying there, and many have wanted to see a relationship between the two. The truth seems to be that wasn't the reason. Colonel Sanguily's son was a doctor at the hotel, and by virtue of the state of almost anarchy existing in those days, he thought that his father, who had just undergone surgery, would be better off there, where he could be by his side and take care of him in any emergency.

The ex-officers were coming and staying with their former boss in protest. The voice passed from one to the other, and soon there were around 800, including those in the Navy, who had been similarly lucky. Perhaps the ambassador's closeness was comforting, but Mr. Sumner Welles packed his bags and left the hotel[45]. I have no doubt that this meeting at the Hotel Nacional took place without any plan, but little by little the idea arose that, if this situation were to continue, the abnormal of the situation would end up producing an international issue, with the probable intervention of the United States.

To understand this, one must place oneself in the context of the circumstances that prevailed at the time. To support his policy, Sumner Welles had succeeded in sending to Havana a flotilla consisting of the heavy cruiser *Richmond*, and several destroyers. If one considers the ambassador's displeasure at so many setbacks; if one takes into account the anarchy prevailing in the country — in some sugar mills the Communists had raised the red flag — if one thinks that the United States had the right, through the Platt Amendment, to intervene militarily when they deemed it appropriate, nothing opposes the idea that, in the face of an act such as that of 4 September, which generated a de facto government containing radical elements, the United States could decide to take the situation into its own hands. Apparently, the US ambassador was considering recommending this decision, and was the commander of the squadron stationed in Havana, Rear Admiral [Charles S.] Freeman[46], who told his superiors that an armed landing would produce a confrontation with the Cuban Army, which in that case the people would undoubtedly support, with the consequent sequel

---

[45] Sumner Welles left the National Hotel in mid-September 1933, after Batista cut off the water, and settled at the Hotel Presidente.

[46] Charles Seymour Freeman (November 19, 1878-February 22, 1969), graduated from the Naval Academy in Annapolis in 1900. During World War I he commanded the ships USS Manchuria, USS Maui and USS Orizaba. Superintendent of the Naval Observatory, 1927-1930. Commander of the naval squadron in Cuba 1933-1934, of the shipyard in Norfolk, Virginia, 1935- 1937, and of the Underwater Squadron of the American fleet 1937-1939. During World War II he was a shipyard commander at Puget Sound until his retirement by age in November 1942.

of dead and wounded, and that this would be detrimental to the newly-released "Good Neighbor" policy.

As a result, the United States was content, for the time being, to refuse to recognize the Pentarky. On the other hand, this did not last long, and all its members resigned in favor of one of them, Dr. Ramón Grau San Martín. Thus, and fearing new complications, the now Colonel Batista decided to liquidate the anomalous situation created by the ex-officers and, in the early hours of October 2, attacked the hotel. The attack consisted of firing at him with all the weapons at his disposal, including the 75 mm artillery. The officers responded with the short number of rifles they had. There were among them several international shooters who made numerous casualties to the soldiers. For several hours, the defenders of the hotel put their hope in the intervention, if not of the United States, at least of the diplomatic corps accredited in Cuba. But nothing happened, and at last, in the afternoon, the ex-officers surrendered. They were concentrated in the gardens facing the back of the hotel and transported in trucks to the military prisons of La Cabaña. When most of them had been evacuated, there was a most unpleasant incident. A corporal, armed with an automatic rifle, suddenly aimed at the mass of prisoners and emptied his load on them[47].

About ten officers were killed at the site, and ____ more wounded[48]. The combat settled once and for all the question of the officers. After a short prison sentence, Batista sent them home, and later, he agreed to a pension which, humanus est! most accepted. They all made their way into civilian life, and I don't know of anyone who didn't do it honestly.

It is fair to note, however, that not all of these officers left on September 4, and that, as time went on, many of these officers re-

---

[47] Lieutenant Ricardo M. Adam Silva (November 3, 1897-May 15, 1995), who was one of the prisoners, stated in his memoirs that "a group of armed civilians, belonging to ABC Radical and some students, opened revolver fire and pistol on us, already unarmed." *La Gran Mentira*, 165.

[48] Ambassador Sumner Welles reported that fourteen officers were killed and seventeen wounded. Among his opponents were eighty soldiers and civilian allies killed and about two hundred wounded.

turned to the ranks. Three of them became generals. I remember at least two who came to colonels, and at least six to lieutenant colonels. One of them, Colonel [Manuel] León Calás, held the positions of director of the Military Academy and the Higher School of War. The secretary of this School, captain [Mario E.] Forest, he was also a former officer. They were our teachers, and we owe them a lot. Teachers in all our schools, from them I received much of my further preparation.

NOVEMBER 8

The new regime was subjected to a new, even more severe test. On the night of November 7-8, the Military Aviation, as well as the garrisons of the Castillo de Atarés, the Dragon Barracks and that of San Ambrosio, revolted. This uprising, under the military command of the commander of the former army Ciro Leonard[49], was made in combination with the ABC, still a powerful organization, which spilled armed groups all over Havana. Many of them occupied the roofs as snipers, others traveled around the city in cars, firing on the soldiers and sailors they found on the way. It was also said, although fortunately it was not true, that the Matanzas Regiment had also taken up arms against the government, and that it was marching on Havana. During the night, a military aircraft tried to bomb the Presidential Palace.

The plane failed to drop its bombs and it seems that it was touched by anti-aircraft fire, going to fall in Matanzas.

That same night we received orders to reclaim the airfield, which, it will be recalled, was north of Columbia Camp, and on a plane below it. Beyond the airport is the Reparto de Miramar and, even further, the sea. From Columbia one descended to the airfield on a gentle slope. The four battalions of Columbia and some elements of the Third took position along the edge of this slope and, at about nine o'clock at night, we received the order to advance. We were given a very large fire and, if there were no darkness, the

---

[49] Ciro Leonard was a veteran of the War of Independence. His biography appears in *Bohemia*, November 19, 1933.

casualties would have been considered. Nevertheless, we had to mourn eleven dead and more than twenty wounded.

Aviation personnel were small but had been reinforced with many Alphabets. My wife[50] says that, as a child, she lived very close to the Miramar Yacht Club, and watched the cars loaded with armed civilians arrive. This aristocratic club was a focal point, as many of its members belonged to the ABC. Once assembled they could easily move on to the airfield, which was one step away.

Under that deluge of bullets, we were jumping forward. That is, we ran ten or fifteen meters and lay down. I remember how, when I was lying down, a corporal named Verdecia, who was marching beside me, was shot dead in the act. Verdecia jumped and, if I didn't turn away, he would have fallen on me. Little by little, now of joining, the mechanic soldier of my company fell. This poor soldier was killed by a shot that came from our own ranks. Looks like when he got in, someone shot, and he got in the way of the firing line.

As the aviation buildings are clustered to the east of the airport, and the advance was on a very wide front, it turned out that battalions 1 and 2, which were to the right of the line, had to advance directly on them, while battalions 3 and 4, further to the left, had nothing in front of them but the airstrips, where there were no defenders. Hence, we received all the fire, while those who advanced without opposition and, after passing the buildings, ended up turning to the right, surrounding the aforementioned buildings. It was then that panic was declared in the opposing ranks, because it was already dawning, and from the control tower and the Almendares Hotel, which was where our adversaries were hidden, they could appreciate that they would soon be surrounded. The alphabets fled, abandoning the aviation soldiers, although we captured a few, plus almost all the military personnel.

The first to enter the main aviation building were Captains [Ignacio] Galíndez and [Gregorio] Querejeta[51], a former Academy of-

---

[50] He refers to his second wife Rosaura Menéndez Hernández de Tejada.

[51] The Afro-Cuban Gregorio Querejeta Valdés (1885-1984) ascended to commander for suffocating the insurrection. On December 24, 1945, when he was in

ficer, who stayed with us on September 4. It has come to my attention that, as we went up to the roof in search of a machine gun that had been harassing us all night, we found that a projectile had pierced his water shirt, next to his soul. As he left the chamber, dragging the bolt with him, he ripped half of the machine gun's face out of him, lying face up in a pool of blood.

The chase lasted beyond the boundaries of the airport, and we entered Miramar. There was a field there called "El Monte de Barreto." Among the weeds we find weapons, equipment, bracelets, etc., in incredible quantities, and that is that the alphabets, in their withdrawal, were stripped of everything that could compromise them.

When I was on the Monte de Barreto, I was ordered back to Columbia. He had omitted to say that having promoted Pedraza to captain, I became a sergeant of the third, and occupied the first sergeant's seat that he vacated. I was also appointed president of the Enlistment Club, a position that was vacated by Sergeant Pablo Rodriguez. As you can see, Pedraza had not forgotten me. It is fair to state, however, that I always tried to do my duty. As a soldier of the Regulatory type, I was, also because of my character, what was known in the service as a 'cot bar', that is, hard in the service. I don't mind being like this, because if you are firm, without being unfair, you end up earning the respect of your subordinates.

Returning to the above, when I presented myself at the Camp Headquarters, I was instructed to prepare the laying of the dead at the Enlistment Club. That's why it was so engraved on me that it was eleven.

Regarding the provincial regiments, all remained faithful. The Navy, for its part, held almost alone a duel to the death all day 8 in the capital. La Cabaña was kept in reserve.

But on the night of the 8th to the 9th the enemy gave us an unexpected gift. Instead of remaining scattered throughout Havana,

---

command of the 7 Máximo Gómez Regiment stationed in La Cabaña, he was appointed and Inspector General of the Army. In December 1948 he was retired for seniority with 44 years of service and an annual pay of $1,920 he enjoyed is his home on Santa Fe beach. His daughter María del Carmen was the wife of Lieutenant Jesús Yánez Pelletier.

making our lives impossible from the rooftops, Commander Ciro Leonard ordered to concentrate all the troops in the Castillo de Atarés. Commander Leonard, for his integrity and intelligence, was one of those men Batista would have wanted to retain. But here he made a mistake by concentrating all his forces in one easily besieged place.

How could Commander Leonard pee like that? Any strategy manual warns the student officer against the false security of strengths. However, this was clearly not the case. During the night, the rebels evacuated Dragons, St. Ambrose and the streets and roofs in favor of the Castillo de Atarés.

The former headquarters of the Edinburgh Dragon Regiment, demolished a year later to build a police station on its site, as well as the former St. Ambrose Hospital, and later Army Headquarters-Master General, were occupied by our troops without firing a shot. Their revolted garrisons had abandoned them.

This castle, which dominates the bottom of the bay, was built by military engineer Augustine Kramer in 1763. Its plant is a regular pentagon surrounded by a deep moat. Beyond the counter-scarf, that is, outside the pit, an embankment, protected by the glacis and with firing pads for the infantry provides an outer line of resistance. To assault him, it would be necessary to climb the hill under the defenders' fire. Then take that outside line, save the moat, and climb the escarpment to the battlements. It was set up for a garrison of eighty men, but on 9 November a crowd of soldiers and civilians gathered in the compound. The hill of Soto, at the top of which is the castle, is round, and can be invested from all angles.

Thus, the Army surrounded the castle and opened cannon fire against it. From the bay, the cruise ship *Cuba* also began to beat it with its four-inch pieces. The castle responded with two 50-caliber machine guns deployed, one facing the land side and the other facing the sea. On the side of the sea his bullets sprayed not only *Cuba*, but also the American destroyers. The sailor was hanging on the rails, watching the fight, when the bullets began to hit the armor. The destroyers lifted anchors and sailed out to sea. The impacts on *Cuba* could still be seen years later.

In Cuba's communist prisons, my co-author Medel met two civilians who had been in Atarés. One was a freshly landed rooster. He was about eighteen years old at the time, and said that curiosity led him to San Ambrosio, and then, knowing how to drive, he drove a truck of ammunition to Atarés. That the number of people inside the castle was such that they practically gave shoulder to shoulder. He paused to watch as a corporal fired the 50-caliber [machine gun] that was hitting the ground. This corporal had a histrionic personality. Every time a target was presented to him, he would turn to the audience, bow in greeting, and show a tracer bullet. Then he turned to the piece, put the projectile into the chamber and fired the tracer to measure the distance. Then, with great deliberation, he fired several bursts. He dismantled a 30-caliber machine gun on the roof of the Single Market and killed and wounded his servants. After each feat, the corporal turned to the audience, who applauded him to anger. The little hen said to herself, "He's a superman." We can't lose with him.

After a wave of applause, to which he corresponded with another bow, he turned the rope toward his piece. But suddenly, he jumped and fell backwards. A bullet had shattered his head. From here, counted the cockerel, already a mature man, the spirit came to his feet. Dead his hero, he felt lost.

The 75 mm howitzers burst into the glaciers of the castle without causing damage, but in the afternoon 60 mm mortars were brought in. The first grenades passed over Atarés, harmless, and people scoffed at them. The other civilian, who in 1933 was a 13-year-old boy, says that he had run away from home and entered Atarés, also out of curiosity. When he saw the grenades passing by, Ciro Leonard, who was very close to him, exclaimed, "They have brought the mortars and are framing the target." Soon they will begin to fall here, and only those under the vaults will be saved. Oh, my God, and to think that I went to France to buy them myself! He then entered the health services and shot himself in the temple. The witness adds that he followed Commander Leonard and witnessed his suicide. And that, when he saw it fall, he ran terrified towards the Plaza de Armas (central courtyard). At that moment, the first grenade had exploded amid the crowd, and that the spectacle was appalling. Shattered bodies and a sea of blood everywhere. People jumped through the outer parapets and ran glacis down in total disbandment, hands up and waving whatever white object they had on hand. The fire ceased; the uprising was over.

THE NEXT DAY

Throughout the republican period, from 1902 to 1933, the United States intervened in Cuba's politics in a kind of covert way but constant way. Although these protests were protested, and the press of that time echoed these protests, and although today it seems incredible and even regrettable, the truth is that the situation was accepted, government after government, as inevitable. Moreover, there was no president for whom it was not a premise to remain in the grace of the United States. What did Batista do the day after the sergeants hit? The same! and with the bay of Havana full of American warships. Small and alone, madness would have been to proceed otherwise. Beginning on September 5, the then Sergeant Batista began to visit the ambassador. On the other hand, it is presumed the anger of Sumner Welles. On August 12, the officers interfered with his plans to replace Machado with General Herrera. Now, the sergeants were doing the same with the provisional government that he had finally constituted. We can also imagine how cold the ambassador would treat the sergeant.

However, the situation was already too alarming, and the President ended up calling Welles on the phone. You can imagine what he said, because from that moment on Welles' attitude became more cordial, even if Washington still did not recognize the de facto government. The convenience of relieving Sumner Welles, who was too involved in the events that took place in Cuba in the last two months, was also evident. Another person was needed, a fresh mind that would dispassionately study the situation and propose the right solution. This man was Jefferson Caffery[52], whom neither passion nor self-love moved, and who

---

[52] Jefferson Caffery (December 1, 1886-April 13, 1974), born in Lafayette, Louisiana, graduated from Tulane University who entered the diplomatic service in 1911. He was American ambassador to El Salvador (1926-28) and Colombia

saw at once in Batista the man capable of restoring order and the principle of authority.

Batista was also eager to please and serve the United States, in exchange, of course, for his permanence in power. Caffery informed his government, and, on his return, he received the order to transmit the following proposition: if Batista eliminated Grau, the students and the communists from power, the recognition and support of the United States was assured.

In the government that was formed in the aftermath of September 4, three well-defined tendencies appeared:

- The Military Trend (Batista)
- The student population (Bachelor's degree)
- The Left Radical (Guiteras)

Of these three trends, the last two, holders of civil power, produced laws that eventually benefited the country, but also their slogans (not paying electricity, not paying rent, not paying telephone), aimed at gaining popular support, were quite demagogic. The militias had also made their appearance (this is a typically communist maneuver). I remember the names of two of these groups: 'Caribbean Army' and 'Pro Law and Justice'. All of them were uniformed similarly to the army.

I said the militias are a communist maneuver. They use them as apparent support for the army, but as they become entrenched in power, the Marxists weaken it by means of laws, dissolving it and replacing it with these militias which, after being purified, become the regular communist army.

All these dangers lurked in Cuba. Thus, when Batista received the proposal of the United States, he hastened to dissolve the militias and to depose the civilian power, replacing it with a president, the colonel of the War of Independence Carlos Mendieta and Montefur, totally subjected to him. From 1933 to 1944 Batista ruled the country with absolute power. The various presi-

---

(1928-33) before taking office in Cuba (1934-1937). He retired in 1955 to reside in Rome and returned to Lafayette a year before his death.

dents: Mendieta, [José] Barnet[53], Miguel Mariano Gómez[54] and [Federico] Laredo Brú[55] were nothing but his creatures. One of them, Miguel Mariano Gómez, believed that he really was the Executive, and Congress, at a sign from Batista, deposed him in 24 hours.

---

[53] José Agripino Barnet (June 23, 1864-September 18, 1945) was born in Barcelona to Cuban parents. Graduated from the University of Havana. He lived in Paris from 1887 to 1902, when he entered the Cuban diplomatic service. He was consul in Japan, Brazil, Germany, and Switzerland before becoming president from December 11, 1935, to May 20, 1936.

[54] Miguel Mariano Gómez Arias (October 6, 1889-October 26, 1950) was born in Sancti Spíritus, the only son of President José Miguel Gómez. Elected several terms to the House of Representatives before assuming the mayor's office of Havana in 1926. Two years later, the constitutional reform overturned the mayor's office and went into exile. He participated in the failed Rio Verde expedition in 1931, was imprisoned, and returned to exile until the fall of Machado. He founded the Republican Action Party and was re-elected mayor of Havana in 1934. He assumed the presidency of the Republic on May 20, 1936. Congress released him on December 24, 1936, for having vetoed the 9- cent law on each bag of sugar produced nationally for the maintenance and expansion of the Civic-Rural Schools. He returned to exile and returned in 1939 again aspiring to the mayor's office of Havana but lost the elections. He retired from public life until he died of brain cancer.

[55] Federico Laredo Brú (April 23, 1875-July 7, 1946) was born in San Juan de los Remedios and graduated in Law in 1895. In the War of Independence, he belonged to the General Staff of the Fourth Corps of Las Villas and reached the rank of colonel. In 1900 he was secretary of the Audiencia de Santa Clara and president of the Audiencia de Santa Clara in 1907. Deputy Prosecutor of the Supreme Court and in 1910 Prosecutor of the Court of Havana. Secretary of the Interior to President José Miguel Gómez (1911-1913) and later opened a law firm in Cienfuegos until 1930. In 1933 he was appointed Secretary of the Interior in the office of President Céspedes and then Vice President of the Republic by election. He assumed the presidency when Miguel Mariano Gómez was ousted, until October 10, 1940. Under his mandate, the Civic Rural Schools and the Civic Military Institute, the Peasant Children's Homes, the National Sports Directorate, the Technical Public Health Service and the National Tuberculosis Council were created. In 1937, the Sugar Coordination Act was established to protect small settlers.

CHAPTER III

FULGENCIO BATISTA

So much has been written about Batista, so well-known is his life, that little more could I add. Judgments about him are usually passionate. He is admired or hated, and it is that with such a figure it is difficult to be neutral. During his second term in office, our relations became very close and, although we have recently disagreed and separated, I always remember him with affection. Now that so many years have passed since his disappearance and since the events he has now witnessed, I believe that I can at least afford to be impartial.

His humble origin is well known. His early years were as poor and as full of need as mine. Like me, he traveled to Havana and joined the Army seeking to improve his situation. As soon as he passed recruits school, he did not waste his time, but learned to read and write correctly, studied shorthand and typing, and ended up winning an opposition for sergeant major stenographer. As his work as a sergeant-major stenographer for the General Staff left him more free time, he founded an academy where he personally taught his specialty. Also, and as I said before, his position in the General Staff led him to meet, in the trials and war councils, personalities who were later useful to him and who, in truth, he knew how to use.

The Spanish saying goes that "what Natura does not give, Salamanca does not lend." Culture is acquired, but intelligence and character are born with the individual. Batista was a true leader. His gift of people and his magnetism were incredible. His soldiers adored him. He also excelled over all the politicians of his time, whom, friends and adversaries alike, he dominated and used.

However, the specific circumstances must coincide for an eponymous character to emerge. Except for the French Revolution, Napoleon would never have gone from being a dark artillery officer. Without the fall of Machado, with its aftermath of chaos, pillage, and disorder, Fulgencio Batista would have perhaps become a non-commissioned stenographer.

I affirmed that Batista, like me, had joined the Army to improve his situation, but the parallel goes so far: military life fascinated me from the beginning. I was never interested in serving on the line, and all my subsequent studies, until I graduated from the War College, were aimed at training me even more as a soldier.

As for Batista, he was a politician par excellence. He was never interested in the Army as a profession. Once past the school of recruits, he did not touch a rifle again, but he was the idol of the Army and, in the absence of popular support, the armed forces were his support base. He knew this well enough and, therefore, he never lost contact with his soldiers, whom he benefited in all he could.

Nor did he allow the troops to be commanded except by men who were totally addicted to him, who owed themselves exclusively to him, and this was at the expense of the technical preparation of the armed forces, because in most cases, these men of trust had little preparation, and under them the spirit of yesteryear languished.

Stop it. The Army could not be allowed to become a mob. As soon as his position was consolidated, the need to restore discipline became evident. Thus, at the dawn of the year 1934 the schools were reopened.

I, for my part, continued in my role as first sergeant of my former company, the second of the 2nd Infantry Battalion, but now I was entrusted with an extra function. In union with another class, and dressed in civilian clothes, we went out at night to patrol the streets. We were located in different neighborhoods of the capital, observing the mood of the population. This was until dawn, and at dawn we returned to Columbia. He barely slept because he had to go on duty.

It was in the days when Grau was still president that the incident of Mella's remains occurred.

Julio Antonio Mella[56] had been a communist cadre, graduated in Moscow. It was he who introduced communism at the University

---

[56] Julio Antonio Mella (March 25, 1903-January 10, 1929) enrolled at birth under the name Nicanor McPortland, is the product of the extramarital union of

of Havana. Bajo Machado had to go into exile in Mexico, where he died in an attack. After September 4, and taking advantage of the chaotic circumstances in which the country lived, the communists tried to produce a blow of effect, burying some ashes that they said were from Mella, and nothing less than in the Fraternity Park. This park had been, since the beginning of the nineteenth century, a maneuvering site of the Spanish Army. Governor Tacón[57] hermoseoed it, surrounding it with fences with monumental entrances. Under the Republic it lost its military function, and Machado made it a beautiful park, in whose center he sowed a fertilized tree with land from all the nations of America. This was the Fraternity Park, of great extension and bordered by colonial buildings.

Taking advantage of the lack of vigilance and the semichaotic circumstances that still prevailed, the communists erected a kind

---

a Dominican tailor and his Irish lover. He grew up between the United States and Cuba during his childhood until he studied high school at Chandler College in Marianao. In 1921 he began studying Law and Philosophy and Letters at the University of Havana, and two years later he founded the Federation of University Students. In 1924 he joined the Moscow-backed Cuban Communist Party and the following year he co-founded the first Central Committee. On September 25, 1925, he was expelled from the university for a year when he slapped Professor Rodolfo Méndez Peñate who had suspended his wife. Two months later he was arrested for a bomb blast at Payret Theater. He was released on bail and fled to Mexico under a false name in January 1926. The Communist Party accused him of being a deserter, of "breaking discipline, tactical opportunism, and relations with the bourgeoisie," and purged him of his ranks. In Mexico he founded the Association of New Cuban Revolutionary Emigrants and wrote for communist newspapers. In 1927 he travelled to Moscow to participate in the Congress of the Red Union International. He was a member of the Stalinist Central Committee of the Communist Party of Mexico, from which he was expelled because of his association with Trotskyists. He was mysteriously murdered in Mexico City on January 10, 1929, while he was accompanied on the street by the Italian communist photographer Tina Modotti, who maintained loving relations with Mella, the Mexican Xavier Guerrero and the Italian Vittorio Vidali. It is speculated that his death was due to a love triangle, the conflict between Trotskyists and Stalinists, or an agent of Machado.

[57] Miguel Tacón y Rosique (January 10, 1775-October 12, 1855), lieutenant general of the Royal Navy, Field Marshal of the Army of Land, First Duke of the Union of Cuba, and senator in the General Courts of Spain. He ruled the island from June 1, 1834, to April 20, 1838.

of cenotaph to enclose the ashes in it. The next day,[58] was marked for burial, the government sent an infantry company (mine), a navy company, an artillery company and Third Party elements. We had no difficulty in disrupting the monument and undoing the demonstration, but once we owned the land, that is, the Plaza de la Fraternidad, they began to set us on fire from the windows and rooftops of the houses that bordered the square. Fearing to return fire for fear of hurting the inhabitants of the houses, we lay down and healed as much as possible behind the trees. Naturally, I didn't want to be hurt, but that didn't stop me from lifting my head occasionally and looking. I remember the luminous points of the shots, which were seen to emerge, here and there, from the surrounding buildings. Also, the bullets that, when hitting the cement of the sidewalks, made sparks pop. Fortunately, we did not have casualties.

Perhaps my performance when the attack on the air force, and from the services that I rendered since November 8, would not have had greater consequences for me, but again Pedraza gaveproof of good memory, and in December 1933 I ascended to second lieutenant *by presidential decree. The ranks of officers had to be filled, just as the first magistracy of the nation, ministries, etc., had to be filled.*[59]

Already restored law and order in the nation, the government and the heads of the Armed Forces began to worry about the urgent preparation of the new officer appointed. Since there were very few former officers of the National Army who wanted to accept the return to the ranks, an offer made repeatedly and with absolute sincerity by the then chief of the Army Colonel Fulgencio Batista. There were cases of former Army officers whom we deeply regretted were not returning. On the other hand, many others, their treatment of the enlisted, as humans, was not correct, even within the strictest discipline. Discipline is for the Army or any other armed organization what blood is to the ~~human~~ animal body. It's his own existence.

---

[58] September 29, 1933.

[59] By December 1933, some 363 sergeants, 26 officers, 32 soldiers, 28 technicians and 63 civilians were already officers of the Army by decree.

Perhaps for many things that have never been written, even the Armed Forces came the revolution of August and September 1933. The ponderous and capable military who could not prevent the revolution from reaching the sergeants, captains, and soldiers of the Armed Forces, were as Cuban as were the sergeants, captains and soldiers themselves. No more, no less.

The people of Cuba tried to get rid of the government that did not want to endure anymore and the enlisted members of the Armed Forces found support in the students and the people in general to seek a change among them; because it was very difficult to achieve this, without changing the concept in the rational, among all the officialdom that existed in the National Army. There were many exceptions among the officers, but many, most, looked at us as things, as objects. In us there was fear as respect for those bosses. Discipline should not be fear but respect and reasoning.

As a man who loves discipline and a lover of the military career, well understood, I believe that the distance that existed between the officers and the troops had to do with the lack of control of the commanders. That is the most powerful reason of September 4, 1933, which was included in the August revolution of the same year.

Much has been written in exile about the case, but also a lot we live those moments, which must be considered as a historical fact that does not admit small things. Or Sgt. Rodriguez or Sgt. Batista or someone else would have had to. The revolutionary force, or part of it, the student body, did not address the chiefs or officers of the Armed Forces, but the troops. He gave his support and helped his leadership. Another event that perhaps detracted from the strength of the National Army officer was the entrance to the National Hotel, abandoning its commands.

On September 4, I do not think it is a quartering as they call it vulgarly, but it was part of the events that happened, and that decided and gave in part, a solution to a chaos that was growing at times, while the only reserve available at the time was the Armed Forces. They were controlled and rearranged by the Sergeants and soon after a clearer horizon began to be seen. We witnessed acts of looting in many places in Havana. We witnessed fires and attacks on the streets because there was no responsible manage-

ment of the authorities. He controlled the Navy and the Army, soon the change was noticed.*

As soon as I had received my promotion, I was sent to Camagüey, and not only I, but a group of second lieutenants, because the diaspora of the officers had left in skeleton the commands of the Rural Guard. For the harvest they asked for reinforcements of junior officers, and there I was, but the fairies did not favor me. While I was assigned to some post, I stayed at the headquarters of Regiment 2 which, like all the others inside, was a cavalryman. And while waiting for me to be assigned to some holding or some sugar mill, I was able to devote myself to my favorite passion: horseback riding. Hours and hours I spent in the chair, jogging and jumping obstacles in the picadero, but as everything has its end, one morning I received the transfer order to Piedrecitas[60].

We expected riots in that harvest, but the country seemed so fed up with riots, that the workers carried out their tasks to the end. In the previous months the Communists, who were few but very active, seized the opportunity of the crisis of authority following the fall of Machado to even organize soviets and hoist the red flag in some power stations, but now they seemed to have vanished.

After the harvest we return to Havana. It must be admitted that these months in Camagüey were a holiday for me. Since the fall of Machado we lived on who lives. We could barely get naked to sleep, as the alarms succeeded the alarms. The last service before I was promoted to second lieutenant, civilian patrol at night and first sergeant by day, had exhausted me. When I returned to Columbia, I felt like a new man.

The events of 1933 had brought about a real mismatch in the officers' corps. Many promotions carried out "revolutionarily," were true mistakes. Others were more successful, but in almost all cases we lacked the necessary preparation. The solution was falling apart: reopening schools. As soon as I was back in my unit (always the 2nd of the 2) I was informed that I would move on to a training course for officers, which would take place at the Castillo de Atarés. This course consisted of 75 officers, chosen

---

[60] Piedrecitas was a hamlet in the municipality of Florida in Camagüey.

from among the youngest. It lasted a year and a half, and again, the inspection of weapons, the scraping of horses, the strenuous exercises of infantry and physical education, and in the afternoons, class in the classrooms.

The course director was Commander Salcedo, one of the former officers who did not cause casualties on September 4. He was also a teacher (and very good, by the way) of horse riding and cavalry. I also remember other professors such as, for example, Captain Fajardo, infantry instructor, and the then lieutenant [Juan A.] Moreno Romani, Physical Education. We had Lieutenant Dr. [Santiago] Codina [Aramburu] for grammar, and Lieutenant Yeste for military history. As for mathematics, our professor was retired Colonel [Fernando] Driggs [Acosta]. The infantry studies reached the battalion school, and the cavalry until the Third. We also received notions of artillery, although without delving much into the subject. Some classmates come to mind who later went far in their career. Genovevo Pérez Dámera[61], later Chief of Staff, was one of them. Ángel Bisset, later lieutenant colonel and shot by Fidel Cas-

---

[61] Genovevo Pérez Dámera (January 3, 1910-June 27, 1992) born in Matanzas. At the end of his baccalaureate, he joined the army as a soldier on July 5, 1929. The Revolution of September 4, 1933, promoted him to lieutenant and he was appointed a field assistant to President Ramón Grau, whom he accompanied into exile in 1934. Then he moved on to Regiment No. 2 of Camagüey where he was professor of mathematics at the School of Recruits. In 1938 he was promoted to captain by opposition and three years later he obtained the rank of commander. When Grau assumed the presidency, he was appointed major general and chief of the Armed Forces in February 1945. In 1948 he was awarded the Spanish Grand Cross of Military Merit by the Spanish government. President Prío removed him for insubordination on August 23, 1949, when he discovered his secret contacts with the dictator Rafael Trujillo. He was later charged in court with miscellaneous embezzlement offences for more than $18 million. However, another court dismissed the charges on 10 January 1951. On December 24, 1951, he was machine-gunned from a car while driving his Jeep in the city of Camagüey. He survived three shots .45 in the neck, shoulder, and a lung. He was elected senator for the province of Pinar del Río in 1954 and 1958. He was granted asylum in the United States on October 21, 1965, and naturalized as a U.S. citizen on August 12, 1974. Sadly, remembered for his phrase: "The journalist is paid or beaten."

tro, was another[62]. Bisset was a great mathematician, and I owed a lot to his teachings.

In those days I was not very healthy. Perhaps the waters of Camagüey did not settle me, or for any other reason, the truth was that a strong colitis was affecting me throughout the course. Despite that, I fought with all my might. A lot had rained since, with a very poor preparation, I had enlisted in the Army. The studies that I was able to do, including the baccalaureate subjects, that I studied at the Institute of Pinar del Río, helped me in an incredible way. In the end, Lieutenant [Miguel] Álvarez de la Noval[63] (Spanish) and I competed for the first place. He was very studious, and only with great effort did I manage to accumulate the points to beat him.

Sometimes, in the evenings, I would sit in the battlements of the Castillo to contemplate the city, which dominated from its height. Less than a year earlier, Atarés had been the center of the November 9 fight. In that central courtyard, where we formed every morning to enter classes, mortar shells had smashed men by dozens. In the health services, which we visited several times a day, Commander Ciro Leonard had skipped the cover of his brains. On the southern slope, in front of the blocks, stood an obelisk that marked the place where, in 1851, 52 American expeditionaries from the Narciso López expedition was shot, including Lieutenant Colonel [William L.] Crittenden[64]. The English were about to oc-

---

[62] Ángel Custodio Bisset Coll was not shot and joined the Rebel Army, being retired in November 1959 with an annual pension of $3,000.

[63] Miguel Álvarez de la Noval (December 13, 1904-February 1, 1985) was born in Asturias, Spain, and emigrated to Cuba in 1916. He joined the army in 1921, married María Consuelo Iglesias in 1927 and became a Cuban citizen on October 14, 1932. Graduated from the Military Academy in 1934 and ten years later was appointed Chief of Public Order Section of the Army General Staff. He obtained his law degree from the University of Havana in 1946. He was head of the Bureau of Investigations in 1947 and in 1951. He received political asylum in Miami in 1959 and the following year he went to reside in Puerto Rico until 1973. He returned to Miami, where he later died.

[64] William Logan Crittenden (1823-August 16, 1851), nephew of the Governor of Kentucky (1848-50) and Senator John Jordan Crittenden, graduated the last of his class of 1845 from the Military Academy at West Point and veteran of the war with Mexico.

cupy this hill of Soto in 1762. Had he done so, the Spanish fleet would have been at his mercy, because Atarés dominates the bottom of the bay. It was because of that experience that the Spaniards built this bastion.

Already towards the end of the course, a jumping competition took place at Rancho Boyeros. I was lucky enough to jump the first, and thanks to my horse, Nero, and the teachings of Commander Salcedo, I managed to make a totally clean tour that earned me the "Colonel Batista" award. *It was then that the problem of the "Bold Lady" began, until my military career was almost unfortunate.*

As soon as I graduated from the course, there were competitions for first lieutenant of infantry. I felt so sure of my knowledge that I introduced myself to them. My only contender was the second lieutenant Alejandro Batista (no relation to the colonel, despite his surname). Lieutenant Batista was a magnificent infantry instructor, and his practical knowledge was vast, though without theoretical basis. Perhaps I will miss something immodest in what I am going to say, but I also had years of experience in the instruction of this weapon and, as a recent graduate in addition to Atarés, I knew the manuals to the right and the other way around. Much of the exam was oral. Sitting the two opponents in front of the court, we answered the questions that were asked alternately. My advantage at all times was so obvious that, at the end, I had no doubt that I had been the winner.

But Lieutenant Batista belonged to the Colonel's escort. The then commander [Raimundo] Ferrer, a former officer who stayed with us, was Chief of the Adjutants and president of the exam board. In a gesture of friendship, he wanted to compliment his boss, and Batista was the winner. How did I feel? What do you mean, how did I feel? I've never had such an unexpected blow. Since he was a soldier, he had always marched forward. Slowly, but always forward, without a major setback.

However, in the midst of it all I had a great satisfaction that largely compensated for the displeasure. At a ceremony that took place in Columbia around that time, Colonel Batista saw me from afar and called me. Grabbing my arm, he took me aside and said, more or less:

—Martin, I know everything that happened. Mundito (Commander Ferrer) is my friend, and in approving Batista, he wanted to give me a satisfaction. But you were wrong, what you gave me is a disgust, and so I told you. I had your file brought in and examined. You're a good officer. I want you, Martin, not to be discouraged. Life is full of this rubbish: charge it to the account of the experience. Prepare for the upcoming competitions and I will see to it that justice is done to you.

Those words from our boss filled me with pride. Someone else heard them, and the matter transcended. Something else caught my attention that day. It had not yet been two years since 4 September. He remembered the Batista of 1933: rather short in stature, thin, falcon. A sergeant and nothing else. Now, his presence was impressive. All those around him, military, civilians, diplomats, were gift giving and full of adulation. And Batista received all those tributes with aplomb, with naturalness, as if all life had been what it was at that moment.

I returned to my routine service as a garrison officer, always in Columbia, always in my company, and remained a second lieutenant, but the Artillery School had just opened. For the first course, those who had the best record in mathematics among the Atarés graduates were chosen, fifteen in total plus ____ from the Navy. Almost no officer likes these courses, garrison officers are made relatively comfortable living. Moving on to a course of improvement means ceasing to have command, returning to the classrooms, submitting again to a discipline almost like a cadet. Studies return, with long hours of work and sleepless nights as exams approach. Upon learning of my designation, I could have moved and gotten the course off my back, but I did not hesitate. The French say that appetite comes from eating, and that had happened to me. Three years ago, I was not a corporal, with the possibility of becoming a sergeant, and perhaps even a non-commissioned officer, already on the threshold of retirement. But now that I was a lieutenant, in the prime of my age, and with the recent opposition, ambition, an ambition that I consider legitimate, had taken hold of me . . . and I went to find my bones in the Battery of La Pastora.

La Pastora is a low-rise battery built in 1735 by the governor [Juan Francisco de] Güemes and Horcasitas[65]. Its location is at the foot of the Fortress of La Cabaña, in the water, and from where the mouth of the bay is dominated. The primitive bronze cannons were replaced around 1840 by the newly invented thick *Barrios* cannons, which, if the Communists have not sent to Russia, are still there. In *September* 1935 he was appointed to the Artillery School. Every day, to the target, we crossed the channel of entry to the bay in the boat of the Morro. Classes were extended from eight in the morning to five in the afternoon, from Monday to Friday. The classrooms, former Spanish barracks, were spacious and airy. For shooting practices we had the No. 1 coastal battery, also Spanish. This battery consisted of four *Ordóñez* 120mm cannons[66]. Its location was on the coast of the North Coast, west of Cojímar. Although the guns were of an outdated model, they were in very good condition. With a range of about eleven kilometers, they were ideal for ballistics studies. Also, over time we went to an artillery firing range that the Army had in the province of Pinar del Río, west of the capital of this name, in a place called Guanito. We carry the lightweight 75mm battery with us.

Among the teachers, I remember retired Colonel Driggs, who had already been my teacher at the School for Officers, and then Lieutenant Colonel [Antonio] Blanco Montalván.

So, the months went by, and the *fifteen-month* course had already expired. There were 26 days until graduation, when the disaster hit me.

---

[65] Juan Francisco de Güemes y Horcasitas, Count of Revilla Gigedo (1682-1766), Spanish general who was governor of Havana and captain general of Cuba (1734-1736) when he renovated the fortifications of the island. As Viceroy of New Spain (1746-1755) he encouraged the colonization of California. Upon his return to Spain, he held the command of captain general of the army.

[66] The Ordóñez Canyon was a coastal artillery piece designed in the late 19th century by Spanish artillery officer Salvador Díaz Ordóñez. The cannons in Havana were used during the Spanish Cuban-American War of 1898.

An offended husband accused his wife of infidelity, and I was the counterpart of that infidelity. Perhaps the matter would not have had greater consequences if this gentleman had not occupied a prominent position. The lord forgave the wife, but I received orders to move immediately to Regiment 1, in the Orient Province. Everything happened so quickly that I arrived at my destination stunned, without reconciling with the idea that my universe was collapsing.

When I presented myself at the Headquarters, at the Moncada Barracks, in Santiago de Cuba, the Chief of the Regiment, Lieutenant Colonel Diego Rodríguez, called me to his presence. This chief knew me well; in Columbia he had been sergeant major of Battalion No. 3. I remember him saying to me: —Hey, Martin, this smells bad. The orders I have are to send you to Imías (the most remote post on the island, near Punta de Maisí). But for starters, tell me the truth about what happened to you.

I told him about the matter with hairs and signs, and at the end, the colonel broke out laughing, exclaiming: —Forgive me, old man, I don't laugh at your misfortune, but the matter is hilarious.

Behold a husband who cannot bear the horns with dignity!

Then, returning to his usual seriousness, he continued: —If it is nothing more than that, it will pass, as all things happen. The mood will cool. Ever since you got promoted, you have two schools in your pocket and you're also a good rider. I, for one, am too lacking in officers to bury you in Imías. Third Squadron 2 has no captain and is commanded by a first lieutenant. Go and take over as second chief. And don't talk about your problem with anyone.

But Colonel Rodriguez was wrong. The husband kept asking for my head, and a few days later I received a confidential letter from the General Staff. I was asked, for the benefit of the institution, to submit my resignation on the grounds of illness or some other personal reason. I was always a disciplined soldier and, as such, willing to obey and endure many things, but not the loss of my career to which I had devoted so many years and my heart entirely. On the other hand, it was strange that, if I was to be eliminated, I had not simply been dismissed "for high convenience in the service," an arbitrary measure, which was generously practiced in our

Army. But it did. I asked permission to consult a lawyer, and the Assistant Captain provided me with Lieutenant Dr. Sigfrido Solís de León. Following his advice, I replied through regulations demanding that, if I had committed a crime, I be tried in private or public court martial. That, if personal reparation was required, I was willing to fight (mourning was allowed in those days) with the offended husband. But I would in no way resign but would defend myself by all legal means at my disposal.

The absolute silence followed this letter. Eleven months I spent in Santiago de Cuba. Every time the mail arrived, I waited for the call from the headquarters to communicate the withdrawal. Amid this uncertainty, time passed until, as I will explain later, I returned to Havana.

Years later I found out what happened. Pedraza, now a lieutenant colonel and chief of police, accidentally learned of the matter. My former first sergeant was, and is, a man of character. I dare say that he was one of the few subordinates with whom Batista measured himself very much, and even feared a little. An assistant of Pedraza, a friend of mine for years, told me what happened. In this case, Pedraza went to see Batista, who, for his part, seemed willing to withdraw. The interview was somewhat stormy, but at last a compromise was reached to leave me alone, although "pro forma" I would remain in "exile" for a while.

And me anxious and restless, not knowing what to stick to. Apart from that, these eleven months spent in Oriente were the happiest of my life, because shortly after appearing as second in command of the squadron, his boss was transferred, leaving me in charge. A whole Tactical Third squadron to myself! A position of captain, being me just a second lieutenant! I wish I had the boys on horseback all day!

The Chief of the Regiment, Lieutenant Colonel _____ was a great lover of baseball. He recalled that, years ago, I had played on the Columbia team, a team that came to be considered semi-professional. Thus, he appointed me director of the team that he had formed in the regiment. Once I had it in shape, we played against civilian novenas from Santiago de Cuba. Then we extended our activities to Bayamo, Manzanillo and Banes, the hometown of Colonel Batista. Sometimes we were successful, sometimes not so successful, but it was always nice.

Until Machado came to power, the Republic maintained many of its colonial characteristics, whose maximum expression was the sugar industry, as the Spaniards had developed it. Machado laid the foundations for Cuba's industrial diversification, but it was Batista's era that gave rise to social problems. It is true that the ephemeral government that emerged on September 4 enacted laws that, in the long run, benefited the Cuban people, but Batista, functioning as an autocrat until 1944, retained these laws and pruning them from their demagogic edges, carried them forward. We must not forget the humble origin of this sergeant. The intimate tragedy of seeing a brother dead of tuberculosis without adequate medical care is later translated in the Sanatorio de Topes de Collantes. The work of the civic-military institutes is understood only through their tormented childhood.

In return for the shortcomings of his own teaching, he made him want to take it to the borders of the Republic. In our time, the illiteracy rate was still very high, especially in the most remote corners of the Republic. The teachers were quite right to be reluctant to go into the mountains, without living facilities and without guarantees for their lives, and without authority to impose themselves on ignorant mounds, who in many cases did not understand or desire this teaching for their children. The solution devised by Batista was to empower high school teachers, high school students and unemployed professionals, appoint them officers and sergeants of the Army, and already under military jurisdiction, and with the prestige of the uniform, send them to the most remote places. There, by imposing their authority, the peasants were obtained more or less voluntarily to build schoolhouses, and they were forced to send their children to school.

The most distinguished students were sent to higher study centers, the so-called Civic-Military Institutes, where they were trained as technicians in various trades. The budget for this work was achieved with a tax of nine cents for each sack of sugar that was produced in Cuba. The resistance to sanctioning this law was what motivated President Dr. Miguel Mariano Gómez was deposed in 24 hours[67].

The assembly of this plan was eminently military. Each regiment was ordered to organize schools to discipline would-be teachers. I was in charge of the one corresponding to Regiment 1. I was given orders to form them militarily and, in fact, in the three months they were with me, I tightened their nuts to the maximum. The aim was to imbue them as much as possible with the military spirit, and to instill in them the gift of command that they would need so much to deal with the peasantry inland. Also, and since they would need to travel on horseback to places where there were no other means of locomotion, I used those of the Third to give them, at least, rudiments of riding.

Time passed, and one fine day I received the transfer order. He would return to Havana, but not to Columbia, but to Regiment No. 5 of the Rural Guard (Fifth Military District). I was assigned to Squadron 2, whose leader was then Captain Pilar Garcia[68]. When I arrived, I was not assigned any mission, except that of constantly riding on horseback: a lot of riding and jumping obstacles. Pilar came to see me ride and had frequent conversations with me, always about equestrian issues.

Little by little the news leaked out: Cuba had been invited to participate in an international equestrian competition to be held in Chile. Colonel Batista attached great importance to this invitation

---

[67] President Gómez vetoed the law on December 21, 1936, and the next day was removed by Congress.

[68] Pilar D. García García (October 12, 1896-January 1983) Born in San José de las Lajas, Las Villas, he enlisted in the Army on April 22, 1915. He was promoted to second lieutenant in 1926. In 1944 he was captain and chief of Regiment No. 3 in Santa Clara when he was retired by President Ramon Grau for his ties to Batista. He participated in the conspiracy of the coup d'état of Batista and promoted the following day to lieutenant colonel. He was head of Regiment No. 4 of the Rural Guard in Matanzas when the Goicouría barracks was attacked by Authentic rebels on April 29, 1956. He was appointed chief of the National Police on March 19, 1958, and suffocated the April 9 insurrection in Havana. On 13 August 1958 he was promoted to Brigadier General of the Army. He went into exile with his sons Irenaldo and Roberto on January 1, 1959, with the Tabernilla and others on the plane that took them to Jacksonville, Florida. He died in Queens, N.Y.

and wanted Cuba to be well represented. Why call me, then? For having won the trophy "Colonel Batista," back in 1935.

The team gradually became more precise. While it cannot be said that I was a great rider, the others were. This was the final organization:

> Team Leader: Captain Rodríguez Sáenz.
>
> Members: Lieutenant [Gerardo] Padrón [Pérez]
>
> Lieutenant Capote.
>
> Lieutenant Diaz Tamayo.

I can hardly argue in favor of horses. After Machado's fall, this kind of event had failed. At the moment, there were no good jumpers. They had to be acquired in haste in the United States. With them we moved to Columbia, where we were allocated a space for accommodation, and part of the Polygon for jumping practices.

I found Camp Deeply Modified. On my departure for Oriente, the renovation work was already beginning. They were now in full development. The former wooden barracks, built in 1901 by the United States Army, gave way to comfortable, spacious, and airy masonry barracks. On the other side of the Polygon the officers' houses, also made of wood, were transformed into beautiful residences.

The General Staff, on the other hand, did not continue in the Castillo de La Fuerza. No doubt remembering how easily he was taken on August 12; Colonel Batista moved him to Columbia.

There he occupied, until 1959, the old building of the School of Application. Thus, the chief remained amid his troops, and not an hour's walk from them.

We're sailing for Chile! A White Fleet ship[69] took us aboard, horses and knights. The journey lasted eighteen days. We played in Colombia, crossed the Panama Canal; we also made stops in Ec-

---

[69] The White Fleet was the steam service of the United Fruit Company that for 108 years, until 2007, transported cargo and passengers in the Western Hemisphere.

uador and Peru, until, finally, we landed in Valparaíso. From there to Viña del Mar, where we were housed in the barracks of the Coraceros Regiment. Magnificent place, and hospitality, royal.

In the competitions that followed, the United States, Bolivia, Chile, Ecuador, Peru, and Cuba were represented. There were only military teams and, once held, we moved to another in Santiago de Chile, where civilian teams took part. We Cubans saved the honor, but little else. Impossible to compete with the formidable jumpers presented by other countries! But competing gives experience, peace of mind, self-confidence. The setbacks in Chile earned us future victories.

I was very impressed by what I saw of the Chilean Army. Extremely rigid discipline, Prussian model. I understand that nothing has changed. It is not surprising that, a hundred years ago, Chileans defeated the Peru-Bolivia coalition. It is the Chilean Army that has saved Chile from communism.

Our absence from Cuba lasted 60 days. This trip to Chile was the beginning of what I came up with as my "equestrian stage." I remained on the team for five years and naturally took part in multiple national competitions. At that time, as soon as we got back from Chile, we started preparing again to compete, now in Madison Square Garden. We went there in November 1938[70]. There, our role turned out to be considerably airier than in the Southern Cone and, when we finished, we moved on to Canada, where we took part in the Royal Winter Fair. At the end, en route again, and now to Mexico, where we appear in new competitions. What a time! How nostalgic it is to remember her! These equestrian events were accompanied by brilliant parties. They would be attended by the best riders in the world, and all enhanced by the presence of beautiful women, from high pan-American and Euro-

---

[70] Díaz Tamayo arrived in New York from Havana in the S.S. Orizaba on October 18, 1938, accompanied by Commander Cecilio Pérez Alfonso and Lieutenants Luis Cantón, René Chipi Córdova, Ángel C. Fajardo, Manuel Hernández, Gerardo Padrón Pérez, and veterinary officer Tulio Figarola. They carried eight horses to compete against the military riders of four other nations at the 55th National Horse Show, Madison Square Garden, New York, November 5-12, 1938. The trophy winners were U.S. Army officers from Fort Riley, Kansas.

pean society. Sometimes, when contemplating myself in that dazzling environment, I could not help but compare my present with my days as an agricultural worker, cutting cane or collecting pineapples for less than two pesetas a day. What a change! How right I was when I smashed my guataca into a tree and enlisted in the Army!

At the beginning of 1939 we returned to Columbia, and I learned that there were prospects for first lieutenant competitions. I don't have to say that I immediately started preparing for them. I was also given the opportunity to enroll in an aviation course, and I did. Here's a new experience. After "flying" (flying alone, without the instructor, for the first time) I managed to accumulate 26 hours of flight. It was then that the chief of the aviation, commander [Rogelio] López Jorge, summoned me to his office and said to me:
—My little son (he said my little son to everyone), if you aspire to be a war pilot, you are welcome, but I just found out that you are also preparing for the competitions for first lieutenant of infantry. Listen to my advice: decide on one of the two things, because you will lack the time to prepare properly, and you will not play a good role, neither here nor there.

López Jorge was right. I was biting more than I could chew, and I made up my mind for the infantry! I was a foot soldier or a horse soldier. As an aviator, I would never be anything but a dilettante.

However, not even in the infantry had my time come. My opponent was the cadet-graduate [Eduardo E.] Martin Elena. The possession of a decoration, granted in those days to this officer by the Mexican government, tipped the balance in his favor by 62 hundredths of a point.

I was still second lieutenant, but not for long. A year later there were again opposition and, at last! I ascended. He had stayed six years in the grade.

This promotion to first lieutenant led to my appointment as Assistant to the Third Tactician. I mean, I went to the cavalry. In many ways this gratified my ego. I had not forgotten that back in 1926, Captain Colin Herrera wanted to enlist me in that unit when, for a moment, Battalion 2 thought it had no vacancies. Now I came to be, practically, the second head of the same, but for me it had an inconvenience: the Help of a unit is an eminently administrative position, and although I transmitted and enforced the provisions of the Commander, I had no direct command of troops. I had a consolation, however, and it was that, as a member of the Equestrian Team, I continued to ride for several hours a day.

WORLD WAR II

As always, I leave it to historians to detail the history of Cuba from 1933 onwards, but I would like, on my own, to say a few words on the subject.

From 1933 to 1944, Batista led the state ship. My opinion is that he did it skillfully. To avoid setbacks, it adhered strictly to the foreign policy of the United States. He even obeyed his slightest instructions. In exchange for his loyalty, and the reassurance it provided to Washington, Batista made multiple concessions to Cuba. Some were of an economic nature; another was the repeal of the Platt Amendment.

In the United States, President Roosevelt had produced a real economic revolution. But as his reforms found strong resistance in the conservative classes, in order to carry them out he was relying more and more on the left. Naturally, if you go too far to the left, you end up running into the Communists, and this is what happened to Roosevelt. The communists make a deal with the devil if it suits their interests. Always few in number, but very disciplined, they obeyed Russia's orders to support Roosevelt to his last consequences, and the president, in need of this support, also clung to them to his last consequences.

In Cuba, the Communists had at all times waged war against Batista. Against him, the students were whipped. Against him, there were riots such that the institutes and the University were closed down again. Later, in 1935, they contributed to a general strike, similar to that of 1933 against Machado. It was believed that this strike would be the final blow against "Sergeant" Batista. However, the strike failed, in what then-Colonel Pedraza had much to do with the government's triumph.

But now comes the good news: suddenly, orders come to the Communists to move into the ranks of the government, and to Batista, from Washington, the "suggestion" to open their arms to these. From that date, until 1944, the year in which Batista left the presidency, they marched, holding hands, and among reciprocal praise, without a cloud overshadowing the idyll.

How to prosecute this fact? Batista is accused of having legalized the Communist Party, and of ministering to several of its members. Correct! The accusation is valid, but I also believe that, if it did not, he would have been in trouble with the State Department.

For the time being, this pairing meant peace for the government. Communists don't recognize morality. For them there is only the "Party line." Their twisted maneuvers, their betrayals, are called "fighting tactics." Our sense of what is good and what is bad is for them a "bourgeois prejudice." Until the integration of the communists with the government, strikes, conspiracies, bombs and attacks followed one another. From this moment on, everything marched on honey flakes, because the "comrades" had no problem in denouncing the allies of yesterday, and in disrupting any attempt against Batista.

Of all these events prior to the Batista-Communismo alliance, I will refer, and I will be forgiven for this sentimentality, to the death of a corporal of the Army by the last name "Man"[71]. This corporal belonged to Regiment No. 4, of Matanzas, and was among the forces of the Rural Guard sent to recognize the presence of suspicious personnel in a former Spanish fort to the west of the city. The detachment surrounded the site, the occupants tried to flee and opened fire upon being told to stop. Man, who remained standing directing the movements of his squad, was hit and fell dead. Two of those trying to escape also died, Mr. Antonio Guiteras and an "internationalist" who accompanied him[72].

---

[71] Marcelo Man.

[72] Antonio Guiteras Holmes (November 22, 1906-May 8, 1935) was born in Philadelphia and at the age of 7 the family moved to Cuba where he graduated from high school and surveyor in 1924 in Pinar del Río. He received the title of Doctor of Pharmacy from the University of Havana on August 20, 1927. On April 29, 1933, he participated in the assault on the small barracks of San Luis,

Much was said about the death of Guiteras who, under Grau, was a minister. On the other hand, its disappearance detracted from the insurrectionary opposition. The death of human beings is always to be regretted, especially if this death is due to the heat of political passions. But let us not forget either the humble soldier: his widow, his mother, his children. Because, believe it, reader, soldiers, usually from the less fortunate layers, have mothers, women and children who need them and who mourn them.

Man's companions erected a simple cenotaph at the site of his fall, which was later destroyed, and in person, by Mr. Eddy Chibás[73].

Oriente. On September 10, 1933, President Grau appointed him Minister of the Interior, controlling the appointment of municipal mayors. On October 25, the Secretary of War and Navy was absorbed by the Government, strengthening Guiteras' command. When Grau's government was overthrown, he created the organization Young Cuba to take power through armed struggle. The group was funded for theft, extortion, and the kidnapping of Eutimio Falla Bonet on April 3, 1935, for a ransom of $300,000. Two weeks later, Guiteras was indicted for the crime along with a dozen of his supporters. When he tried to flee the island on May 8, 1935, Guiteras and Venezuelan revolutionary Carlos Aponte Hernández were killed during a shootout with the Army and fifteen supporters were arrested.

[73] Eduardo Chibás Rivas (August 20, 1907-August 16, 1951) was born in Santiago de Cuba where he attended the Dolores School and later the Belén School in Havana. His father, a wealthy engineer, was Minister of Public Works in the interim government of President Carlos Manuel de Céspedes. He entered the University of Havana in 1926 and was listed on the University Student Directory. During the struggle against the Machado regime, he suffered imprisonment and exile with his father when they were both accused of planting bombs. He joined the Authentic Party in 1936. He was elected as a delegate to the Constituent Assembly in 1939 after a mysterious attack where he received a small-caliber line shot in the side. Elected to the House of Representatives by the province of Havana in 1940. Elected senator for the same province in 1944. In 1947 he founded the Cuban People's Party (Orthodox) and the following year he failed in his presidential aspiration. In 1950 he was elected senator of Havana in the by-elections to fill the vacant record of the late senator José M. Alemán. His weekly shrill radio denunciations during 1943-1951 against government corruption, real or imagined, provoked controversies and duels. The blind agitator was slightly wounded in sword duels with Senator Santiago Rey Pernas (1945), Minister of State Alberto Álvarez, Senator Francisco Prío Socarrás and Minister of Labor Carlos Prío Socarrás (1947) and Senator José Manuel Casanova (1949). Sentenced to six months in prison in 1949 for falsely accusing three Supreme Court justices of bribery. President Prío pardoned him after a month. Unable to prove his accusation that Education Minister Aureli-

How did that dead man, that soldier who had fallen in the line of duty, bother Lord Chibash? I received my gratitude to Mr. [Pedro E.] Pérez Mejides. This journalist was the only one, to my knowledge, who in full reaction against Batista wrote an article on the subject. It was published in *Bohemia*, and in it appears Mr. Chibás destroying the small funerary monument[74].

I hope I'm forgiven for this digression. Let us now return to the subject.

It is well known that, in 1917, the declaration of war by the United States against Germany brought with it a similar declaration by Cuba. In 1941 history was repeated. Germany had not offended us at all on either occasion, but that does not detract from the fact. Both Menocal in 1917 and Batista in 1941 acted on the geopolitical principle of finding our destiny inextricably linked to that of the United States. The question of whether or not Cuba would send its troops to the front appeared on the table. In anticipation that this would be the case, a Cuban military mission was sent to the United States naval base at Guantánamo to receive combat training in a naval infantry unit. The group consisted of eight junior officers and eight sergeants. Because he was the top grader, I was in front of him. I remember the names of some of its members: second lieutenants [Francisco] Tabernilla, the two brothers Valdés Jiménez (one from La Cabaña and another from Columbia), Radillo, Lage, Ramos and Marrero. This last godson of then President Batista.

[Two pages of the four-page manuscript are missing here, from 67 to 70. The period covers the time he divorced his first wife and remarried.]

Dr. Ramón Grau San Martín was undoubtedly the figure of the moment. The demonstrations of jubilation bordered on delirium.

---

ano Sánchez Arango had stolen school funds, he took a bullet in the lower abdomen during his radio show. He convalesced in the hospital for eleven days and died of internal bleeding after receiving a blood thinner. He never married.

[74] The monument to Corporal Marcelo Man was a small concrete column, two kilometers from El Morrillo, a few meters from the river Canímar. Chibás destroyed it on May 8, 1946, on the eleventh anniversary of Guiteras' death, in repudiation of Batista, who had been out of the country for more than a year.

In the inaugural parade, in front of the Palace, I remember a poster with the images of Martí and Grau. The sign that accompanied them read: "God enlighten you, Cuban dreamer!" A cartoon also appeared in the press in those days. You could see two men in it. One of them wiped his sweat with a handkerchief, saying, "What a barbarity! How hot it is!" And the other replied: "Don't worry. Let Grau go up."

It should be noted that all these expressions of enthusiasm were generally peaceful. However, here is an episode that I witnessed, and that shows to what extent, at times, the mob can be cruel and unconscious. On January 28 of each year a school stop was held in the Central Park of Havana. Students from public and private schools paraded along the Paseo del Prado, flowed into the Central Park and laid flowers before the statue of the Apostle Marti. On January 28, 1945, as the students of the Civic-Military Institute, the work of Batista, approached them, many spectators shouted all kinds of insults at them. The performance of the police was poor and did not dare to intervene. The boys and girls who made up the contingent, very disciplined, continued their march. The voice of the instructors was heard among the shouts and denoutions: "Stand firm! Stand firm! Face forward! Face forward! Stand firm! Stand firm!" until you pass the park and go out again to the Prado. I can imagine how those little hearts would beat, frightened like birds, without knowing what was happening, or why they were mistreated in that way. In fact, the students of the Civic-Military Institute were poor children, mostly orphans. Their only crime was to be advantaged pupils in their respective home schools. For them Batista, Grau, the Authentic, were as alien to them as the planet Mars. What imprint would such a terrible experience leave on their souls?

The work of the historian is arduous. It requires patient research work for which I have neither time nor vocation. I prefer to let my memories work with their subjectivisms, their successes and inaccuracies, although as seen in the course of what I have written, I often rely on some text to give greater consistency to what is narrated. See, for example, how I view the 'genuine' process from its inception until 1952.

In 1926, Communist infiltration began at the University of Havana. Manipulated by them, the student agitation against Machado was becoming more and more marked. They fought firmly, they had their heroes and their martyrs, but when Machado fell, their background and their youth meant that they were not taken into consideration. In forming a government, Sumner Welles thought more of mature, conservative men. It is said that, when the students were mentioned to him, the ambassador replied: "What these boys have to do is return to the classrooms!"

What frustration! How could they think that they would return to their desks, as if so many years of conspiring, bombing and carrying out attacks were a summer holiday? His age and circumstances were different. By the time the university was closed, the vast majority of his economically able peers had continued their career abroad and were already professionals. They were just... revolutionaries.

The sergeants' coup, by calling them to form the civilian part of the government, turned out to be a golden opportunity for them. For a short time, they and other more radical elements liberated the exquisite elixir of power. Oh! Months later, when Batista expelled them from the government, they were again, as they say, "on the street and without a key." They had to make their way through life without a trade. Nor was the type of individual who threw himself into student struggles the most appropriate to learn one, devote himself to it entirely, and join the peaceful and hardworking citizenship.

The immediate solution was the ease that the university gave in those times to finish studies. Through three or four month courses, part of the lost time could be earned. And what career do you study? Well, of course, the law. The Spanish proverb reads: "The lawyers live from fools and fools." The legal profession is not a technical profession in the sense of, for example, engineering. In the United States they are not recognized for any special treatment and are called 'Mister'. In France, the term 'Maître' is used to refer to craftsmen. As far as I know, only in Cuba were they "doctors." Just by memorizing a series of texts, we obtained a doctorate in law at our university, and let's not delve too deeply into the question of how some of them obtained their degree. Let us say, however, that their quality as "revolutionaries" was of great value to them. Whether or not they later exercised the career was something else and, in truth, some of those boys never went to a law firm.

But in their few months of government, they had enacted very good laws (others not so good) that had gained them popularity, and always with the communists as subtle mentors, they founded the *Cuban Revolutionary Party*. The members of this party called themselves the only authentic revolutionaries; hence the name that always distinguished them. It was not long before they were joined by the most popular layers and a lot of middle class. The Communists made common cause with them in their new stage of struggle, now against Batista, but in 1935 they passed to the government with weapons and baggage, which the real ones never forgave them.

In 1944, the real people came to power with incredible credit. I dare say that they had in their hands the political regeneration of Cuba. Failure to do so led to the spiritual collapse of the country that had long been expected of them. This could be seen in the indifferent acceptance of the people in the face of the coup d'état, of which I was one of the protagonists.

Over the course of the days, the credit of the real ones began to decrease. From page 350 of Márquez-Sterling's History of Cuba, the painful progression of its deterioration is clearly exposed. Well, although, as a result of the Second World War, Cuba's economy continued to boom, the political inexperience of the rulers soon began to manifest itself, aggravated by the weakness of the Executive before his family and friends. In a press interview in Miami, a government minister[75] openly stated that he had taken

---

[75] José Manuel Alemán Casharo (January 20, 1905-March 25, 1950) Son of General José Braulio Alemán Urquía, secretary of Public Instruction and Fine Arts of the government of Machado. He served in the ABC organization and was imprisoned in 1933. During Batista's presidency he was an obscure employee of the Ministry of Education, head of the Personnel, Assets and Accounts Section financed the construction of the ballpark later called BobbyMaduro, and through

more than $100 million, and when reporters asked him, "How could you possibly take so much money?" He replied, smiling: "Well, very simple: in suitcases."

Several members of the government organized gangsters to settle their differences with a clear shot. Grau granted police appointments to many of these individuals, thus protecting them in their activities. Anyone who rereads the press of that time will be able to get an idea of the tragic situation the Republic was going through, and to what extent gangster gangs became powerful, since there was a time when so many appointments were granted and so many excesses were allowed, that the authority escaped from the hands of the President. In Orfila, Marianao, two rival factions whose members held official positions within the security forces, clashed in a battle that lasted for hours. One of the chiefs, Morín Dopico, and his wife were killed[76]. Several of his supporters also fell, including one named Armando Tró[77]. The battle ended only when, acting on his own, Army Chief[78] ordered a tank company to intervene.

In another of their Marxist backwardness, the real ones began to meddle in Central America. Nicaragua, Honduras, Guatemala, and

---

the Ansana Corporation invested in multiple real estate and land. He died of Hodgkin's cancer at his home in Alturas de Miramar, Havana.

[76] Antonio Jesús Morín Dopico (December 10, 1916-1980s) expelled from the University of Havana for being leader of the "bonche" of gunmen. He was unharmed and his pregnant wife, Aurora Soler, fell when she left the house under fire. Morín died in Havana in the 1980s.

[77] Emilio Tro Rivero (June 18, 1918-September 21, 1947) sentenced to one year in prison in 1935 for unlawful association and sabotage. He served in the National Revolutionary Alliance (ANR) and in 1939 was a member of Acción Revolucionaria Guiteras (ARG). He was arrested for the attempted murder of police chief Mariano Faget in 1941. He fled to Mexico and from there to Los Angeles, California, on September 1, 1942, where he enrolled in the U.S. Army. During World War II he never saw combat and was assigned to the Combat Personnel Replacement Centre in Toome, Northern Ireland, where he was naturalized as a U.S. citizen on April 21, 1944. Upon returning to Cuba, he organized and led the nationalist Revolutionary Insurrectionary Union (UIR) in which Fidel Castro was a member. On July 8, 1946, Tro murdered the secret police officer Julio Abril Rivas and the head of the Public Works Police Bruno Valdés Miranda.

[78] General Genovevo Pérez Dámera.

Costa Rica were affected by the activities of the "Legion of the Caribbean," financed by Cuba and composed of Cubans and other "internationalists." Authentic government was also contested with the Dominican Republic. In Cayo Confites, in northeastern Cuba, a force of revolutionary students and regular unemployed was concentrated (among them was Fidel Castro). His mission was to land in Santo Domingo and overthrow the then President Trujillo. This force set sail for its destination on a ship that, fortunately, was intercepted by a Navy frigate. I understand that, also in this case, the head of the Navy acted on his own, given the absence of orders from the Executive and the seriousness of the matter. Finally, in the recreational estate of a government minister (the same one who took the money in suitcases) the Rural Guard occupied a real arsenal, destined for Caribbean adventures.

All of these cases have some family resonance. They remind us of a little of the current adventures of communism in Central America and in Santo Domingo in the time of President Johnson. Actually, they have their point of contact. The political education of the student generation of '33 was due to the Marxists. Some of them had even served in the ranks of the Party. In the 1940s they were rabidly anti-communist, but they still knew not how to act but how they had been taught.

In 1948 there were new elections, won by Dr. (also of those lawyers) Carlos Prío Socarrás. This was Grau's candidate, and the circumstances in which those elections were won are well explained on pages 350 to 352 of Marquez-Sterling's aforementioned work. It cannot be said that there were electoral irregularities in Estrada Palma or Menocal. What is positive is that things continued as before, and in some cases even worse.

Grau did the same with one of his oldest champions, also lawyer Dr. Eduardo Chibás. For years, this, from a radio station consumed an hour on Sundays, from 8 to 9 p.m. Before 1944 his voice was raised in favor of the Authentic Party and its boss Dr. Grau San Martin. Then, gradually, his broadcasts adopted an increasingly pronounced tone of criticism, until he launched accusations against the government after accusation of the worst things imaginable. There was no fraud, theft, illegal trade or smuggling that was not reported, and the accusation was substantiated with the corresponding evidence. At the end of the administration Grau undertook it, even more viciously, against Prío. His terrible verbal picket was demolishing, week after week, the government building. He also founded a political party he called "Orthodox," because of the correctness of its intentions. Chibás promised that, once they won the next elections, he would sweep away all that "herd of thieves." And to put more emphasis on his intentions to sweep, his supporters tied a broom to the mudguard of their cars. Among his plans was to prosecute and confiscate property that had been misused. Naturally, the radical nature of their aims attracted the Communists, who soon received orders to join orthodoxy[79]. Chibás died in 1951, because of a shot that he himself unlocked in the belly, but the party had already acquired an alarming strength. An example of what could be expected was when, in 1950, President Prío nominated his brother Antonio for Mayor of Havana. As a contrast, an immense majority of voters voted for their opponent, Mr. [Nicolás] Castellanos[80]. That night the capital was illuminated and there were celebrations in the streets. The symptom couldn't be more ominous.

---

[79] Eduardo Chibás and the Cuban People's Party (Orthodox) always maintained a political line opposed to communism and not to agree with any party.

[80] Nicolás Dionisio Castellanos Rivero (December 6, 1911-February 10, 1985), born in Matanzas. Mayor of Havana 1948-1952. Exiled in Miami on December 16, 1960, where he later died.

CHAPTER IV

THE ARMED FORCES 1944-1952

If something did not interest the real ones it was the Army, because how can we forget that it was this army that marginalized them from power in 1933? In 1944, when Batista handed over the government to them, he also handed over this Army to whom, before leaving, he urged them to obey the new administration elected by the people of Cuba. A boss tried to protest and was promptly withdrawn. The others simply obeyed.

It was this moment when the real ones, if they had greater experience, could have taken over the hearts of the soldiers. It wasn't that hard. The military only knows how to obey his immediate superior. In exchange for his obedience, he hopes that his person will be respected, in his degrees, in the things he believes in. The leaders who at that time held the command were, of course, the product of September 4, but they were also apolitical, and as leaders, men of little importance. He would have agreed to leave them in his command, then withdraw them, little by little, for years of service.

Far from this, Grau adopted the method of inviting them to lunch at the Palace and, after lunch, returning to their barracks, finding that they had been removed. None of those generals had the slightest roots in the troop, and their disappearance did not excite anyone, but the way Grau followed was somewhat mocked, and the press, in festive echo, was responsible for ridiculing the fact. For us, so respected under Batista, that was the first grievance.

Why did Grau appoint Commander [Genovevo] Pérez Dámera as Chief of Staff? Because he was the only officer I knew. Their relationship dates to 1934, when Grau, after his deposition, went into exile. By order of Batista, the then Lieutenant Pérez Dámera accompanied Grau into exile. The way the lieutenant carried out his mission earned him the recognition of the former president, and this paid his dividends in 1944.

That the exaltation of this commander to the generalate and chief of staff violated the order of precedence, military ranking and ethics did not give Grau cold or heat. What mattered was to have at the head of the armed institution a man who owed himself exclusively to him. Now the President could sleep peacefully and he, once this delicate matter had been resolved, left us alone.

Before moving on, it should be noted that Batista was not too scrupulous about promotion and staging, but Batista could do things with the soldiers that were forbidden to others. He was "of the house" and knew how to speak to them and leave them satisfied.

In my opinion, the command of General Pérez Dámera showed, for the moment, a positive balance. No other Chief of Staff, except President Batista himself, enjoyed such absolute freedom of action. He used this freedom to the full. Batista's attitude to the soldiers was always to please them; that of General Pérez Dámera, to train them and modernize his equipment. The Managua Camp, built during the war to house the conscripts of the Compulsory Military Service, or Emergency Service, as it was called, became the headquarters of the General Schools of Classes and Recruits. From then on, the regiments sent the newly enlisted personnel and aspiring officers and sergeants to Managua where, with greater means than in their parent units, they received higher and more uniform instruction. The School of Cadets also moved from El Morro to Managua. The buildings, picaderos, shooting and maneuvering fields, begun under Batista, were completed in Grau's time and, in 1945, the move took place. A little historical touch: Managua, about 20 kilometers southeast of Havana, was used in 1762 to keep in custody the prisoners taken from the English who besieged Havana. Also, a ship captain named Don Ignacio de Madariaga[81] organized and maintained from there the supply of the capital. According to the chronicles, he did an excellent job.

---

[81] Juan Ignacio de Madariaga Aróstegui (18th century - March 30, 1771) was wounded in a naval battle against the English in Cabo de San Antonio, Cuba, on December 12, 1744. Madariaga delegated to Governor Juan de Prado the government of the interior of the island during the siege of Havana by the English.

For us it was the Military Academy Center, although in general, the entire Army received the vigorous jolt of General Pérez Dámera. Also, during his tenure we were free from interference from politicians. This general felt a visceral aversion for them and for the journalists, of whom he said: "Journalists are beaten or paid." The press took revenge by ridiculing him in cartoons or comments, but without daring to go any further, because the president's support was absolute.

Although the army's readiness increased dramatically, it should not be inferred that General Pérez Dámera was popular with the soldiers. His treatment of subordinates was arrogant and despotic. His famous inspections, which multiplied throughout the garrisons of the Island, brought terror to the hearts of the bravest. Unexpectedly, the same thing fell on the command of a regiment as on a distant post commanded by a corporal or a sergeant. Upon arrival, the inspection officers entered, without ceremony, the various units, scrutinizing even the smallest details of the armaments and administration books. Errors, irregularities, were punished with transfers and withdrawals, with no other legal procedure than the general's disposition. Public was the anecdote that, when the caravan of vehicles of the general and his entourage appeared in front of a barracks, the sentry, instead of shouting: — Corporal Guard: form the Guard! "Chief of Staff!" he cried out in anguish: "Help!"

When the Grau government passed to Prío, General Pérez Dámera was ratified in his position. For a while, things went well between the two. Moreover, and as a courtesy of the general, an increasing number of soldiers went on to work, as free labor, on the estates of the President (and of the Army Chief himself, who, by the way, had rounded up a small fortune). Naturally, this recharged the service of the line troops, who saw their numbers diminish in favor of dozens and dozens of soldiers who were on special duty. During the Republic, there were always special services, but never on the scale that, beginning in Grau's time, lasted until 1952.

As a result of the naval combat of 10 June 1770, he expelled the British from the Falkland Islands.

There is no doubt that General Pérez Dámera managed to have the Army in a fist, until he could say, as in fact he said or was attributed to him: "The Army will do what I command it." But in the long run, that confidence in his own strength was fatal to him. The government's discredit was growing. Street attacks and fighting between the various groups continued to be more and better. It was then that some mischievous little devil brought to the general's mind the idea that he was the one called to redeem Cuba. Didn't he have in his hands the real source of power that rifles are? And this idea was reinforced by the president of Santo Domingo because, in effect, as long as the real ones remained in power, the disturbance of the Caribbean would not cease, and Trujillo saw in a Cuban coup the solution to this problem. I do not know how far the agreements between the two arrived, but it is true that General Pérez Dámera sent an Air Force plane to the Dominican Republic. There was a colonel in him, a man the general trusted. Although I never knew what they agreed to, nor what message it brought back.

However, the President vented the danger. Prío was not without personal value. He also knew how to use the surprise factor and acted accordingly. The general was spending the weekend on his estate in Camagüey when he received a phone call from the President himself. He was, at that time, in his own office in union with his brothers and his military assistants.

From this office of the Chief of Staff, in the Columbia Camp, where he arrived unexpectedly, he informed General Pérez Dámera that he had just signed a decree withdrawing it. He appointed in his place Brigadier General Ruperto Cabrera[82], who himself promoted to Major General, and since General Pérez Dámera had eliminated all the generals, except Cabrera, Colonels

---

[82] Ruperto Cabrera Rodríguez (March 27, 1900-December 2, 1986) born in Baez, Santa Clara. His son, Captain Mario Cabrera Bosque, was an airman for the Army Air Force. On March 20, 1951, he was awarded the Legion of Merit medal by President Harry Truman for "outstanding meritorious conduct in the performance of outstanding services to the United States government from June 1950 to February 1951. He sought asylum in Miami in 1968 where he later died.

[Otalio] Soca Llanes[83] (Assistant General), Elias Horta[84] (Headquarters-Master General) and [Quirino] Uría[85] (Inspector General) were promoted to Brigadier General.

General Pérez Dámera accepted his retirement in a sporting spirit. Asked by the journalists about the reason for this act by the President, he replied: —The President withdrew me because he wanted to.

Here's what things are. If the Chief of the Army were in his post and the President was arrested, the soldiers would have obeyed him without hesitation. Such was the existing discipline and fear that this chief came to inspire. Conversely, when the troop experienced the retreat of General Pérez Dámera, its jubilation was indescribable. I saw soldiers hugging and crying with joy in front of the Columbia barracks.

The Army now entered a quiet stage. General Cabrera was a gentle man. Nothing centralizing, he let his subordinates act, among whom, by the way, were very capable men. One of the new generals, Horta, was a man of incredible probity. Of modest origin, and a product of September 4, it had opened step by step. Chief of regiment for several years, finally reached the generalate on the occasion I have referred. He was entrusted with no less than the custody of the army's wealth: that is, the Headquarters-Master General. Why didn't Prío study better the character of the man he intended for that position? Because once in office, Horta made the

---

[83] Otalio Soca Llanes (December 1, 1905-January 25, 1978), was a sergeant in the Army who was promoted to captain after the Revolution of 1933 and in 1943 was colonel-in-chief of the Aviation Corps. In March 1945 he was assigned to the command of Regiment No. 4 in Matanzas. On the night of March 10, 1952, he went into exile in Miami. He later returned to Cuba, returning to Miami on July 31, 1964, where he later died.

[84] Elias Horta Suarez (August 4, 1892-?) born in Melena del Sur. In 1945 he was colonel and head of the Eighth Infantry Regiment, being transferred on 24 August 1949 as head of Regiment No. 7 "Máximo Gómez."

[85] Quirino Uría López (June 15, 1907-January 29, 1984), a native of Los Palacios, Pinar del Río, was a general of the Army when on September 22, 1949 he was appointed chief of the National Police, a position he held until he returned to the Army on September 4, 1951. His son landed with the 2506 Brigade in Playa Girón and was captured. He sought asylum in Miami, where he later died.

Army budget his own, and minutely kept track, in pesos and cents, of the last penny that was spent. If he were a little more flexible, if he had listened to certain suggestions that were made to "sotto voce," Horta would have made many people happy, and he would have ended up a millionaire. Far from that, he opposed unnecessary expenses, dubious purchases, suspicious supply contracts.

Medel, co-author of this book, recalls that as he was General Horta's aide-de-camp, he came to see him as the chauffeur of the mistress of one of the most important characters in the government. This driver was the bearer of a message, in which the general was asked to have the lady's car repaired in the workshops of San Ambrosio. The general replied: — Lieutenant, tell that driver to go to the garage, to have the vehicle fixed there and to charge the arrangement to my personal account. As for the gentleman, you call him personally and tell him that he knows very well that in the Army workshops private cars are not repaired.

A man of this temperament was a bone pierced in the throat of many people: it was not long before it was removed. He was replaced by Colonel [José H.] Velázquez [Perera], who ascended to the generalate, but fearing that Velázquez would turn out to be another Horta, was sent on secondment to the 7th Artillery Regiment. The CPR position Quartermaster was occupied by a more adaptable subordinate[86].

In 1948, the War College was established. Its function was to train the officers chosen for the higher grades. The minimum grade required was that of captain. I submitted my application, and it was accepted. The course lasted two years. In the first of these, we use the premises of the Aviation Officers Club as a classroom. Then we passed to the Castillo de Atarés, of so many memories for me.

The students were eighteen, although over time three of them caused casualties. The studies were military, historical, social and economic. The professors were the best available to the Army and

---

[86] In 1950 Colonel José H. Velázquez Perera was head of the "Máximo Gómez" 7th Regiment and Brigadier General Elías Horta Suárez was Army Headquarters-Master General.

the University of Havana. Among the first, I remember Lieutenant Colonel [Manuel] León Calás, and the captains [Mario E.] Forest, San Martín and Codina. As for the university students, the doctors [Herminio] Portell Vilá, [Ramón] Infiesta, [Rafael] García Bárcena, Massin, Valdés, Vivo, Lavin and Mosup. The studies were extremely rigorous, to the extent that to keep up we hardly had time to sleep. I lost a portion of pounds, but at last I was able to get to the end and graduate, I don't remember if in the third or fifth place.

Great importance was given to that first course. Graduation was in Columbia in the mid-1950s. The ceremony, very lucid, consisted of a great lunch at the Officers' Club. Graduates sit at a long table, to the right and left of the President of the Republic, and the rest of the crowd in others. In short, all this meant for me an increase in salary; they also increased our chances of promotion. As a badge, a plaque was created that we would wear at the height of the warrior's left pocket. This badge provoked jealousy, and in the long run, in order to please certain characters, various high-ranking officers were allowed to use it "honoris causa." Vanitas vanitatum!

I returned to Columbia, returned to my unit, and resumed my life as a barracksman, that is, the routine of guard changes, inspections, exercises, maneuvers, and unit administration.

These periodic absences of the Second Company of Battalion 2 already added up a good number since my enlistment in it, back in 1926, and my return was never without emotion: it was like the return of the prodigal son. Of the personnel who were in your ranks when I enlisted, very few were left. The retreats, deaths and transfers, with the consequent replacements, had been renewing the staff, but the spirit and the daily movement were the same. If the recorders existed at that time, and if we could have captured what we could call "military sounds" of 1926 and 1951, we would see that they were more or less the same: the hitting of the butts on the pavement, the hammering of the bolts when, on returning from the exercises, the soldiers unloaded the rifles. The heels in the way of the officers. Through the window of my office came the rumor of rolling platoons.

Then, hour by hour, the horns of the guard corps: pray brightly and splash everything with their short and repeated notes. "Call of the Guard," "Call of officers," "Water, feed and scratching." Then, as the day fell, the martial echoes gradually transformed into long, piercing moans: "Retretta," "Turning off the lights," "Call to Headquarters," "Silence" and something that struck me emotionally from the day I first entered the Camp: the loudness of the command voices. Years went by and I was always impressed. Oh, Army! Army! . . .

But yes, there had been changes. For example, a soldier without a warrior could not be conceived until the Second World War. Now we were all in shirts. The changes in the regulations of the American Army were reflected in ours. In closed-order formations, the showy but very complicated Prussian school gave way to those taken from the ancient Greek phalanx, much simpler, which allowed easier control of the staff and the concentration of more men per unit of space. The following diagram will give you an idea:

	c o o o	c c c c
	o o o o	o o o o
		o o o o
	c o o o	o o o o
Ropes (C)	o o o o	o o o o
		o o o o
	c o o o	o o o o
	o o o o	o o o o
		o o o o
		o o o o

Arms movements had also been simplified. The new semi-automatic Garand rifle was a more delicate weapon than the old Springfield. It required, therefore, a less energetic handling. However, this does not mean that the entire Army received the Garand. This did not reach us until last March 10, 1952, and not for all units.

This is how my life went, and now, with the "Brévet" of the War College, I began to prepare for competitions for commander.

We have said that the armed forces were sometimes entrusted with functions very different from their own, which were intended to make up for the shortcomings of other departments. See this case: the bus company covering transport services for the Havana public was called 'Allied Bus'. Although it was a particular entity, the vitality of its services made the government take a great interest in it. Each bus had its driver and a driver. This gave the exit and the stops of the buses by means of a bell, and charged the tickets, marking what was charged in a mechanical device. Among the various irregularities that had been occurring in the company, the drivers marked less than they charged, then sharing the profit between them and the driver. The disorganization and lack of control reached such an extreme that the bus leadership asked the government for help, which it delegated to the Army, and the General Staff delegated to Colonel [Antonio] Bilbatúa[87], an officer of the former Army. Bilbatua selected a group of officers. Among those selected I was myself and, due to my degree, I was in charge of the operation. I established my command post at the main offices of the Allied Omnibus, located in Belascoaín and San José. This operation took months: the evil was deep, and we had to act energetically. Over time, however, the machinery began to roll smoothly, and the tension of my work diminished. It was then the event that shook my life to its roots. Let Dr. Márquez-Sterling recount the event:

> Nobody had their lives insured, and politicians much less. Jorge Quintana published in *Bohemia* a very interesting study on gangsterism, and showed with numbers and cases that the Republic was dissolved along that path. This streak of attacks and crimes reached its climax when being killed by a gang, in the sight of

---

[87] Antonio Bilbatúa Sanz (1899-) born in Bilbao, Spain. In 1930 he was a cadet at the School of Officers when he accompanied 23 cadets to a course at the Military Academy in West Point, N.Y. He was a colonel and military chief of Santa Clara province in 1952 when he refused to second Batista's coup d'étatand was withdrawn. On July 26, 1953, he was detained for a few days, together with his brother Jesus, to investigate whether they were involved inthe assault on the Moncada barracks, which was negative.

passers-by, the former minister of government of Grau, Alejo Cossío del Pino[88], owner of the Radio-Chain Plant Havana, shot while talking in a cafe on the corner of Belascoaín and San José with the representative Radio Cremata[89], who miraculously saved his life...

I was in my office that day, as usual, when I heard the shots. I looked out the window and saw people running and hiding behind the columns of the arcades. The head of the Traffic Section, Mr. Fernandez, knocked on my door, and together we went down to see what was going on. Mr. Cossio del Pino was sitting on one of the sidewalks of the bar and fell flat on the counter. Blood was beginning to flow from the wounds on his back. Disgusted, I went back to the office and phoned my battalion chief, letting him know[90].

The next day I went to Columbia to pour gasoline into my car and, finding myself in the gasoline bomb, I met a former comrade in

---

[88] Alejo Cossío del Pino (1902-February 12, 1952) born in Avocado, Havana, his origin was a butcher, mechanic and owner of the country restaurant Topeka near Arroyo Arenas. He was councilor of the municipality of Havana (1936-1940) and elected representative to the Chamber of Deputies in that province by the Authentic Party in 1940. He was appointed Minister of the Interior of President Grau in May 1947 and resigned six months later. He was president of the Radio CadenaHabana plant when he was shot 18 times by two UIR members at 8:15 p.m. in the Strand Bar, and three others were injured.

[89] Radio Cremata Valdés (November 15, 1904-July 1, 1998) was born in Santiago de Las Vegas. Graduated in Law from the University of Havana in 1928. He devoted himself to the defense of workers' unions and unions, advising some. In 1933 he was appointed secretary of the Municipal Administration of Havana. Elected to the House of Representatives in 1936 by the Republican Action Party, he was secretary of the House in 1940. Two years later, he joined the Liberal Party and was elected senator. In July 1953 he was appointed secretary of the Batista regime's Advisory Council. He went into exile in Miami on May 19, 1959, and obtained U.S. citizenship on January 2, 1973. He died in Miami.

[90] It could not have been the murder of Alejo Cossío del Pino, which occurred on February 12, 1952. He confuses it with the attack on January 10, 1951, on Antonio Bayer and López Joffre, the head of political information for the newspaper *Tiempo en Cuba* by Rolando Masferrer. Bayer and three employees of the newspaper were machine-gunned at Corbón Bar, located on the corner of Industria and Bernal, by UIR members after 7:30 PM. Bayer died with 39 bullet holes and his companions, and the bar clerk were injured. Bayer was the son of the late captain of the National Police of the same name and a member of the Revolutionary Socialist Movement (MSR) led by Masferrer.

arms, Captain Venegas, to whom I lied about it. I was so impressed, I added phrases like this: "But how long will these things continue to happen?" Possibly I added even harsher concepts, but always on the confidential plane of old friends.

There was everything, but after three days, orders came to my work to present myself in Columbia, at the headquarters of the Regiment. The Assistant Captain brought me in the presence of the Chief of the Regiment, Colonel [Urbano] Matos Rodríguez. I greeted him as if he were a subordinate and he, severing the gesture, ordered me to hand over my pistol and accompany him to the General Staff. We made the entire journey without a word and, once in the General Staff, we went up to General Cabrera's office. He told me to sit in one of the leather armchairs in the office, while he sat in another and Colonel Matos at a certain distance, who kept his eyes on me. General Cabrera referred to me, almost point by point, although with some adjunct, the conversation we had with Captain Venegas, telling me that this constituted a criticism of the government, that my attitude had been subversive, etc. I tried to explain to him that everything had been a conversation with a comrade, based on our old friendship, and how impressed I had been before the murder, almost before my eyes, of Mr. del Pino. The general ordered that my gun be returned and that I remain at my home until further notice.

Days later, I saw the news of my retirement published in the newspaper, "for years of service." Here is the text of the decree, signed by the then Minister of Defense, Dr. (lawyer) Rubén de León:

PRESIDENTIAL DECREE
LIEUTENANT ARRESTED IN LA CABAÑA ...
VARIOUS TRANSFERS

> First Lieutenant Juan Carrillo Ugalde [sic] was arrested in La Cabaña prison, as he met yesterday.
>
> It was also learned that the Second Chief and Territorial Inspector of the District itself, Lieutenant Colonel Ángel González[91],

---

[91] Ángel González Alfonso (June 1, 1890-January 1976) was born in El Vedado, Havana, and enlisted in the army in 1912. The year ascended out and when the

and more than twelve officers of that command, were transferred to Pinar del Río and other territories, respectively.

The President of the Republic, Dr. Carlos Prío Socarrás, signed a decree endorsed by the Minister of Defense, Dr. Rubén de León, ordering the retirement, for years of service, of the captain of the Army Martín Díaz Tamayo, as it was said unofficially[92].

It occurred in the first days of February 1951[93].

---

war of the Chamberlain was appointed first sergeant He participated in the uprising of august 1933 against President Gerardo Machado and in the subsequent September 4 revolution where he was promoted to lieutenant. He helped stifle the November 9, 1933, uprising in Havana and the following year he was appointed assistant captain. During World War II, when the Compulsory Military Service was created, he was promoted to commander-in-chief of a battalion. President Prío appointed him lieutenant colonel when he was assigned to La Cabaña. He was territorial inspector and second head of the "Ríus Rivera" Regiment in Pinar del Río when on June 4, 1951, he passed with equal charge to Regiment No. 10 of Infantry of the Emergency Service. On 10 March 1952, he was appointed as a supervisor of the Castillo del Príncipe prison in the capital. In December of that year, he was appointed second head of Regiment No. 1 in the Moncada barracks in Santiago de Cuba where he remained until he retired from the army in 1955. He arrived in exile in Miami on February 20, 1966, where he later died.

[92] The Emergency Committee of the Council of Ministers had announced on 7 February 1951 that it was proposing "the dispatch to Korea of three companies of the Cuban Regular Army, to fight for the cause of democracy under the banner of the UN." The newspaper Alerta reported that Captain Martin Díaz Tamayo and Lieutenant Manuel Ugalde Carrillo were excluded from the ranks of the Army because they were "heads of sedition" against the proposal. José Duarte Oropesa points out that "Martin Díaz Tamayo and Manuel Ugalde Carrillo caused their exits from the Army cadres for alleged differences and disagreements with the proposed armed expedition to Korea." Herminio Portell Vilá contends that "there were some protests in the barracks and certain officers and soldiers were discharged" for opposing fighting under the UN flag in Korea. «Cuba will send 3 companies to fight in Korea», *Diario de la Marina*, February 8, 1951, page 1; José Duarte Oropesa, *Historiología Cubana* From 1944 to 1959, volume III (Miami: Ediciones Universal, 1974), 147, 199; Herminio Portell Vilá, *Nueva Historia de la República de Cuba* (Miami: La Moderna Poesía, 1986), 620.

[93] The note appeared in the press on February 18, 1951. Brigadier Francisco H. Tabernilla Palmero says in his memoirs that the coup had been prepared since the beginning of 1951 and that "Ugalde Carrillo, who at that time was a lieutenant and was in the plot, spoke to another comrade and he denounced him and there the first suspicion was created by the high command. Díaz Tamayo, who was captain at the

I received the withdrawal card on March 10, 1951.

For me that super injustice upset me. I was married, I had an eight-year-old son, retirement was a misery, I had used all the best of my life in the army, which I adored and never forgot, precisely because of what he has to watch over and support the country and for the same of all the institutions that make the nation great. The army was part of my home, my school, and my relationship with the Church and God.

Like all human beings, I have had good and bad times in my life, but there is no doubt that this blow was the worst of all, and I will never admit that it was deserved. So many years of work, of effort, of sleepless nights trying to improve, to make my way, but always within the Army, my great love, the only area I knew. I, accustomed to order, discipline, uniform, to obey and be obeyed promptly . . . The military, by our way of life, we form, with our women and children, a world apart. To deprive ourselves of that world is to deprive ourselves almost of the air we breathe, and that's what happened to me. It was then that I understood the tragedy experienced by so many others like me in all the years of the Republic, dismissed like this, without investigation and without record, "for high expediency in the service." What a terrible thing not to be able to return to a barracks, to be excluded from the treatment of my former comrades, for whom a retiree was something like a stinker. *Although the military did not have a vote in Cuba, this could be one of the reasons why politicians were less interested in a better deal with the military, even though the military had many family members who did have the right to vote. I had to leave the army because of pressure from the grown-ups, who did the most damage and were better paid.*

There was also the economic question. On March 10, 1951, I received my retirement card, and my pension began to arrive, which was not enough to support my wife and son. My savings began to go, which were not many, because the captain's salary was nothing

---

time, committed another indiscretion. So there were two or three more." As a result, Batista suspended the conspiracy until the end of 1951. Gabriel E. Taborda, *Palabras Esperadas: Memorias de Francisco H. Tabernilla Palmero* (Miami: Ediciones Universal, 2009), 48-49.

of the other world. I had the relief of not paying rent because the house was owned by my wife[94], but I repeat, with my own pension I could not live, and I began to look for additional sources of income.

A former friend, Mr. Eugenio de Sosa Chabau moved his relations and obtained for me a position of collector in the Central Station of the Allied Buses, Avenida de Rancho Boyeros. My job was to receive the money from the taxis that made the station service, which totaled about a hundred. I also regulated their departures and took them time until their return. This job allowed me to go on living but, although I tried to hide it from my wife, my mood was going from bad to worse. He reflected again and again: this is how a government called "democratic" threw an old servant into the void. In any regular army, when a military person commits a crime, an investigator is appointed who collects all the data related to the crime, initiates a file with them, and submits it to the Legal Body that, in turn, initiates or does not initiate the case. The Regulations provide all means for the defendant to defend himself, as is the case in civilian life. However, our "democratic" government adhered to the comfortable practice of retirement for years of service or for high convenience of service.

10th OF MARCH

One good day in October 1951, a former comrade in arms appeared at my work, also withdrawn by identical procedure. Martin —he told me— General Batista knows your case, and he begs you to go see him[95].

---

[94] He resided in the house of his mother-in-law, Aurora Hernández de Tejada y García, which had been manufactured in 1927 by her husband. After her husband's death, the widow made the legal arrangements for the dwelling to remain in equal parts between her and her daughter.

[95] Batista's brother-in-law, Roberto Fernández Miranda, states in his memoirs that he was the one who took Batista's errand to Díaz Tamayo, "who worked at night at the Bus Terminal Station." He adds that they had several meetings at the Kuquine library and that "in one of them Díaz Tamayo objected to General Tabernilla, present there, being appointed head of the Army General Staff." Fernández says that Díaz Tamayo then told him that "In proposing this I commit-

I was dumbfounded. He knew that Batista was in Cuba, that he was a candidate for president for the next elections, but that was all. That he remembered me, who he was so far away from in his years in government, amazed me. So, I told the emissary, who answered me: Well, you are wrong, Batista knows you well. Go see him, he won't weigh you down.

I asked him for three days to think about it. He came back after those three days. "What have you decided?" he asked.

—All right, I'll go see him. I wouldn't read anything into that.

He instructed me to come in at dawn, between 1: 00 and 2: 00. The interview would be at his Kuquine estate, where he lived. He specified that I enter through the front cover of the property, that is, the main entrance.

Actually, I didn't explain myself that much mystery. Batista was legally in Cuba and I, a civilian now and a free man, could see him when I felt like it.

It is worth summarizing here the trajectory of former President Fulgencio Batista in all these years: following the custom of previous presidents, as soon as he handed over power to Dr.

Ramón Grau San Martín, he took the plane and left Cuba. Abroad, his divorce took place and his marriage to his second wife, Mrs. Martha Fernandez[96]. He then made a journey through several countries of Spanish America, establishing, at the end of his itinerary, his residence in Daytona Beach, United States (the house in which he lived is today a museum). During the four years of Grau

---

ted a real recklessness, because I earned the enmity of General Tabernilla who never forgave me."

[96] Martha Fernández Miranda (November 11, 1923-October 2, 2006), daughter of Spanish immigrants, married Fulgencio Batista on November 28, 1945, when he was in Mexico, and she was in Havana. Batista began the divorce of his wife Elisa Godínez in Mexico on September 6, 1945, and ended it in Cuba on November 10. Martha spent her honeymoon at the Waldorf Astoria Hotel in New York. They established residence in Daytona Beach, Florida, until returning to Havana in 1948 on the ferry because Martha had a phobia of flying. The couple had five children when they left Cuba in 1959 and eventually settled in Spain. After Batista died in 1973, Martha resided in West Palm Beach, Florida, until her death due to Alzheimer's.

he did not attempt to return to Cuba, but for the elections of 1948 he ran and was elected, in absentia, Senator of the Republic. Parliamentary immunity enabled him to return safely from many inconveniences, but not from, for example, terrorist attacks. For this reason, he surrounded himself with an escort of former faithful. He settled in Kuquine, an estate he owned about ten kilometers west of Havana. From there he founded a political party, called the United Action Party (PAU) and launched his candidacy for president in 1952. Batista was counting on the people, fed up with the Authentic disorder, to vote for him, even if he were like a lesser evil. The elections for mayor of Havana in which Antonio Prío was a candidate demonstrated the extent to which the vote would be against the government. What he did not take into account was that, with the appearance of the Orthodox Party, the popular vote would go towards that third position. In my opinion, his chances of winning were always minimal, if not null.

These are the conclusions I have come to later. What I thought at the time was that Batista, knowing the difficult situation I was in, called me to offer me some kind of help, or to work for him in the political campaign.

I arrived in Kuquine at the appointed time. Two or three men from his escort were standing guard at the entrance, and when I identified myself, the front page opened and I entered with my "little cacharrito," leaving it right there. One of the escorts led me to the library, which is behind the dwelling house, inviting me to sit in an armchair in the office. Little by little Batista appeared and, it must be said, I was moved. How many memories! The former president symbolized all those years of power, of security, that had already passed and that would not return. In addition, Batista possessed a magnetic personality. He was a man born to command, a command he exercised with quiet dignity. All this influenced to produce in me that emotional state.

I find it impossible to reproduce exactly the conversation we had, but I can say that he followed the logical pattern. That is, first the effusions, the generalities, the memories, the anecdotes. Then, little by little, the sentences became concrete. And it was these, more or less:

Batista:—Well, what do you think about how things are in the country?

Me: —Very bad. You see the fact that gave rise to my retirement. That's the way it goes.

Batista: —And what does the Army think?

Me: —We are quite disgusted. We've been mistreated a lot.

Batista: —What do you think the troops would do if I stood before them?

Me: —About those in the interior of the country I can't say, but Columbia would follow him without hesitation

So far, as you can see, there is nothing definitive or compromising, but once this point was reached, and given my answer, it was to the point.

You've only been out of Columbia a short time, and you know a lot of people there. Would you like to draw me a map of the interior layout of the camp? I would also like a list of officers and soldiers who could be counted on.

I started reciting names to him, but he interrupted me saying, "No." Do that calmly and in writing.

He added not to come back until he warned me. That he would send someone to see me at work, and that he would receive instructions. That next time he would come at night as he had done today. "If you see policemen," he said, "don't worry. But watch out for Military Intelligence Service (SIM) patrols. Commander [Clemente] Gómez Sicre[97] is very careful.

When I was leaving, I asked him what would happen if the conspiracy transcended, as had already happened with others. Batista replied with a smile:

---

[97] Clemente Ricardo Gómez Sicre (February 7, 1912-May 17, 1983) born in Matanzas. Subsequently implicated in Colonel Ramón Barquín's frustrated Conspiracy of the Cigars in 1956. He died in Miami.

—I'll be fine. Prío is not afraid of me, but of the Orthodox. If these win, they take away even the shirt he's wearing. We're going to get the chestnuts out of the fire.

I have always believed that there was an agreement, tacit or express, between Batista and Prío. President Batista was extremely discreet and never revealed, at least in front of me, anything to that effect, except the words I have just quoted. The whole conspiracy, until its culmination in the coup d'état, was carried out in the greatest reserve, but not so much that it was not leaked enough to alert the secret services. I know that they submitted more than one report to President Prío, which was not answered. The then Commander of the Police, [Rafael] Salas Cañizares[98], Chief of the Police Radio Section, was in charge of the custody and surveillance of Kuquine, and the crew of the persecutors were openly fraternizing with the staff of the farm. It will be said that Salas acted on his own, but all that personal at his command, he did not see or did not speak? Moreover, in the early hours of the night of March 10, one of the conspirators, perhaps repentant, called the President. It was one of his aides who answered. The person insisted on talking to the President, but the assistant replied that this was impossible and, finally, the person told the assistant what

---

[98] Rafael Ángel Salas Cañizares (January 16, 1913-October 31, 1956) was born in Cruces, Las Villas, where he studied and graduated as a telegraph artist on September 18, 1930. He joined the Army on September 26, 1933, and obtained the rank of Corporal in the Signal Corps. He was discharged after three years to join the National Police as a guard in the Central Division. In 1938 he was assigned to the Third Station and two years later he was transferred to the 14th Station and placed in service on the Plana Mayor. In 1940 he ascended after studies at the Academy and belonged to the Transit Service until ascending to the rank of sergeant on March 1, 1945. On 3 December 1947 he was promoted to second lieutenant of the Radio-Motorized Section and six months later was first lieutenant. On 14 November 1951, he was appointed Inspector of the Motorized Patrol Service. For his participation in the coup d'état on 10 March 1952, Batista appointed him colonel-in-chief of the National Police. Two months later he was promoted to Brigadier General. On October 29, 1956, in pursuit of the assassins of Colonel Antonio Blanco Rico, he entered the Haitian Embassy with a colonel and two assistants where ten revolutionaries were, six of whom had participated in the attack on the Goicouría barracks. A gunfight broke out and Salas Cañizares was mortally wounded in the intestine below his bulletproof vest.

would happen. This one thanked him and there was everything. Did the message come at the hands of the President? I understand you did, but nothing happened.

I understand that everything I have just said will mortify some, and more than one Cuban of the time will consider it a heresy, but with the greatest respect, such is my opinion, and so I express it.

As General Batista had ordered me, I drew a plan of Columbia, pointing out the current arrangement of the units and other dependencies (I learned later that the President had made an assignment similar to the then First Lieutenant Salas Cañizares, but not being Army Chambers, I was unaware of the interiority of the latter and his report had gaps). I also compiled a list of Columbia staff, which could be referred to. Later, I waited.

The one who came to see me after about two weeks was Dr. [Antonio Nicolás] «Colacho» Pérez[99], member of a well-known Cardinal family. As is well known, Nicholas was later Minister of Defense. I have to say here that he was the most efficient and active of Batista's collaborators in the conspiracy. Colacho and I changed our views and he, on his own, gave me concrete instructions as to interviewing the staff I deemed appropriate. He also set me a date to attend a meeting in Kuquine.

Regarding the former, several accepted, others were frightened and refused to take part in the conspiracy. Also, perhaps, some gave me away, because a few days later a SIM car began to stand guard in front of my house. This surveillance continued until 10 March. This guard made my outings difficult, especially the night ones, which were the ones I used for my contacts. I had no choice but to return every day of my work, park the car in front of my

---

[99] Antonio Nicolás «Colacho» Pérez Hernández (August 6, 1902-August 24, 2001), a native of Cárdenas, served in the ABC organization and had the difficult and dangerous mission of coordinating relations between civilians and military personnel, both in active service and retired, during the conspiracy of the coup of March 10. He was a senator on 1 January 1959 when he was imprisoned in La Cabaña and five months later sentenced to 20 years in prison for his participation in the coup d'état. He arrived in Miami on January 19, 1968, where he naturalized as a U.S. citizen on 11 June 1993. He died in that city.

house as if I were going to retire to rest and then, at night, jump over the wall that separated the bottom of my house from the neighbor, and walk away. So, sometimes I would do my rounds by bus, sometimes in a friend's car.

Sometimes, being essential to use my car, he made me accompany my wife, as if we were going to the cinema or to some visit. By the way, I remember that Rosaura[100] had a fractured leg at that time, and inside the plaster cast she hid the compromising papers.

The date of my second visit to Kuquine has finally arrived, as there were four of them, in total, that I made before the coup.

Those in attendance were, generally Colacho, the retired naval officer (later admiral) [José] Rodríguez Calderón[101], General Batista himself, and myself. On one occasion, the then Joint Chief of Staff, General [Francisco] Tabernilla[102], who at that time was re-

---

[100] His second wife Rosaura Menéndez Hernández de Tejada (July 17, 1917-August 14, 1993).

[101] José Eduardo Rodríguez Calderón (March 14, 1901-November 15, 1987) was born in Santiago de Cuba and was orphaned as a father. He attended Colegio de Belén and entered the Navy on December 13, 1926. He was chief engineer of the shipyards of Casablanca, Cuba. He was a frigate captain in 1945 when he was retired by President Ramón Grau. His support for Batista's coup d'état earned him the rank of Rear Admiral and Chief of Staff of the Navy. He was promoted to Admiral on 19 June 1956. He left Cuba on the plane with Batista in 1959 for Santo Domingo and arrived in Miami on September 8, 1961, where he stayed away from all political activity. He naturalized as a U.S. citizen on November 12, 1971. He was murdered at home along with his niece granddaughter by her husband.

[102] Francisco José Tabernilla Dolz (January 28, 1888-April 22, 1972), a native of Havana, joined the Army as a cadet on June 14, 1921. In 1930 he was a lieutenant when he accompanied 24 cadets to a course at the Military Academy in West Point, N.Y. He supported the September 4 Revolution and was named head of Artillery Regiment 7. In 1941 he was a quartermaster of the Army and the following year he was promoted to brigadier general. Forcibly retired on December 29, 1944, when President Ramón Grau purged the Batista Army and accused it of "ignoring superior orders." He accompanied Batista into exile in Florida. Shortly before returning to Cuba with Batista, he sent a letter to the *Diario de la Marina*, which was published on October 24, 1948, denouncing the rumors that he was returning to conspire against the government. He said that "he will not follow any path in his country other than that of a legal nature." His

tired, attended. It was precisely on that night, when during the conversation I made a slip that earned me the subsequent and constant enmity of General Tabernilla. This is what the mistake consisted of.

When we were discussing the future distribution of command, Batista asked me directly, and only me, who I thought should be the Army Chief. Without much thought, I suggested the then Colonel [Eulogio] Cantillo Porras[103]. Naturally, I was considering exclusively the professional side of the issue. Colonel Cantillo was of the appropriate age, and he was supposed to be very skilled, given the specialization studies he undertook in various academies of the American army. General Tabernilla, although coming from a distinguished family, and being an officer prior to September 4, did not, in my opinion, possess any of these conditions. In my

---

performance in the coup d'état of 10 March 1952 won him promotion that day to major general. He was Chief of Staff of the Army and in 1957 took command of the Joint Chiefs of Staff. In 1959, he settled with his family in West Palm Beach, Florida, where he later died.

[103] Eulogio Amado Cantillo Porras (September 13, 1911-September 8, 1978), born in Mantua, Pinar del Río, graduated from high school in 1928 and was a surveyor until joining the Army on October 3, 1933. In the year he was a sergeant and entered the Cadet School in September 1937. Graduated at three years of second lieutenant and assigned to the 7th Artillery Regiment. In 1942 he was promoted to first lieutenant and took courses in coastal and anti-aircraft artillery in the United States, where he was added to the 602 Anti-Aircraft Artillery Regiment in Long Island, NY. The next year he was captain of a heavy weapons company. After two additional courses in the US, he was appointed director of the School of Cadets in 1947. He was promoted to commander by opposition in 1948 and the following year was appointed chief. of the Aviation Corps, with the rank of lieutenant colonel, and a member of the High War Tribunal. In 1951 he obtained the rank of colonel and after the coup d'état of Batista was appointed assistant general of the Army with the rank of brigadier general. In 1954 he was head of the Infantry Division and two years later he was a member of the Joint Chiefs of Staff of the Army. He received the rank of major general on December 3, 1957. From April to August 1958, he was representative of the Joint Chiefs of Staff in the Bayamo Area of Operations and became chief of operations in the Santiago de Cuba Area from September to December 31, 1958. On January 2, 1959, he was arrested and then sentenced to four years in prison by a Revolutionary Court. However, he was held in prison until 20 April 1967. He left for Mexico on April 17, 1968, and a month later arrived in Miami, where he later died.

opinion, his real aptitude was for Minister of Defense, a well-paid position, but with few responsibilities.

I explained all these reasons with the greatest good faith, for having Batista invited me to express myself with complete freedom. I, who am a man of little talk, that night I talked more about the bill. I did not take into consideration that he was deeply wounding General Tabernilla, and contrary to the President's plans. Tabernilla never forgot an offense, and as for Batista, if he had inherited anything from Machado, it was his suspicion of professional officers. Neither objected to anything at the time, and even the decision was reached that Tabernilla was Chief of the Army for the first six months only, then passing to the Ministry of Defense. As for Cantillo, he would be given the leadership whenever, accepting the reality of the coup d'état, he approached to occupy it, because Colonel Cantillo, Chief of Aviation for those days, had not been initiated into the conspiracy. It was delegated to his brother, the then retired colonel Carlos Cantillo [González][104], but he did not dare to speak to him, and the result was that, by March 10, Eulogio Cantillo knew nothing about him, and this was about to upset our plans.

Another thing I ignored at the time was the close friendship that united Batista with Tabernilla, dating back to 1933. If he was more aware of it, he would have acted with greater tact. But, well, I was ignorant of all those things, and I didn't judge humanity as I judge it today either. Keep in mind that I was always a line soldier and did not look beyond the headquarters of my battalion.

---

[104] Carlos Manuel Cantillo González (October 27, 1907-January 31, 1992) born in Guane, Pinar del Río, is the son of a member of the Rural Guard. He joined the Army as a cadet on October 14, 1925. In 1944 he was retired by President Grau and was engaged in real estate in Miami. After the coup d'état, he was appointed Military Attaché at the Cuban Embassy in Mexico on April 26, 1952. Two weeks later he became head of the Accounts and Payments Section of the Army General Staff. He was colonel on 8 November 1956 when he was appointed head of the Military Intelligence Service. He later became a brigadier. On May 19, 1959, he was sentenced by a revolutionary court to 20 years in prison for implicating him in the death of Pelayo Cuervo. A week later he received an additional 30-year prison sentence for his participation in the Batista coup d'état. He arrived in Miami on August 19, 1970. She applied for U.S. citizenship on March 29, 1976, but was denied two years later. He died in Miami.

Let us therefore return to the action plan. It consisted of two parts: political and military. I'll explain the policy first.

Assuming that, fed up with disillusionment as it was, the Cuban people would accept, if not enthusiastically, at least indifferently the coup d'état. It was not the question of a popular reaction that we should be concerned about at the moment. However, in the long run, free elections would have to be held and power handed over to the victor. That is, both the people of Cuba and the United States government would tolerate perhaps two or three years of de facto rule, after which it would return to normalcy. Not only did General Batista understand this, but he also made it clear to us. We were more concerned about what would happen to the military if a regime that was averse to us took power. Batista explained that the return to normality would be made with all kinds of guarantees for those who now helped him. And that's how it went.

As for the coup itself, the plan took shape, and as it was fulfilled with such precision, in its development the reader will see what it consisted of. It should be noted, however, that it was since the Day Officer, who in every army has command of the unit for 24 hours, was in the plot. It would be the Day Officer who would facilitate our entrance to the Camp. The night of March 10 was set for two reasons: one of the conspirators, Captain [Dámaso] Sogo[105], was the Officer of the Day. The other reason is that being Sunday, al-

---

[105] Dámaso Sogo Hernández (December 11, 1903-January 19, 1982), born in Avocado, Havana. Orphaned by parents, he learned to play the trumpet and joined the Army as a musician on February 6, 1925. He was made an officer with the September 4 Revolution. After the coup d'état, he was promoted to lieutenant colonel. Appointed colonel and head of the 5th «Martí» Regiment in Havana on 18 May 1953; head of Regiment 4 on 17 April 1954; head of Regiment 5 on 20 August 1954; presided over the War Council against the accused in the Conspiracy of the Cigars in April 1956; head of the Inspection Section of the General Aid on 13 April 1957; supervisor of the National Pine Island Prison on 12 August 1957; head of the 10th Infantry Regiment of the Emergency Military Service on 26 September 1957; head of Regiment 7 on 24 March 1958; and assigned to the Directorate of Operations G-1 of the Army General Staff on 23 October 1958. He was a brigadier on January 1, 1959, when he obtained political asylum at the Mexican Embassy and emigrated to Miami, where he naturalized as a U.S. citizen in April 1981, and died there.

most all the bosses would be absent or resting in their homes within the same Camp. That it should be in the morning, because at that deeper hour the dream of the garrison. The reason for the hour, 2:40, was due to a decision by General Batista. I don't know what motive he had.

CHAPTER V

THE DAWN OF MARCH 10, 1952

We have said before that the Columbia Camp sits on a plateau; from whose northern rim a slightly sloping slope descends to the sea. From the southern part, and from the limit of the Camp, the terrain rises again to the Marianao Road. There, the level stabilizes. A large avenue starts from Marianao Road and will die in the Camp. Through this avenue we descended in the early morning of March 10. We had gathered next to some existing water tanks on the Causeway, a little to the east of the Avenue, and from there we left. In the car of the head was, at the helm, the captain [Luis] Robaina[106]. Alongside him, retired Lieutenant Francisco «Silito» Tabernilla[107], and at his side, Roberto Fernández Miranda[108], the

---

[106] Luis Robaina Piedra (June 21, 1902-October 10, 1989), enlisted in the Army on September 10, 1924. He was captain on March 10, 1952, when he was promoted that day to Brigadier and Headquarters-Master General. Appointed Inspector General on 30 April 1956 and obtained the rank of Major General on 5 December 1957. Batista's father-in-law, with whom he went into exile on January 1, 1959. He settled in Miami on March 3, 1960, where he later died.

[107] Francisco H. "Silito" Tabernilla Palmero (August 22, 1919-January 20, 2015), a native of Guanabacoa, enlisted in the Army on September 7, 1937, and retired with the rank of first lieutenant in 1945 under the government of Ramón Grau. After Batista's coup d'état, in April 1952 he was promoted to lieutenant colonel and colonel three months later. He was head of the Joint Tank Regiment in 1955 and appointed brigadier general on 5 December 1957. He was head of the "General Alejandro Rodríguez" Infantry Division on 18 September 1958. He went into exile in West Palm Beach, Florida, on January 1, 1959, where he later died.

[108] Roberto Ramiro Fernández Miranda (June 7, 1922-September 26, 2009), a native of Havana, enlisted in the Army on May 29, 1929. He was retired with the rank of captain in 1944 by President Ramón Grau due to his friendship with Batista. After the 1952 coup d'état, he was promoted to colonel and head of the Presidential Palace. The following year he was appointed colonel and on December 5, 1957, he reached the rank of brigadier general. On January 30, 1958,

brother-in-law of President Batista. In the back seat we were Batista, on the right, and me on the left. Batista wore a military jacket that I had provided, and one of my old junior officers hats[109]. I wore my captain's uniform. After us, in the second car, came the captains (active) [Jorge] García Tuñón[110], lieutenant [Pedro] Bar-

---

he was assigned head of of Artillery. He went into exile with Batista and became a U.S. citizen on January 27, 1972, in Miami, where he later died.

[109] Roberto Fernández Miranda confirms this version in his memoirs by saying that Kuquine "left in several cars, in one was General Batista with Díaz Tamayo, "Silito" Tabernilla and me . . . Díaz Tamayo had brought uniforms and hats for General Batista and for me. " Roberto Fernández Miranda, *Mis Relaciones con el General Batista* (Miami: Ediciones Universal, 1999), 116. The biography by Edmund A. Chester, *A Sergeant Named Batista* (1954), pages 227-230, contradicts this version. Chester points out that Batista left Kuquine in the second car driven by Captain Luis Robaina and accompanied by Francisco Tabernilla Palmero and Roberto Fernández Miranda. It indicates that Tabernilla was the one who handed the military jacket to Batista. Díaz Tamayo is omitted from the biography. Tabernilla notes that Batista after leaving Kuquine moved to another car driving Robaina and did not accompany him. Gabriel E. Taborda, *Palabras Esperadas: Memorias de Francisco H. Tabernilla Palmero* (Miami: Ediciones Universal, 2009), 51.

[110] Jorge García Tuñón (July 22, 1913-January 25, 2004) was born in Paris when his father Conrado García Espinosa was there on a mission. In 1932 he studied six months at Georgia Industrial College in Barnesville, Georgia. His performance in the March 10 coup made him general and head of the Infantry Division in Columbia. The intrigues of General Francisco Tabernilla Dolz soon transferred him to the headquarters of La Cabaña and later appointed Military Attaché at the Cuban Embassy in Chile. He was retired from the Army for "health reasons" on November 27, 1952. The US Embassy received reports that the withdrawal was because the general was in contact with Aureliano Sánchez Arango and was offered a million dollars to lead a revolt by December 15. His brother Pedro, a lieutenant colonel and director of the School of Officers in Managua, was also retired. Colonel Pedro Barrera believes it was a false rumor created by Tabernilla. Jorge and Pedro were detained for a week after the attack on the Moncada barracks on July 26, 1953. The former general founded with his three brothers the prestigious Caribbean Military Academy in Havana. In June 1957, he met with William Wieland, head of the Caribbean Bureau of the Washington State Department, and they discussed how to overthrow Batista. Subsequently they met again about fifteen times. He obtained political asylum in Miami with his wife and daughter on July 17, 1957. Two months later he received a letter ordering him to return to Cuba to face charges of conspiring to foment a rebellion. When he didn't return, he lost his retirement. In January 1958, he handed a document to Wieland pointing to Fidel Castro's totalitarian and communist ideology with plans to dissolve the Army and create a militia by taking power. He remained in exile in Miami and joined the

rera Pérez[111] and captain [Víctor] Dueñas Robert[112], this last one dressed in civilian clothes.

When we reached the height of a small park to the right of the Causeway, we were joined by five or six female police pursuers. In each one there was a guard as a driver, one or two soldiers and a retired officer. I remember among them the captains [Manuel] Larrubia [Paneque][113], Pilar García, Aquilino Guerra and the first lieutenant Hernando Hernández.

---

organization Fuerzas Armadas de Cuba en el Exilio, whose military coordinator was Martin Díaz Tamayo. He naturalized as a U.S. citizen on June 21, 1963, in Miami and died there.

[111] Pedro Antonio Barrera Pérez (December 27, 1921-December 28, 1974), a native of Artemisa, joined the Army as a soldier in 1942 and two years later graduated from the School of Cadets with the degree of second lieutenant. In 1947 he was promoted to first lieutenant and in 1952 he was commander. After the coup d'état of 10 March, he was appointed lieutenant colonel. Barrera was the controller of the Allied Omnibus Cooperative in 1953 and three years later he was promoted to colonel, being military chief in Bayamo, Santiago de Cuba and El Macho. In 1957 he was sent to Caracas as a military attaché and chargé d 'affaires. There he was surprised by Batista's fall. He emigrated to Panama and arrived in Miami on April 5, 1960, proceeding to New York where he worked as a housekeeper. Barrera naturalized as a U.S. citizen on August 23, 1965, and died at Jackson Memorial Hospital in Miami.

[112] Victor Manuel Dueñas Robert (April 15, 1912-August 28, 1992) born in Matanzas, graduated from the School of Cadets on July 15, 1941. He was captain on March 10, 1952, and was promoted to lieutenant colonel after the quartering. He was supervisor of the Havana Prison in 1954 and two years later head of Regiment 2 of the Rural Guard. Appointed Colonel on December 5, 1957. He was sentenced to ten years in prison by a revolutionary court on May 29, 1959. He died in Miami, where he was a bank security guard.

[113] Manuel A. Larrubia Paneque (January 1, 1898-April 15, 1959) was a native of Alto Songo, Oriente, a former government official of Machado who actively participated with Batista in the restructuring of the Army on September 4, 1933. He was a commander when he was forcibly retired by President Grau in 1944. When Batista returned to Cuba in 1948, Larrubia led some 300 men who protected him in public events and his presidential campaign throughout the island. He lost his candidacy for Representative for Havana del PAU in the 1950 elections. His participation in the March 10 coup d'état and his arrest of General Ruperto Cabrera promoted him to lieutenant colonel and head of the Army Air Force. Appointed colonel three weeks later, on May 1, 1952, he was relieved of his post and appointed director of the Military Academy by the influence of General Francisco Tabernilla Dolz, who wanted to put his son Carlos in charge of aviation. In 1956

First Lieutenant Salas Cañizares stayed in the park in his patrol car, constantly communicating with the headquarters, which he showed that he was providing various services.

Colacho stayed in his apartment, from where he kept in telephone contact with the first medical lieutenant Gustavo Márquez Cárdenas, who from the Camp infirmary constantly informed him about the situation. Colacho asked: How is the girl? Is she being calm? Has she improved? And the answers agreed: —The girl is calm. The "Girl," of course, was the Camp. The one who was «better», «calm», meant that there was no newness, and that the garrison rested in the peace of God. If there was an inconvenience: "The girl is wrong," Colacho would have notified us immediately.

Exactly at 2:40 we arrived at Post No. 4. There arose an inconvenience. Captain Sogo, Officer of the Day, was not on site to facilitate our entry. Predicting that something like this might happen, we were carrying in the second car, as I said, several active officers. The stakes gave us the stop! We paused. One of us pulled out his head and told him that we were carrying a sick man for the medicine cabinet, and that the doctor was waiting for us. In that, from the second car, Captain Garcia Tuñon got out of the way, and clarified: — All right, pose, let them pass!

And when he saw that officer and all of us in uniform, plus the pursuers who followed us, he presented the gun in a sentry and gave way to us. We were finally inside! It was then that Sogo appeared shouting, "Let them pass, go!" Go ahead! Go ahead! Here comes the second part. Our car headed to the Regiment Headquarters (where Colonel Matos had arrested me months earlier). In this headquarters there remained during the night an administrative guard composed, generally, of a lieutenant and one or more typ-

---

he was appointed Military Attaché in the Cuban Embassies in Nicaragua, Costa Rica and Panama José Antonio Lugo Abreu, Carlos Prío's emissary to Generalissimo Rafael Trujillo in 1956, pointed out in his memoirs that the Dominican dictator informed him that Larrubia, and other Cuban officials conspired with him to overthrow Batista. He returned to Cuba in November 1958 and took command of the Rural Guard post in Cabaiguán, Las Villas, where he fought the rebels. He was shot by Castroists at the Santa Clara Regiment 3 range.

ists, in case there were any new developments. When we arrived, they were all sleeping on their legs.

The officer turned out to be Second Lieutenant Galvez, a former friend of mine. I shook him gently, saying, "Galvez, Galvez, wake up." The lieutenant opened his eyes, stared at me, as he finished waking up, exclaiming then:

—Hey, Captain, what are you doing here? And I answered him, saying,

—Look who's here.

He looked back, and when he saw Batista, he jumped from the cot, exclaiming with laughter and tears:

—General, you're finally back! You finally remembered us!

Batista was a very even-handed man, but Galvez's emotion was a good symptom, and I think he got excited too, but to hide, he ended up answering him in a casual tone.

—Let's go! Let's not waste time! Wake up the staff, we have a lot of work to do.

The soldiers, upon awakening, reacted in a similar way to the lieutenant, and within moments they were typing in their machines the telephones that we dictated to them, notifying the regiments of the command that we had assumed this.

In the meantime, the pursuers crossed the Polygon and went to the houses of the chiefs, to arrest them and prevent a reaction. The chiefs to be arrested were as follows:

- Major General Ruperto Cabrera, Chief of Staff.
- Assistant General, Otalio Soca Llanes.
- Inspector General, Quirino Uría López.
- Chief of Regiment, Colonel Urbano Matos Rodriguez.
- Inspector General of Regiment 6, Lieutenant Colonel Policarpo Luis Rodríguez.

Standing in front of each house, the pursuers' staff simultaneously knocked on the front door. He ordered time, and all the calls were answered, either by the same bosses or by their wives. The instructions were to, as soon as the door opened, penetrate quickly, albeit without unnecessary violence, and seize the persons concerned. Once arrested, they would be taken to the private home of General Batista's mother-in-law, in nearby Reparto Querejeta, near Fifth Avenue, holding them there until further notice.

Everything went great. Lieutenant Colonel Policarpo Luis Rodríguez opposed a moment of resistance. Those who detained him, his former companions, convinced him, saying, "Don't be like this." We don't want to hurt you. Don't make us act differently.

Colonel Matos, whose house was immediately at Post No. 13, as he left, he shouted to the sentry: — Post, they take me prisoner! But the soldier, located on the outside of the cover, either did not hear it or did not want to hear it.

The next step was to send the troops to the Polygon, without weapons, and to inform them that General Batista had assumed the government of the country, and that the figures of the deposed government, even the military leaders, were already traveling to exile (the latter was not true, but it was thought that it would give greater purpose to the "fait accompli"). Those in charge of waking up the troops and bringing them out, as well as reading them the proclamation, were our men, previously instructed about what they had to do. I remember, for example, the then First Lieutenant [Pedro] Rodríguez Ávila[114] and the Second Lieutenant [Manuel] Varela Castro[115], both in the Tank Company. To Captain [Juan]

---

[114] Pedro A. Rodríguez Ávila (May 13, 1906-February 1983) born in Yellow, Matanzas, joined the Army on April 16, 1935. He was first lieutenant on March 10, 1952, when he was promoted to colonel and brigadier general at the end of the year. Appointed Lieutenant General and Chief of the Army General Staff in January 1958. He accompanied Batista to the Dominican Republic on January 1, 1959, and then went to Miami on April 25, 1960. He was naturalized there on September 6, 1972, and died there.

[115] Manuel Varela Castro (January 26, 1923-May 15, 2011) was a lieutenant on March 10, 1952 when he was appointed commander and chief of the mixed tank battalion. He was a lieutenant colonel in April 1956 when he was sentenced to six years in prison for being the second-in-command of the Conspiracy of the Pure. On his release on 1 January 1959, he took command of the fortress of La Cabaña, which he handed over to Ernesto "Che" Guevara after two days. On

Rojas [González], in Battalion No. 1, Sergeant Third [Carlos] Besada[116], in the Auxiliary Arms Company of Battalion No. 3, and First Lieutenant [Juan G.] Chirino [Fall], in the Signal Corps. Also Sergeant Major Gabriel Ulloa Fránquiz[117] in Battalion No. 2 Infantry.

When the Command of the Regiment, which was where we were, gave the order, we saw little by little the soldiers half asleep go out and form in front of the barracks, in front of the Polygon. And reality surpassed our calculations. As soon as the proclamation was read, the troop broke into Batista alive. The movement had triumphed! Everything was now ready for the next step, which consisted of me going to occupy the General Staff, and temporarily occupying the position of Assistant General. My mission would be to telephone all the commanders of the Republic, inform the regiment leaders of what happened and ask them to join or, otherwise, to hand over the command to the subordinate they deem appropriate and withdraw to their homes.

For those who are unaware of the layout of the former Columbia Camp, it is worth reminding them that the Regiment Headquarters building was located towards the center of the Polygon, and that of the General Staff at the west end of it, half a kilometer away.

September 13, 1960, he was granted asylum in Miami, where he was a real estate broker and a construction entrepreneur. naturalized as a U.S. citizen in 1976. He was buried in Woodlawn Memorial Park South.

[116] Carlos Miguel Besada Valdés (July 25, 1916-March 22, 1992) was sentenced to death by a revolutionary court in Remedios on February 25, 1959, for the death of rebels on August 15, 1958 when he was captain of a Rural Guard barracks in Las Villas. The sentence was commuted to 30 years' imprisonment. He received an additional 15-year sentence on 1 June 1959 for his participation in the 1952 coup d'état. He died in Cocoa, Florida.

[117] Gabriel Ulloa Fránquiz, native of Agramonte, Matanzas. In May 1959 he was convicted, due to the testimony of former lieutenant Aquiles Chinea Álvarez, of having killed three Granma expeditionaries, Humberto Lamothe, Eduardo Reyes and Oscar Rodríguez, in the combat of Alegría de Pío, and sentenced to 30 years in prison. The former lieutenant received an additional 15-year sentence for his participation in the coup d'état on 10 March.

Rodríguez Ávila sent me, to occupy the General Staff, an armored car (scout-car)[118] and several armed numbers.

When the warning came to me that the car was waiting for me, I was in the office of the Chief of the Regiment, where General Batista would establish his headquarters for the time being. It was he who said to me: —Your transport has arrived. Go over there. So, I went there.

I remember that, as I went down the stairs (the office was on the high floor) that leads to the small lobby, I stumbled from hand to mouth with Brigadier General Uría and Soca Llanes. The three of us had been soldiers and ropes together. Soca and I appeared in the same decree promoting sergeants. Now it was up to them to be victims of the circumstances, as I was a year before. I could not help but feel sorry for his predicament, and more so being, in a way, one of the protagonists. When they saw me, they stood up and I greeted them with affection. I asked them if they needed anything, and if General Batista knew of their presence. They responded to my greeting somewhat tense, but they shook my hand with outpouring. They replied that they believed that Batista already knew that they were there, and that they were waiting for orders. We say farewell. I wished them luck. It was the last time we saw him.

As I rode in the scout-car, I was joined by Sergeant Ulloa, who, from that moment on, began to act as my assistant. Captain Garcia Tuñon also got in the car, telling me that he wanted to accompany me. I did not understand this, because García Tuñón had the specific mission of assuming command of Regiment No. 6, but I told him nothing until I reached the General Staff. There I called him apart and returned him to where Batista was.

As in the Command of the Regiment, there was an Administrative Guard in the General Staff, and no security device. This guard consisted of an officer and several typists, ordinances, and a motorcyclist. In truth, they seemed completely alien and even indifferent to what was happening in the Camp, a few steps away from them. Officers and soldiers slept or watched from the landing of

---

[118] M-3 Scout Car armored car with capacity for seven people, it carried a 50-caliber machine gun and two 30 caliber ones.

the staircase the hustle and bustle, the cheers, and the movements of the garrison. I communicated to the Guard Officer, a commander who had already entered in years, that he was coming to occupy the General Staff. He objected for the time being, but at last he gave in and put himself at my command. I then placed sentries at the entrance and went up to the Adjutant General's office, which was on the third floor.

I confess that I was impressed when I entered the office. Large, furnished in the Chippendale style. I had always entered him by appointment by the Chief, standing before the desk, in the attention position, while the general gave me some order. Only a day before it had been General Soca Llanes' private preserve, and now I was entering it, as owner and lord. How easy coups could be! How strange that was to me, and what consequences it had for the Republic!

But well, I couldn't get lost in reflections. She had to work. I sat at the desk and picked up the phone. My first call was for Regiment No. 8, "Riús Rivera." I spoke to his boss, Colonel [José] Fernández Rey. He seemed to rejoice, but when I asked him to join, he asked me until eight in the morning to answer. Indeed, he called me shortly before eight, making himself available to General Batista.

In the other regiments, that is, No. 5 (Havana), No. 3 (Las Villas), No. 2 (Camagüey), No. 7 (Holguín), and No. 1 (Santiago de Cuba), the colonels did not abide by the coup d'état, but handed over the command peacefully. With Regiment No. 4 (Killings) I had some difficulty. His colonel was [Eduardo E.] Martín Elena[119], old

---

[119] Eduardo Ernesto Martin Elena (October 13, 1909-October 14, 1982), born in Alba de Tormes, Salamanca, Spain. He was a military attaché in Washington and a member of the Inter-American Defense Board. He sought asylum in Miami on August 22, 1960 and was the military chief of the Revolutionary Democratic Front (FDR) of Antonio "Tony" de Varona. The CIA agent, E. Howard Hunt, in his memoirs Give Us This Day described Martin Elena as "a strict discipline without humor, incapable of having a good relationship with the troop, who was booed when he visited the Trax base where the 2506 Brigade was trained." In January 1961, the colonel resigned from the FDR when he was not appointed military commander of the 2506 Brigade and was not informed of the plans for the Bay of Pigs invasion. He naturalized as a U.S. citizen on November 13, 1975 in Miami and died there.

acquaintance of mine, and recently deceased in this city (Miami). Also, as you may recall, I had been my opponent in the first lieutenant competitions. Very regulative, Martin Elena began to list the reasons why it was not possible for General Batista to take power. According to him, the coup contravened several provisions, both Constitution and of the Regulations. I replied that both the Rules of Procedure and the Constitution were next to me, in a desk drawer, and that the realities were different. So, we stayed for a few minutes, he arguing and quoting paragraphs, subsections, etc., until I decided to hang up. I then called the Chief of the Infantry Battalion who, as you will recall, had replaced the Thirds after 4 September. Fortune accompanied me. The Battalion Chief, Commander Aguilar, had stayed overnight in the Unit. I explained what happened and, when I said that I agreed with the coup, I explained Martín Elena's attitude. I ordered him then to take command of the Regiment, avoiding, however, any violence. There were no problems: Commander Aguilar appeared before the colonel with several officers, and he handed over the command. However, when Aguilar informed me that he was already in control of the situation, I told him to send Martín Elena to me in custody, which he immediately completed.

Then I called my wife. Rosaura was already quite restless with my comings and goings. She, to please me, had cooperated with me in everything I had asked, but in such a nervous state, that the night of the coup I decided not to tell her anything. So, when I picked up the phone, the first thing he asked me was, "Where are you?" My answer was: — Well, here, in the General Staff. What do you think?" Then she explained to me: — When you called me, I thought we were scared to death, Mom and me. Indeed, what would have happened if the coup had failed? I don't even want to think about it, but I can say that we wouldn't have had a great time.

DURING THE 10TH OF MARCH

March 10, itself, was Monday. In the morning, the staff began to report to work, encountering the situation created. We had agreed in Kuquine that the officers would be disarmed and taken to the Officers' Club as they presented themselves. This was done, but the enlisted men were arriving at their respective units and, of course, at the General Staff. To these, and then to the officers as they were arriving from the Officers' Club, I made them come in several groups to my office and, officially, I communicated what happened. I remember ending up saying to them, "Some of you may not agree with the change of government. Those who are in that case may retire to their homes, and they will not be disturbed. Those who agree will take an oath of allegiance to the new regime. And I don't remember anyone refusing to take the oath[120].

It would be about nine o'clock in the morning when Cantillo arrived, communicating that he was coming to take charge of the General Aid. I confess that this surprised me. We had agreed that Cantillo would be Chief of Staff, if he accepted the coup, and that Tabernilla would be Minister of Defense. Until two days later I did not have the explanation of what had altered the plans, and later President Batista himself told me in great detail.

As I said earlier, Carlos Cantillo, the brother of Colonel Eulogio Cantillo and a retired colonel himself, had been charged with putting Eulogio in the background of what was planned. As things happened, Carlos did not think it appropriate to communicate anything to his brother, and perhaps it was for the best. The then Colonel Cantillo would possibly have disagreed with the conspiracy, and he would have reported it to General Cabrera. As far as I know, the first news Cantillo had was a call made to him on Batista's orders shortly after the arrest of the generals and colonels at their homes. In this call he was informed of the success of the coup (I repeat that Batista took it for granted that Cantillo was aware of the situation), the telephone call added the order that Cantillo be kept at his home until further notice. Now the surprised was Cantillo, who far from staying in his home as requested, went out through the back of his house facing the airfield, jumped the parapet and ran downhill towards his unit. When he

---

[120] As a result of the coup d'état, Major General Ruperto Cabrera Rodríguez; Brigadier Generals Otalio Soca Llanes, Quirino Uría López and José H. Velázquez Perera; Colonels Eduardo Martín Elena, Francisco Álvarez Margolles, and five others; 22 Lieutenant Colonels, 11 Commanders and 10 Captains were withdrawn for disaffection.

arrived at the Air Force he found a real confusion. His brother Carlos Cantillo had appeared at the meeting and, upon communicating that there had been a coup in Columbia, the staff present were enthusiastic, but Captain Mario Cabrera (son of the general), controlled the situation in favor of his father and arrested Carlos. The arrival of the Colonel Chief of Aviation put some order into that. Colonel Cantillo was not sympathetic to the coup, but he realized that while Columbia was in Batista's possession, he could do little. So he mingled, calmed Cabrera, and waited.

Once Batista heard that something was wrong with the air force, he sent the later Colonel Larrubia with some personnel, and with orders to send him to Cantillo. Larrubia defined the issue, and putting Cantillo in a vehicle, he sent him to Columbia.

Once in the presence of President Batista, he tried to convince him, and for more than three hours he argued with him to accept the coup. He didn't want to; it seemed disloyal to his former superiors. He finally asked to speak with General Cabrera, and Batista agreed. I understand that General Cabrera acted with great wisdom. I am informed that the essence of what he advised was as follows: —Look, Cantillo, you have to be realistic. Our moment has passed. You are a great officer with a magnificent future, and you can do much good to the Army.

Take advantage of the opportunity that is given to you. I absolve you of all responsibility.

But now it was Batista who, observing Cantillo's hesitations, began to doubt whether it would be wise to entrust him with anything less than the command of the General Staff. It was Colacho who offered the formula: Cantillo's services should not be dispensed with, who is considered the most brilliant officer in the army. Given his organizational ability, he would be optimal as a General Assistant. The Old Pancho (Tabernilla) can occupy the Headquarters for six months until seeing how Cantillo is doing. In the meantime, I would occupy the Ministry of Defense.

I don't know if Colacho offered himself to the Ministry of Defense. I say this because I have been told so. In any case, the issue is irrelevant because, as I note elsewhere in this book, the Cuban Ministry of Defense was a sinecure and had no influence on the management of the armed forces. Batista accepted Colacho's formula without a second thought. It was basically what he wanted. Tavern was unconditional and this quality, more than any other, was what he wanted in a position like that. See what things are: Walking time Tabernilla was Colacho's worst adversary, and who after all made him leave the government.

Late in the morning General Tabernilla arrived at the General Staff and took office. In Kuquine we had agreed that he would not take part in the coup, but that he would wait at his home, together with his sons Carlos and Marcelo. Only the eldest, Francis, "Silito," entered Columbia with us. After this entrance, Lieutenants [Pablo] Miranda and [Manuel] Ugalde Carrillo[121] went to find the general at his house and took him to La Cabaña. Tabernilla had been head of La Cabaña for several years, and the staff knew him well, and although the Artillery Regiment was expected to join the coup like the others, his arrival was supposed to overcome any unexpected difficulties. Inside La Cabaña there were several officers and enlistments won for our cause, and when I called them from the Helpline to tell them of our success in Columbia, they did what we had done, that is, to announce to the troop that Batista had taken over the government. The reaction of the enlisted was also similar, and the arrival of General Tabernilla reaffirmed the

---

[121] Manuel Antonio Ugalde Carrillo (June 13, 1919-March 21, 1980) Born in Rhodes, Las Villas. He enlisted in the Army on September 3, 1941. He was first lieutenant when he was retired in February 1951 with Martin Díaz Tamayo for opposing the sending of Cuban troops to Korea under the UN flag. The coup d'état of 10 March promoted him to lieutenant colonel. Two weeks later he briefly served as Field Assistant to the Army Chief of Staff and on March 27, 1952, held the position of Chief of the Military Intelligence Service (SIM) until March 27, 1954. On April 20, 1954, he was sent to the Cuban Embassy in Santo Domingo as a Military Attaché. Appointed Field Assistant to the Minister of National Defense on January 10, 1955 and became Executive Officer of the Armed Forces Advance and Insurance Fund on May 7, 1956. Four months later he was assigned as supervisor of the National Pine Island Prison and on 9 August 1957 became head of the Infantry Division. He was promoted to colonel on 5 December 1957 and two weeks later was appointed chief of operations in the Sierra Maestra. On 23 October 1958 he was head of the 7th. Military District. He went into exile in Santo Domingo with Batista on January 1, 1959, and later went to the United States, where he naturalized as a citizen on May 26, 1976. He died in Los Angeles, California.

fact. The same can be said of the Police and the Navy. In the Police, Salas Cañizares occupied the Headquarters with his men, and Rodríguez Calderón obtained the same result with a group of young officers that he and Colacho had captured.

I attribute the complete success of the March 10 coup to multiple factors, including the fact that the fruit was literally ripe, and we only had to pick it. From a tactical point of view, the capture of Columbia, the strategic heart of Cuba, was definitive. Batista's magic name did the rest.

One point remains to be addressed: the Presidential Palace. Batista gave orders not to touch him, not even to approach him. Nor that they bothered President Prío. He trusted that Prío would act as he did. I mean, disappear from the scene without causing any trouble. Dr. Prío was informed of the events shortly after these occurred. He immediately went to the Palace, and soon a number of civic delegations, including students, began to arrive, offering their support and urging him to resist. I must admit that if the President had stayed in the Palace, he would have put us in a predicament. However, Prío had no interest in defending himself, and those who invited him to do so were opposed, so that as soon as he could he slipped out of the Palace and took refuge in an Embassy[122]. The garrison, which consisted of an infantry company and a police detachment, was informed that the President had gone out for a moment to organize the defense, and that he would return to fight alongside them. As for me, knowing Batista's thought in this regard, I neither called the Palace nor ordered any action against it. What for? Palace would fall for himself.

Unfortunately, a police lieutenant, last name [Julián] Negret, at his own risk, appeared in front of the Palace in a pursuer and intimidated the surrender. Sergeant Sócrates [Álvarez Barrios][123], of the Presidential Escort, stepped out of the garages. There was then an exchange of shots, where Negret was killed and Socrates wound-

---

[122] The Mexican Embassy gave safe conduct to his country and from there Prío went to Miami Beach, Florida.

[123] Sócrates Álvarez Barrios (November 5, 1920-February 1, 2007) was born in Bacuranao, Havana. He died in Miami.

ed. It is a gross mistake to believe that Socrates was the author of the shots that touched Negret. These were apparently due to the head of the Presidential Assistants, Colonel [Vicente] León[124], who fired at him from a terrace on the first floor, adjacent to the Council of Ministers' Hall. In turn, the persecutor's occupants fired at the visible target. This target was Socrates. Fortunately, the sergeant survived and today lives in Miami. Colonel León caused a casualty in Playa Girón.

After this incident, the garrison of the Palace was left alone, in the uncertainty of not knowing what was happening. It was in the morning hours that a tank company made its appearance. It was commanded by the then captain [Miguel] Álvarez de la Noval, the same one who competed with me for the first place, when the course of Atarés, back in 1935. The second in command was the then second lieutenant José Raúl Corzo Izaguirre, recently deceased in Venezuela[125]. The captain asked to speak with the head of the garrison and explained the situation. He informed him that the president had taken refuge and that, if he were forced to attack them, policemen and soldiers would die in vain, since nothing had to be defended . . . And this is the end of it. Days later I was sent to the Palace to investigate the events. I congratulated the garrison on their loyalty. Almost all these personnel continued to serve the new government. Four of them died during the attack on the Palace on March 13, 1957.

Returning to March 10, when Colonel Cantillo relieved me as Assistant General, I introduced myself to General Tabernilla, who had already begun to serve as Chief of Staff. He offered me the position of chief of his assistants. I thanked him for the honor, but I declined. One of the reasons was that I knew from Batista that I

---

[124] Vicente F. León y León (April 5, 1917-April 17, 1961) was born in Palmira, Santa Clara. He enlisted in the 2nd. Signal Corps Company on April 5, 1934. He entered the School of Cadets in 1938. He was captain in August 1948 when he participated in the delegation of President-elect Carlos Prío who traveled to Guatemala. Two years later, as commander, Prío appointed him his field assistant and chief of the Presidential Palace Guard. Married to Isabel Bécquer. He was administrator of the Focsa building in Havana during 1956- 1960. Member of the 2506 Brigade and died in combat at Playa Girón.

[125] José Raúl Corzo Izaguirre (September 9, 1916-June 9, 1983).

was destined for another position. Another was that I lacked a vocation for that position. He always threw the line and the command units at me. Also, with my exaltation to the generalate, that stage would be left behind. To finish the narration of my conversation with Tabernilla, while I refused the honor of being head of his aide-de-camp, I asked him for authorization to remain in the vicinity of the General Aid until everything normalized.

What led me to this request was the confusing situation that was taking place throughout the building. As the day progressed, the number of officers and enlisted, and later civilians, arrived and swirled in halls and offices. General Cantillo, pressured by a multitude of applicants, could hardly work. There were individuals who claimed to have entered with Batista the night before. Others, who were close friends or childhood companions of Batista. Almost everyone came to ask for promotions or some other kind of benefit. Psychologically, I don't think he was yet fully immersed in the situation, nor did he know who was who. There were also soldiers, especially officers, who showed in a veiled way their dissatisfaction with the coup. For all this, already in the evening, I picked up the phone and called the SIM and requested the then first lieutenant Barrera Pérez. When he was in the machine, I asked him to send several pursuers with some numbers, an order that he immediately complied with. The SIM people arrived and without many glances cleared corridors and offices, taking, in addition, arrested those who could not justify their presence in the General Staff.

Also, that night we again had difficulties with aviation. Captain Mario Cabrera, appeased since the previous morning, created problems again. It would have been easy to settle the matter using some energetic measure, but no one really wanted to hurt him, because Mario was, and is, an excellent boy. On the other hand, perhaps the information of what was happening in the Air Force arrived somewhat bulky to the General Staff. I then asked General Tabernilla for authorization to take the scout-car that had been at my disposal since the previous morning and go and see what was happening. When I arrived, Larrubia had already managed to convince Cabrera to stay calm. So, I returned to the General Staff, and since I had not slept for 48 hours, I collapsed more than I lay down on a couch of the Helpline and rested for a few hours.

There is now the question of promotion. On the 11th someone approached me and informed me quietly: Hey, we are making the decrees. You'll be promoted to colonel. At the same time, he added the names of others whose performance in the coup had been rather passive. These would be promoted to brigadier generals. As these decrees were made by order and under the direction of General Tabernilla, I interpreted it (and I continue to interpret it) as a bad disposition of the latter towards me, dating from that night in Kuquine when I insisted that it be Cantillo and not him the head of the Army. I did not comment, and I waited for events. It seems appropriate to me to repeat that the reason for my conspiracy was my retirement, and that if I did not call General Batista, I would not have thought to do so either. Winner now, logically I expected an improvement, and a colonel was more than I dreamed of receiving. What, then, to worry about? I simply felt curious about the evaluation that had been made of my services. It will be remembered that in the meetings at the President's estate, only the people I already mentioned took part, that is, Colacho Pérez, then Admiral Rodríguez Calderón and myself. General Batista's contacts with the other conspirators were made through us. General Tabernilla attended only one of our meetings and remained at his home until after the coup. So. . .?

Batista, however, did take all these things into account. He had already become head of the government and was now to sanction the appointments. When he saw the Decrees, he simply returned them, saying to the messenger: Tell old Pancho to do them again, and that Díaz Tamayo must be a brigadier general.

So on the 12th, the appointments finally appeared. General Tabernilla remained chief of staff with the rank of major general. Cantillo was confirmed as Adjutant General. General [Luis] Robaina, who drove the car that President Batista and I drove into Columbia, was named Headquarters-Master General. I became Inspector General. All three of us received the rank of brigadier general.

These four positions were traditional in the Army, but now two were created that did not exist before. The 6th Infantry Regiment, based in Columbia, was always more effective than a unit of its kind. It will be remembered that he always had a Tactical Third (cavalry), a mountain battery (four 75 mm cannons) and a section of machine guns. During the war he had also received light tanks (Stuart) and medium tanks (Sherman). General Pérez Dámera acquired two 25 mm anti-aircraft batteries in France (16 fire hydrants, if I remember correctly) and received a light 75 mm battery from the United States.

After 10 March, the infantry was separated from all the supporting weaponry I have just mentioned, and the Mechanized Regiment was created. The two regiments were grouped under the name of "division," under the command of a brigadier general, García Tuñón, for whom the square was created. The Mechanized Regiment was under the command of another brigadier general, Rodríguez Ávila. As for the Military District of La Cabaña, it was under the command of Brigadier General [Juan] Rojas. Allow me now this little vanity: of all these general officers, I was the only graduate of the War College. Cantillo also had several courses on his record and, although I'm not sure, I think he had studied at the United States School of Command and General Staff.

This promotion represented for me something I never thought to achieve, even in my most feverish dreams. Because of my temperament, because of my limited ambition, I would have become a lieutenant colonel over the years. No more. The way he disposed of my life by retiring, changed my destiny in the way I least expected. What's more, if Batista hadn't quoted Kuquine, I would never have thought of conspiring. Do not think that I will blame him alone for the blow, or that I will shed tears of regret for my participation. I have said, and I will repeat here, that the conditions were more than created, and that every Cuban, in his measure, is responsible for him. I, who was practically born with the Republic, witnessed how president after president, with his entourage of senators, representatives, governors, mayors, and important officials, looted the treasury and incurred electoral fraud. Coup by coup were destroying the morale of citizens. From 1902, public affairs followed a downward curve that was accentuated, administration after administration, until its final crisis in 1959. In Cuba there are all the greatness and all the miseries of the Spanish people. We Cubans criticized those who did and dismantled in power, until we had the opportunity to do the same. Of course, there were probate citizens and blameless officials, but an honest official was a hindrance, a living accusation to others, so they were isolated and dispensed with at the first opportunity.

As the Cuban people are intelligent and hard-working, a very strong affluent class came to constitute itself on our island. The men who were part of it, businessmen and, therefore, men of order, men of character, could have saved the country, as they did internationally in the economic order, but our bourgeoisie turned away from the politicians with disgust, and instead of managing them, they ignored them. Now an anecdote comes to mind that illustrates the point: an ingenious owner was summoned to the Palace by Grau. The answer was as follows: "Tell the President that I am a very busy man. If you are interested in seeing me in my office, I will gladly welcome you."

Nothing would have been better for most of our politicians than to serve those who repay them in such length. But as Lenin rightly said, the bourgeoisie does not have the instinct for preservation. While the different governments of Cuba, bad or worse, respected the principle of ownership, this bourgeoisie ignored them. When Fidel Castro appeared on the horizon and they saw what was coming over them, with the greatest naivety in the world they believed they could buy him by sending him food and money to the Sierra Maestra. Then, when Batista fell, they gave Porfia more money, tractors, pregnant cows and land for agrarian reform. How the communists would laugh to see with what humility, with what anxious gaze the rich deposited their tributes at the feet of the god of hatred! What a face their blindness came out of! They're served!

Orestes Ferrara called Cuba a country of pork rinds and coffee with milk. On the contrary, I think that Cuba has always had elements of great value in any of the fields of human activity. However the village is a child and needs to be run by professionals. When we took power, the leaders of public opinion were [José]

Pardo Llada[126], Chicho Pan de Gloria[127] and Clavelito[128]. Of course, there were some serious press, such as the *Diario de la*

---

[126] José Pardo Llada (July 27, 1923-August 7, 2009), a native of Sagua la Grande, Las Villas, studied law at the University of Havana, but did not finish his degree and was dedicated to journalism. Despite his hoarse voice and dragged err, he became an announcer. From his program on Unión Radio and his articles in *Bohemia* magazine and the newspaper *Diario Nacional*, he severely criticized the Authentic governments. On June 2, 1945, he denounced Eduardo Chibás in the newspaper *Mañana* as a "little gangster" and later served in his Orthodox Party. On September 18, 1948, he was slightly wounded in a sword fight at the Capitol with Authentic Representative Menelao Mora, whom he had offended on the radio. The following year, on September 14, 1949, he fought with Colonel José Caramés, head of the National Police, whom he also insulted on the radio. Elected House Representative for the Orthodox Party in 1950. Due to his constant radio offenses, the Ministry of Communications of the Prío government closed his program on August 28, 1951. The US Embassy in Havana had him listed as a vocal left-wing extremist and sympathizer of the communists. In June 1953 he participated in the Montreal Pact between the Authentic and the Orthodox, so the following month he was erroneously implicated in the assault on the Moncada barracks and went into exile on August 13, 1953. He returned to Cuba on March 26, 1954, denounced the Montreal Pact, and led the Cuban Nation Movement to aspire to elections. In August 1956 he created the Revolutionary Nationalist Party after a trip to Bolivia, from which he adapted the name. Despite his previous opposition to the armed struggle, at the end of December 1958, he appeared at the rebel headquarters in the Sierra Maestra, where Fidel Castro did not receive him and ordered that he be assigned in the kitchen to peel potatoes. On 7 January 1959 he was appointed Minister of Communications the cabinet of President Manuel Urrutia. He later established a radio hour with Max Lesnick Menéndez, praising the Castro regime, the shootings of his enemies, denouncing "Yankee imperialism," and premiering the slogans, "Cuba yes, Yankee no," and "Fidel, shake the tree." Main witness in the trial against Joaquín Martínez Sáenz. In August 1959 he accompanied Ernesto "Che" Guevara on a tour of India, Indonesia and Japan. On February 1, 1960, the United States was denied a tourist visa "because of its previous communist affiliation." He replied that it was "an honor" not to have a "garbage visa" because "he had rather ungrateful memories of America." Two weeks later he said he had documents proving that the Americans blew up the USS Maine in 1898. On March 26, 1960, he denounced Luis Conte Agüero as "an enemy of the Cuban revolution and a professional anti-communist" and applauded the closure of the entire anti-government press. Three months later, four men and three women were arrested for conspiracy to murder him. On July 9, 1960, while at the wheel of his car in front of the traffic light at the corner of L and 19, he was shot by Roberto Cruz Alfonso and Balbino Emilio Díaz Balboa. He was unharmed and an escort was injured. The attackers, whom he accused of being mercenaries paid from Miami, were then arrested. He identified them in court and asked that

Marina and some other publication. What about everyone else? Won't I know how most journalists changed their tone when a good sum was put in their pocket? By the 1950s, public morale was at its lowest level since the inauguration of the Republic. It had to happen what happened. As Batista sat in the presidential chair, much could have been done to restore this morale. Eight years ago, the people had believed in Grau. The frustration had been terrible, but not irreparable. Batista knew this well. He described to us the need to limit his stay in power. The coup d'état would be a salutary warning that freedoms, if they are not known to be used, will eventually be lost. Then came the reorganization of the parties and a democratic exit through elections in which he would not take part. We dealt with this point quite a bit! But nothing was done, and while the principle of authority was restored, and wise measures were dictated that led to the economic boom, Batista gave no political exit. He dedicated himself, however, to rehabilitating his private economy.

Let me now touch on this point, albeit in passing. The fact that I did not enrich myself in the generalate (and opportunities were left to me) will not make me a judge of those who did. If I never

---

they be shot as an insult to the enemy, and so it was. Two months later, in a televised program, he denounced for two hours and twenty minutes the American press, including the UPI, the *Miami Herald* and *Time* and *Life* magazines. He traveled to Moscow on November 1, 1960 and returned the following month, praising the communist system. His opponents nicknamed him "The Red Parrot." He deserted to Mexico on March 11, 1961, abandoning his wife and daughter in Cuba. Two years later, unable to enter United States, he settled in Cali, Colombia, where he contributed to several publications and was a radio commentator. He naturalized as a Colombian citizen in 1974, created the Civic Movement, and in March 1982 was elected to Congress by the department of Valle del Cauca. He was also Colombia's ambassador to Norway in 1983 and the Dominican Republic. He returned to Cuba as a tourist for nine days in 2004 through the efforts of his friends with Fidel Castro. He died in a hospital in Cali.

[127] A fat short, bizarre and coryphic president Carlos Prío Socarrás.

[128] Miguel "Clavelito" Alfonso Pozo (September 29, 1908-July 21, 1975) born in Ranchuelo, Las Villas. Propagator of the *décima campesina* who became famous with his radio program "Put your thoughts on me." He asked his audience to place a glass of water on the radio to receive positive energy that would solve his problems. He failed in his aspiration to be a Representative for the Authentic Party. He died in Havana.

touched a penny of the sums I had at my disposal, it was simply because doing so was not in my way of being. I have lived long enough to know something about the human being: man is a predator. Honesty is a condition that society has instilled, generation after generation, as a necessity to be able to live together. But the beast is within us lurking. It is logical that he jumps when he is given the opportunity. And what better opportunity than the one that offers a top position in the government, that abstraction that does not protest, and without fear of judges or prosecutors? President [Andrew] Jackson, the father of administrative corruption in the United States, coined his famous phrase that "To the victor belongs the spoils." In our latitudes, dropping state funds into private bags is accepted practice, and no one is shocked by it. On the other hand, the Cubans did not invent garlic soup, and some rulers south of the Rio Grande make us appear as angels. Americans are more subtle, but the scandals that erupt at every turn in Congress and other branches of government are outward manifestations of great underground currents, just as volcanoes are a pale sign of the fire that devours the bowels of the planet.

Money is a force, and, like all forces, it can do much good, though mismanaged, it can destroy its possessor. The water that quenches our thirst drowns us. The electricity that lights us up, lightning us up. Receiving a fortune without being mentally prepared for it can lead to disaster: flattery rocks us, all the pleasures are suddenly given to us, friends grow wild around us.

The examples are too frequent and well known; see only the recent case of Alemán's son (the one who took the money in suitcases), and the more recent one of Kennedy's son. As for President Prío, who was plagued by millions when he left power, he showed an incredible lack of imagination. Instead of moving to Europe and alternating material pleasures with intellectual enjoyment, he stayed in Miami surrounded by flies, cheap counselors, and flatterers. We know it's sad end[129].

---

[129] Carlos Prío Socarrás was financially ruined and shot himself in the heart at his residence in Miami Beach, Fla., on April 5, 1977.

Batista was more skilled. With its coffers overflowing with doubloons, the old Europe opened its doors to him. It was received by the rulers, they called it "Excellency," a coat of arms appeared to him that traced his nobility back to I do not know how many generations. Batista read, wrote, left several books that, although reflecting only his point of view, are not without interest. He bequeathed a fortune to his widow and to each of his children, and even better, he passed on the art of preserving it. He died quietly, surrounded by his own, at the end of a rich and intense existence. The soldiers who fell to keep him in power, and even to protect his escape, are dead and buried. But that has been happening for centuries. It is in the natural order of things, and things will change... when the human heart changes.

I trusted Batista as a possible return to my infantry captain position, which I was. No revenge or revenge, as I've said a thousand times. And there are my powerful accusers back in the day. Tell them if I bothered them when I was more than them. I never did, even though President Batista called me to the office and asked me if I wanted to establish any injunctions against those who had accused me. With that same philosophy I participated in March 10; to work, to help with what I learned in military schools, including the War College. I was the only one of the generals on March 10 who was graduated from it. There was a small group of officers from other grades who had that diploma. I only remember the commanders Manuel Hernández Hernández, [José] Triana Tarrau and [Cándido] Curbelo del Sol, the lieutenant colonels Nelson Carrasco Artiles and Félix Pérez Montoya, and another group of about ten to fifteen.

SINCE THE TWELFTH OF MARCH

I don't know if the pull *I* just pulled is appropriate. I simply let the pen run, and I'm going to leave it like this, but resuming the course of the narration, on the 12th there was a serious incident in the 7th Regiment of the Rural Guard, in Holguin. A small group of officers were dissatisfied with the coup d'état and tried to revolt and take over the unit. It was not at all difficult to reduce it and, what was optimal, there were no casualties. I was sent to investigate the facts and to take whatever action I deemed appropriate. Once there, and after hearing the parties, I considered that the attitude of the head of the sedition had been hesitant, and I replaced him with his immediate subordinate. The head of the sedition was remorseful. I recommended his immediate retirement, as did the rest of those involved. The General Staff approved my measures.

I also took notes of everything I saw and heard. The factor common to all of them, as in the similar cases that followed, was the dissatisfaction, especially among academic officers, with the way promotions were distributed.

It is logical to think that there would be rewards for those who, more or less directly, acted in the coup. These, in turn, would stimulate the collaborators of all confidence, which were not so many. As for the bulk, it would benefit from general measures, such as the salary increase that was issued on the same day 10. Unfortunately, some bosses took it upon themselves to distribute degrees to friends and protégés. Batista could have controlled this, but he was too political and let it happen. What's more, he did the same thing. There were sergeants who came to commanders. Naturally, officers who had reached their grades after many years of study and sacrifice, could not happily contemplate that a subordinate would now send him. This was especially true of academy officers, who were always sensitive in terms of ranking. The culmination of their discontent was the conspiracy of Colonel [Ramón] Barquín[130], in 1956.

---

[130] Ramón Barquín López (May 12, 1914-March 3, 2008), born in Cienfuegos, joined the Army on November 15, 1933. He graduated as an officer from the School of Cadets in 1940 and studied at the War College in Mexico during 1943-46. In September 1950, he was Lieutenant Colonel in the General Directorate of the Military Academy, when he was transferred to the Engineering Section of the General Assistant General Staff. He was Military Attaché in Washington, D.C. In 1952 and was promoted to colonel after the coup d'état of Batista. Arrested on 14 April 1956 for leading the Conspiracy of the Cigars and imprisoned in the Isla de Pinos National Prison until 1 January 1959. Named ambassador to Europe until he defected in 1960. He was military coordinator of the People's Revolutionary Movement (MRP) in early 1961. He moved to Puerto Rico shortly afterwards where he established a youth military academy in Guaynabo, where he died.

Meanwhile, General Batista passed his royals to the Officers' Club, on the opposite side of the Polygon. For the time being he was only a 'Head of Government' and, days later, President. I also learned that in the early morning of March 10, when they began to call different personalities to form a government, the scare they experienced turned out to be capital, and it was not until they saw it well cemented in power that they went, free of charge, to sacrifice themselves for Cuba. Of course, there were exceptions, and I am pleased to note that. It was well known that, instead of the Constitution, statutes had been established and that, instead of the Congress, an Advisory Council had been established[131]. All this had a provisional character.

My office in the General Staff was very close to that of the Adjutant General, and as soon as I took office I began to work. For the time being, my duties consisted of conducting periodic inspections of the regiments and conducting service-related investigations. There were also other types of special inspections, motivated by special circumstances as well. As the months went by, my functions increased. My next appointment was as President of the Military and Naval Circle, a position I held for five years. This was followed by the creation of a loan and insurance agency for members of the Armed Forces (CASFA). I was its organizer and director from 1954 to *April* 1956 *when we were transferred to Regiment No. 1 Slaughterhouse for "service needs."* In 1955[132] I went to the United States invited by the army of this country. On

---

[131] The Consultative Council was created on April 2, 1952, after more than thirty countries recognized the Batista regime. The United States waited until March 27 to do so. The council was composed of 80 members, chosen by Batista, representing all sectors of the nation, whose sole function was informative. Its members included its president Carlos Saladrigas Zayas; vice president Gastón Godoy Loret de Mola; Generoso Campos Marquetti, an Afro-Cuban veteran of the Liberation Army; Eusebio Mujal Barniol, head of the CTC; worker leader Raquel Valladares, one of the seven women on the council; writers Claudio Benedi Beruff, Mario Cobas Reyes, Rafael Esténger Neuling, politicians Anselmo Alliegro Milá, Radio Cremata Valdés, and journalists Ramón Vasconcelos Maragliano and Gastón Baquero Díaz. The council ceased to exist on January 27, 1955, after the country returned to the 1940 Constitution and there were free elections.

[132] The visit was from May 17 to June 4, 1955.

that occasion I visited different bases and toured twenty states. I oversaw the assembly and organization of the Bureau for the Repression of Communist Activities (BRAC). For this I passed a very interesting course at the CIA. All these things I will refer to in due course. For now, I will go back to 1952, still at the threshold of March 10.

I had just debuted as Inspector General when something very curious happened to me. My former professor at the War College, Dr. García Bárcena, requested an audience to see me. I received it with real pleasure and the conversation began in a very pleasant way, but shortly after talking, he snapped at me: —why didn't you tell me? Since I didn't know what he was talking about, I begged him to tell me what he meant. He ended up trusting me that he and other university professors had been conspiring with the military (he even named one of those who entered Columbia with Batista and me), and that, if everything was already arranged and coordinated, why did we have to go and find Batista, who he had expressly vetoed? At the moment I thought the doctor was joking, but as I continued talking, I saw that he was very serious. I felt disappointed, but I had no choice but to explain things to him as I knew them: that Batista had been the one who originated everything and that, on the contrary, it was he who had made us call. That we had organized and established contacts to a greater or lesser extent, but that Batista was always the flag without which the conspiracy would not have had the least chance of success. We said goodbye to García Bárcena and I, but gradually he performed an act in line with his line of thought. With a group of unarmed youths, he tried to take the Columbia Camp. We arrested them all, although they were released later and, fortunately, there were no personal misfortunes. During the interrogation, Dr. García Bárcena stated that he had large cores of troops inside the camp, which we could not verify[133].

---

[133] Rafael García-Bárcena Gómez (June 7, 1907-June 13, 1961) belonged to the University Student Board of 1930, founder of the Authentic Party and member of the executive council of the new Orthodox Party in 1947. Professor of Philosophy at the University of Havana. After being expelled from the War College after the Batista coup d'état, he founded the Revolutionary Nationalist Movement (MNR)

It was more painful to me what happened with a former comrade in arms for whom I felt true affection. He was one of those who entered through Post 4 with President Batista and me. His conduct had earned him a high position. We agreed on a meal at the Columbia Officers' Club, and on a separate note he expressed his dissatisfaction with the way the grades had been distributed. He objected to General Tabernilla being the Chief of the Army. I told him that was a decision of the President. My interlocutor continued in his thirteen, and proposed that we join forces to carry out a coup d'état where true justice would be done, and that already in his command the conditions for this were created. I answered him bluntly that what he said to me was very serious, and that I was obliged to give an account of his words. Indeed, I located General Tabernilla and informed him of the fact. The next day the President summoned us to his office. We were present the Chief of Staff, the chief who had spoken to me and me. In the presence of the President I repeated his words and he was forced to admit them, but the President did not want to be harsh and merely moved the officer and then withdrew him.

Why do these things have to happen? I come back to the point that prosperity, suddenly overtaken by those who are not prepared for

---

on 20 May 1952, with members drawn from the Orthodox Party. One of his followers, Mario Llerena, declared in his memoirs that García-Bárcena had been contemplating a putsch before March 10, 1952. The assault on Columbia would be carried out by armed students who would unite junior officers who would take over the camp and the MNR would take over. The conspiracy was an open secret since two months earlier, on February 13, 1953, the U.S. Embassy in Havana described it to its State Department and its embassies in Mexico, Guatemala, the Dominican Republic and Venezuela. Hours before the uprising, on Easter Sunday, April 5, 1953, García-Bárcena and the leadership of the MNR were arrested in an apartment in Almendares and 46 followers in a house in front of Post 13 of the Columbia camp. General Francisco Tabernilla Dolz ridiculed the plan as "The Blade Strike" and "the work of a mad poet." On May 21, 1953, García-Bárcena was sentenced to two years in prison, thirteen followers received minor sentences and 54 others were acquitted. Some members of the MNR joined the group organized by Fidel Castro for the attack on the Moncada barracks on July 26, 1953. García- Bárcena was released under the general amnesty of May 1954. On January 20, 1959, he was appointed press secretary of the revolutionary state ministry and extraordinary ambassador. He resigned as Ambassador to Brazil on December 26, 1960, six months before his death in Havana.

it, can lose it. What else could we aspire to, men like us, mere junior officers until recently? We were now in the very first positions. Is it that, as the French say, appetite comes with eating? In any case, it was not the last of the series, as we will see.

It is appropriate to quote Machiavelli, when he writes that conspiracies, even if they fail, always do harm, because they introduce precedents, doubts and fissures in what must be unquestionable. In my view, this first conspiracy called into question the monolithic quality of the Armed Forces. But it also affected us in other respects. Quoting again the author of *The Prince*, he writes that most of the evils of this world come from not being man either completely good or completely evil. With his mixture of absolutism and benevolence, Batista showed that his government could be attacked with minimal risk. For example, I'm sure Colonel Barquín, expecting a severe punishment if he was caught conspiring, would have thought twice before doing so.

Another thing: the case I just reported reaffirmed Tabernilla in command. We do not know if the President had sent this general to the Ministry of Defense after six months, as I was given to understand, but from that moment on the matter was not discussed again. Moreover, surely now in his position as Chief of Staff, he gradually moved to place his pawns in key positions. This will also be dealt with in due course.

ON 20 MAY 1952

Since ancient times there have been military parades. They are demonstrations of power intended to impress some potential enemy, possible allies, or the people themselves. The Romans had two types of parade: the "Triumph," given to generals who returned victorious from a great campaign, and the "Ovation," reserved for more modest achievements. In the first case, the general passed in a squadron at the head of his troops. On the platform of the car was the driver, and a slave who whispered in his ear every moment, "Remember that you are nothing but a mortal," so that he would not become too vain. At the ovation, the general rode his warhorse.

On 20 May 1952, the President considered it appropriate to offer a test of soundness. Delegations from around the world were invited. The culmination of the events to be held around that date would be a major stop, involving as many units of the Armed Forces as possible. About ten days before the date, I was notified that I would head the parade. Why me? Because until that time, still in Cuba, the magazine officer was parading on horseback and, even though a large part of my military life had served as a foot soldier, my fondness for cavalry was known to all.

In the blocks we had magnificent specimens destined for the high chiefs. I preferred *Lucero*, my riding from when I was assistant to the Third. Although a little old already and with a rude appearance as he meditated in the blocks, as soon as he felt the rider on his loins he transformed into a beautiful print of posture and creativity. We hadn't seen each other in a while, but I think it was with mutual delight that we galloped for hours and hours along the polygon.

Traditionally, the troops were located along the entire length of the Malecon and on both sides of the Paseo del Prado. The head of the column leaned against the Central Park. When the march broke down, the troops began their progression, passed the presidential gallery in front of the Capitol and were going to break ranks in the Fraternity Park. There they took trucks and buses back to their barracks.

The same was done on May 20, 1952. I, who had made that tour so many times, first as a soldier, then as a lieutenant and finally as a captain, could not help but feel like a dream when I considered that day to be the chief who would lead the soldiers of the Republic before the President, before his Supreme Chief, and who would receive his greeting, unit by unit, before breaking ranks. With all this in mind, the reader will be able to imagine my emotional state when, as in a dream, I stepped on the stirrup, jumped on the chair and broke the march. My main plane followed me: assistants, master barracks, trumpet, messengers. And here are the human speeds. Soldiers were never well seen by the people. However, that day, as I went up the Prado, the crowd cheered us without reserve.

At one point, an object hit me on the shoulder and fell to the ground. I did not look away, but a policeman from those who formed the fence picked it up, and the object was delivered to me, days later. It contained a key, wrapped in scented paper. On the paper, in very fine print, the following message: "Here is my address and the key to my apartment. Come see me tonight. I will be yours." I don't know how the thing transcended, but the truth is that Dr. [Andrés Domingo] Morales del Castillo[134],

Minister of the Presidency, at every moment exclaimed in the presence of President Batista, who in turn laughed willingly: —On the day of the stop, General Díaz Tamayo had the keys rain down.

After passing the presidential rostrum, I took my position. Before me I saw all the troops, a Navy regiment, police units, armored forces, light artillery, anti-aircraft artillery, the Third, and finally, infantry, infantry, infantry. From all of them I received the greeting. When they passed me, the regiments, battalions, companies shot down banners and scripts. Only the national sign remained erect. The officers greeted me with their sabers. I, for my part, corresponded with mine, as determined by the rules of procedure. *Matiotes, matiotetom, dapanda matiotes* (Vanity of vanities and always vanity) cried the ancient Greeks. That is true, but what else does the human being live on, apart from the bread he eats? I, for

---

[134] Andrés Domingo Morales del Castillo (September 4, 1892-June 1, 1979) was born in Santiago de Cuba where he studied elementary and high school. Graduated in Law from the University of Havana in 1915. He held several positions in the judiciary from 1916 to 1934, being judge and magistrate in Palma Soriano, Holguín, Santiago de Cuba, Pinar del Río and Havana. In 1934 President Mendieta appointed him Secretary of Justice. He then became a judge of the Supreme Court of Justice until Batista appointed him Minister of Finance in 1940 and soon after became secretary of the Presidency. Elected senator of the Province of Oriente by the Liberal Party in 1944. He incorporated the PAU DE Batista in 1949 and after the 1952 coup d'état he was appointed secretary of the presidency and of the Council of Ministers. He was interim president from August 14, 1954 to February 24, 1955 at the Batista to avail himself of the electoral license required by the 1940 Constitution to become president. Batista reappointed him secretary of the presidency and of the Council of Ministers in 1955. Four years later, he accompanied Batista into exile in the Dominican Republic and Portugal. In 1960 he obtained political asylum in Miami, where he later died at home because of an embolism. He never married.

my part, confess that never or after, in my entire existence, did I feel that vanity so full as that day.

I will be told, "Well, what battles were you victorious from?" I regret to answer that in my military life there was never an Austerlitz, nor a Solferino, nor a Maltiempo. Simply, to the conditions that the medium proposed to me I faced them as I knew, and I solved them as I could. I wish I could offer something more to the reader but, as there was nothing else, I am satisfied with my achievements.

CHAPTER VI

THE ARMED FORCES 1952-1958

I was never attracted to politics. I have come to take an interest in her, here in exile, out of mere instinct for preservation. It is logical that it was, because, how could I think of presidents, or if Congress voted or not such or such a law, after twelve hours of work in the sun? Before me, only the furrow that had to be pulled extended and, when night came, I collapsed more than I lay down in what I had as a bed, whether it was jergón, hammock, or colombina.

My joining the Armed Forces didn't change that state of affairs. In the barracks, the political issue was always taboo. The fact that the army was used politically by the president did not mean that the soldiers analyzed the fact. The order was carried out militarily, and the matter was no longer discussed. They say that the soldiers are men of schizoid temperament, that we flee to the realities of daily life, with their struggles and ups and downs, and we are going to take refuge in that great maternal cloister that is the barracks. There, the government guarantees us the daily pitanza and a salary, in exchange for our dog loyalty. SEA As far as I am concerned, my mind never departed from the roll call, from the inspections, from whether I entered the guard, from the next maneuvers . . .

In the personal order, the question of helping my mother was in first place, but it was a great comfort to me the sports I always played in Columbia and the studies I did to complete my instruction. Be a corporal! Here's another one of my big goals! How hard I fought to reach it! And how eager to be a sergeant! I came to get it at the end of 1933, after November 4th. But that date had another unexpected achievement in store for me: a promotion to second lieutenant. Then came the courses: that of officers, in Atarés, and that of artillery, in the Battery of La Pastora. After my eleven-month stay in Santiago de Cuba, my equestrian stage began, between 1936 and 1939.

In that period, I traveled all over America, as in a beautiful dream. And let's not forget the oppositions: it was in oppositions that I won my first lieutenant and captain degrees. And what much it represented for me, in prestige and economically: my brévet as a graduate of the Higher School of War. What more could I wish for? I could well say, like Quevedo:

> Let others speak of the government
> Of the world and its monarchies,
> While my days are ruled
> By butter and tender bread.[135]

I had to come to that retreat in 1951, to get out of my ivory tower and push me into the conspiracy.

It is true that Batista did not allow the military to interfere in the politics of the country. Moreover, he did not even let them address the issue in his presence. Here is something that never took away my sleep, and I was able to devote myself exclusively to the duties of my office.

In his open letter to former President Batista, dated August 24, 1960, General Tabernilla accumulates on his former head indictment after indictment which, for the most part, are absolutely true. One of them is that Batista did not allow his subordinates to make military decisions, being the one who ordered each one of the plans. Neither a promotion, nor a transfer, nor a movement of troops took place without his consent. Tabernilla informs us that he, as Chief of the Army first, and as Chief of the Joint Chiefs of Staff later, had no authority, and that he was there, simply, "painted on the wall." But what does General Tabernilla complain about? That's why he was placed in such high positions. In this, the President followed his old pattern of appointing men to the top positions who owed themselves to him and who did not dispute his authority.

---

[135] Translated from poem "Ándeme yo caliente" by the Spanish lyric poet Luis de Góngora (July 11, 1561-May 24, 1627).

General Tabernilla also electrocuted the former president, accusing him of being a voracious thief, but this is as if the pot told the casserole that it has a flecked bottom. Why, instead, did the general not devote himself to quietly enjoying the pennies he saved in seven years of uninterrupted bliss?

You can't cover the sun with a finger. Only Batista could have dealt the March 10 coup. Without him, we meant little to others. The effect of his name and person upon the troops was electrifying. Batista's successes in the economic order raised the Cuban's per capita and his credit abroad. Failures in his policy led Cuba into chaos. Batista was everything in his two periods of government. No one can argue with this. Why, then, his obstinacy, once in exile, in publishing justificatory memoirs and in charging others with his own faults? The betrayals and conspiracies of some subordinates are the work of frightened men who, because of the height in which they were, saw the disaster coming and tried to save themselves. Those who were faithful to him in spite of everything are dead. As for me, the bad will that General Tabernilla always had for me ended up working in my favor, because, by getting Batista to withdraw, he avoided having to make any decisions.

In my opinion, Batista's error curve follows this path:

- Not to hold free elections (without him as a candidate) in a reasonable time.
- Not physically eliminating Fidel Castro when he had it in his hands.
- Release Fidel Castro, allowing his passage abroad.
- Allow Castro to disembark in Cuba, when the General Staff knew the time and place where he would disembark.
- Allow Castro to survive the landing, pushing him into the Sierra, instead of capturing him.
- Subsequently, prevent the troops from encircling and capturing him when they had the opportunity.

- In the 1958 elections[136], to force the presidential victory of Andrés Rivero Agüero[137], when everything indicated that the solution was Dr. [Carlos] Márquez-Sterling.

That I wasn't to the liking of some bosses may be my own fault. My character is rather withdrawn and does not invite intimacy. Nor did the position of Inspector General help to win me friends, as I was often entrusted with investigations that, when crystallized, scratched the skin of many. I remember a case of silk smuggling. The magnitude of the event was such that despite the tolerance with which these things were looked at, it was necessary to do something. One fine day General Tabernilla called me. According to him, the *Chief* (Batista) wanted me to investigate the issue of smuggling. Of course, I had so many missions on my head that he, Tabernilla, thought I wouldn't have time for it. If I thought it was too much, I had nothing more to say and he would tell the president.

Even today I am not sure if my answer was intelligent or not, but these were my words: —If those are the wishes of the Lord President, I will consider them an order and, as such, I will fulfill it; time is of the least. But that, you know me and you know that I will get to the bottom of it. Nor are you unaware that smugglers climb the Palace stairs every day.

---

[136] The presidential election was held on November 3, 1958.

[137] Andrés José Rivero Agüero (February 4, 1905-November 8, 1996) was born in a bohío about Burene, in the Municipality of San Luís, Oriente. He studied high school in Santiago de Cuba and obtained a law degree from the University of Havana in 1934. During the first government of Batista he held the positions of Minister of Health and Agriculture and ambassador to Peru during 1943-1944. In the second Batista regime he was appointed Minister of Education in 1952 and Prime Minister in 1957. Elected senator by Pinar del Río in 1954 and president in the controversial elections of 1958 that did not recognize the U.S. government. He went into exile with Batista in 1959 and settled in Miami, where he later died. His brother Nicholas was killed by the rebels on July 1, 1958. His half-brother Luis Conte Agüero was an opponent of Batista. His son Carlos Rivero Collado was an infiltrated Castro agent who from Cuba denounced the exile in the press and in his book *The Nephews of Uncle Sam* (1977).

Naturally, the general did not like what I said, and ended the interview with these sentences: —Okay. I'll tell *Titón* (Colonel Tabernilla) to inform the *Chief.*

I never heard of it again.

The president was always kind to me. He never had a reproach for me, not a word out of tune. As the birth of my daughter Roraima approached[138], the first lady, Mrs. Martha Fernandez, offered my wife a *Baby Shower* in Kuquine. We were surprised the magnificence of the party and the quality of the guests, as well as the attentions that Mrs. Fernandez had with my wife. The proper thing was that I asked the president to be him and his wife the godparents. But I didn't, and the best man was my eldest son. Why did I act like that? —I don't have a good response. Let's just say it was courtesy. Batista never made the slightest comment about it in my presence, but it must have hurt him. What a clumsiness of mine! What shall I do?

All these things contributed to me gradually isolating myself from my classmates. On the other hand, my position required an active social life. Official acts, ceremonies, gala dances, receptions and cocktail parties were frequent, and I was expected to attend most of them.

I was also often invited to Kuquine and the President's residence in Columbia, where baskets were played on weekends. Indeed, in his aforementioned letter, General Tabernilla states that Batista wasted his time playing, instead of devoting it to more urgent matters. I don't think so. It is true that the sessions were long, especially for me, who liked to spend the evenings in my family. The truth is that the President played only when circumstances allowed, and rather as a distraction.

These evenings followed a pattern. First, the President and his guests sat down to watch boxing on television. Then the food came and, finally, the game began. Batista felt at ease among his most intimate relatives and collaborators. He was in a good mood. The stakes were pennies, but the President was cheating

---

[138] Roraima Díaz Menéndez was born on September 1, 1953.

anyway, almost always in combination with some of us. In the end, already late in the morning, he would mend his mischief with a cold dinner.

THE MILITARY AND NAVAL CIRCLE

This was an institution dating back to the 1920s. It had about 1,150 members and their families. Of these, about 800 were officers and some 350 civilians.

I received the position of President of the Circle in 1953 and was there uninterruptedly until my retirement in 1958. Although it was one more responsibility, I liked the appointment because it was perfectly in agreement with my temperament, and I say this because sports played a prominent role in this activity.

The Board consisted of the Chairman, Secretary and Treasurer, as well as members up to 27 members. There was no Vice President. In proportion to the members of the club, two thirds of the managers were military and one third were civilians. When I arrived, I found an enthusiastic and efficient directive, and I had little or nothing to change in it: we always worked in the greatest harmony.

As for the building, it occupied a narrow area, enclosed between the Spanish Casino and the Havana Yacht Club. Our relations with these two clubs were always cordial, but the need to find another more suitable place for the Club House became more and more evident. It was the President who made the final decision to build a new one. A point east of the *La Concha* Public Spa was chosen for this purpose. The new Circle opened its doors in 1957. It cost more than $100,000, and the expenses were partly covered by the sale of the Old Circle to its neighbors, who were thus able to expand their respective beaches. The construction works, as well as the budget, were carried out by engineer [Manuel] Pérez Benitoa, in-law of the Prime Minister.

In my references to my "equestrian stage" I omitted to say that for a while I had also dedicated myself to polo. The experience was exciting, though short-lived. Jumping and polo are two completely different forms of riding. In jumping, the rider's function is to guide the horse, but guide him gently, without unduly gravitating on his back, without hindering his movements. Touching the reins out of time, however slight, can confuse the beast, causing it to break down an obstacle rather than save it. The pole, on the other hand, is extremely violent. The rider, possessed by the demon, communicates his fury to the running animal; he brakes dry, turns, rushes against other players, colliding with them to get them away from the ball, object of all that frenzy. A few tugs on the brake and the sudden changes of direction, at full gallop, exhaust the poor animal, which ends up bathed in sweat and the mouth dripping foam.

The pole is of Hindu origin. Being India a colony of England, the British officer observed the Maharajas practicing it, and soon introduced it into their paintings. From England it passed to the West. When the American occupation (1899-1902) the American cavalry officers played it in Columbia, and I am told, they tried to induce the Cuban officer to do so. At the moment they were not successful, and it is explained: the pole is called "the sport of kings." Only wealthy classes can practice it, because each rider must have a block of very expensive horses, very specialized in the game, and that are renewed frequently. At the end of the war, Cuba was ruined. There was no wealthy class, and the budget of the first governments was very modest. When the business class reappeared, and with it the economic well-being, the pole also made its appearance. Soon the Army also had its equipment, and good riders were never lacking.

As for me, when my enthusiasm was greater, a bucket of cold water fell on my head. Just like when I started simultaneously preparing for the competitions and studying aviation, my boss called me a chapter.

"Lieutenant," he told me, "If you continue playing polo, you're going to cancel out on the jump team: choose one of the two things!" And the polo is over! But I kept liking him. My status as President of the Military and Naval Circle allowed me to be useful to the various *teams*, military, and civilians. Among the players I made good friends, including Mr. Gustavo de los Reyes Delgado[139], creator of the famous *Santa Gertrudis* cattle. In 1959, Gustavo was stripped of his property and thrown into the communist prison. A cellmate of the co-author of this book, Claudio Medel, they lived together in La Cabaña and Isla de Pinos for several years. Medel recounts that Gustavo used to tell him: —These communists are imbeciles: they have taken away some cattle that will soon be gone, but they have not taken away my brain. If I'm released, wherever I go, I'll be rich again.

And that's how it went. Today he owns four haciendas in Venezuela with more than 30,000 head of cattle. And this proves to the fullest the fallacy of communist dogma. The businessman is the true creator of a country's wealth. If he is limited, if he is suppressed, the country stagnates. *Sublata causa, tollitur effectus*[140].

THE CASFA (ARMED FORCES SAVINGS AND INSURANCE FUND)

One of Batista's ideas regarding the Armed Forces was the creation of CASFA. As the trade of arms, well handled, does not enrich anyone, it was the case that the kind of troop, when discharged, was left in a difficult economic situation. This institution made a sum of money available to the retired, or to the next of kin in the event of death, which allowed them to meet the first expenses, and even to achieve a balance in life. Also, in case of emergency, they were lent sums that they then paid in comfortable monthly instalments.

As military salaries had risen on 10 March, CASFA's capital was formed on the basis of savings and interest earning discounts deposited in banks in the capital.

The readiness to create this institution came directly to me from President Batista. At the moment I did not know what to think, because I had no experience in the matter, and that must have been the work of an expert.

---

[139] Gustavo de los Reyes Delgado (November 29, 1913-March 17, 2014) was born in Havana. Arrested by the Trinity Conspiracy, prisoner number 25,507.

[140] Once the cause is suppressed, the effect disappears.

In the case of the Military Circle, I took charge of an efficient organization, composed of gentlemen who worked with the greatest disinterest. In this case, the obvious occurred to me, that is, if I could find the right staff, the problem would find its solution. Fortunately, those staff showed up.

To the General [Aristides V.] Sosa de Quesada owed the drafting of the decree-law that established the organic basis of the Bank. Other lawyers, among whom I remember Captain Auditor Pedro Díaz Landa came to my aid, and accountants, almost all military, but some civilian friends of mine from other times. Both the regulations and the calculations of future income and expenses were exhaustive. Thus, possible casualties were established for the next five to ten years, considering ages and unforeseen accidents.

The primitive law was later supplemented by another, for not fulfilling all the requirements that the president desired.

Basically, CASFA was organized as follows:

1. To avoid future misinterpretations with money, the Bank was placed under the supervision of the Court of Accounts of the Nation. And when I moved to Oriente in April 1956 and was relieved as a director, I was pleased that this very Court of Auditors placed us first or second among the best-organized government agencies[141].

2. The President of CASFA was nominally a civilian. My position was as vice president.

3. All members of the Army, Navy and Police benefited. When I handed over CASFA, there were about two million pesos in two banks in the capital. Also, the two houses that housed the offices and other dependencies, two almost new cars, several thousand pesos in modern electronic machinery and a large amount of first-rate furniture. The loan facility was also functioning, which was the responsibility of each military officer. I was succeeded in the Directorate by General [Luis] Robaina [Piedra], to whom I handed over the organism in full operation in 1956.

---

[141] Díaz Tamayo was appointed president of CASFA on December 18, 1952.

THE CASE OF THE MONCADA BARRACKS

Here is something well known, which has had so many consequences on the destinies of America, and who knows if even the world. It all began on Sunday, July 26, 1953, when a former university agitator, named Fidel Castro Ruz, attacked the headquarters of Regiment No. 1 in Santiago de Cuba, Province of Oriente. To do this, he concentrated a little more than a hundred men in a farm near the city. The members of this group came almost all from the western provinces. They came to Oriente by groups, mixed with the public that came to Santiago to celebrate the carnival. From the farm they set off in several cars, dressed as soldiers, and with a very heterogeneous armament.

When they got to the Post Office, they killed the sentry[142]. But still dying, he had this time to sound the alarm. Raul, Fidel Castro's half-brother[143], stood by the door and directed the entrance to the camp, while Fidel Castro verified that those who were coming in the rear vehicles would stand and run towards the door. Then, when they all passed inside the camp, the two brothers fled and placed themselves under the protection of the Bishop of Santiago, Monsignor [Enrique] Pérez Serantes[144].

The Moncada Barracks consisted of several narrow building bodies on its front and about thirty meters deep. These buildings, of two floors each, faced a large maneuvering area. Upstairs, they communicated with each other through a corridor that ran all along them. There were the soldiers' bedrooms. On its ground floor were the premises, such as the main barracks, offices, and workshops. Passing the front page that gave access to the camp, the assailants found the first building. Some tried to break into the ground floor, probably looking for weapons. Others went up the stairs to the upper floor hallway and entered the bedroom. There

---

[142] The Corporal of the Guard Isidro C. Izquierdo Rodríguez.

[143] He crosses out the reference to half-brother because in the army it was rumored that Raúl Castro's biological father was the commander Narciso Campos Pontigo.

[144] This version is false. Only five rebels entered the barracks. Monsignor Pérez Serantes did not intervene until August 1, 1953, when he witnessed the surrender of Fidel Castro. Raúl Castro had been captured in San Luis four days earlier.

were few soldiers sleeping in it because most of them were not on duty or in the Guard Corps, but those they found were killed when they tried to get up. Then, through the windows, they shot at the neighboring bedroom, knocking down several men who, in smaller cloths, ran to the gunsmiths to take the guns.

But this is where his luck came in. Colonel Ardant du Picq[145], in his Studies of Combat, states that the soldier, when he starts shooting, stops advancing. Once sheltered in the bedroom the assailants, lacking direction, stopped. The guard, when reacting, first dominated with his fire all those who showed themselves in front of the building. Then a caliber machine gun.30 covered the guard and the garrison members who advanced along the street or, on the upper floor, along the corridor. Many assailants had crowded into the barber shop in front of the bedroom, and they were all killed. The others were lined up by the rifle station throughout the barracks. Others fell as they tried to flee through the back of the building. Those who were able to escape were mostly captured in the following days in various places in Santiago. As for the Castro brothers, Monsignor Pérez Serantes presented them, after obtaining from the President a guarantee for their lives[146].

Here's the first of Batista's big mistakes. Leave alive, and then amnesty the main perpetrators of that attack where 20 soldiers perished[147].

Moncada was the event that made Castro known, and the basis of his later renown. And what about the wrong to the relatives of so

---

[145] Charles Jean Jacques Joseph Ardant du Picq (October 19, 1821-August 18, 1870) was a French army officer and military theorist whose writings had a great effect on French military theory and doctrine.

[146] This is the official version of the government that was forged. The detailed history of these events appears in: Antonio Rafael de la Cova, *The Moncada Attack: Birth of the Cuban Revolution* (University of South Carolina Press, 2007).

[147] Fifteen soldiers and three policemen were killed in the Moncada barracks, in addition to twenty-three soldiers and five policemen wounded. In the simultaneous attack on Bayamo barracks, one policeman was killed, and two soldiers were wounded.

many fallen soldiers? And how would the other soldiers judge the impunity granted to the murderers of their comrades?

That same night I received orders from the President to fly the next day to Santiago de Cuba. My mission would be to impose the medal of distinguished services, posthumously, on our murdered comrades. He would also, on behalf of the President, preside over the burial.

Colonel [Alberto] del Río Chaviano[148], head of the No. 1 Regiment, led me on an inspection by the Moncada. The corpses had already been lifted, and the blood washed. The bedroom looked tidy again, but the entire facade of the company, as well as the iron railing of the corridor appeared riddled by the machine gun's impacts.

After the burial, the colonel took me to the farm located on the Morro road[149], place from where the attack had started. About ten men had been left there for various reasons and, when the Army arrived, they resisted. Their lifeless bodies lay everywhere. One of them looked like Castro, and del Río Chaviano, for a moment, he thought it was him. Actually, Castro was never exposed, either there or in the Sierra. When the Russian Bashirov sent Castro to Bogotá[150], back in 1948, to cooperate in the famous *Bogotazo*, he

---

[148] Alberto Roberto del Río Chaviano (July 4, 1915-April 26, 1978), a native of Sagua la Chica, Las Villas, joined the Army on November 23, 1933. He was married to Francisco Tabernilla Dolz and captain on March 10, 1952, when he was promoted to colonel. Two months later, he received command of the Eastern Military Department. Appointed Brigadier General on 5 December 1957. He was head of Regiments 6 and 7 of the Rural Guard and on September 18, 1958, he obtained the command of the Third Military District. When Batista ordered his arrest, he fled to the Dominican Republic on December 27, 1958, where he had a cattle herd that was later expropriated by Trujillo. In 1963 he resided in Dallas, Texas, being a Spanish teacher until moving to Miami shortly before dying of marrow cancer.

[149] The farm was near the village of Siboney, opposite the Morro, eight miles east of Santiago de Cuba.

[150] Salvador Díaz-Versón Rodríguez (November 6, 1905-February 15, 1982), argued in "When did Fidel Castro become a communist?" published in the Miami newspaper El Mundo on October 19, 1960, that Fidel Castro, at the age of seventeen and being interned in the Belén Jesuit school, was controlled by Soviet intelligence agent Gumer W. Bashirov. He wrote that the Russian sent Castro

did something similar. That is, as soon as the riots broke out in the Colombian capital and the police reaction came, Castro ran to the Cuban Embassy to seek refuge. The then-ambassador had the weakness to admit him as a political asylum seeker[151].

1953 AND 1954

These two years were relatively quiet for me. Apart from my routine work as Inspector General, as Chairman of the Military Circle, plus the organization of the CAFSA, only three extraordinary missions, two of them with diplomatic jurisdiction, marked the period.

In 1953 I flew to Mexico, attending the Independence festivities as an Extraordinary Ambassador. The then president, Mr. [Adolfo] Ruiz Cortines, was extremely kind to me. Mexico was already familiar to me, because, as you will remember, in 1938 the equestrian team had come there. Even in 1953 the inconveniences afflicting the capital still did not exist: I am referring to overpopulation and air pollution produced by industries. In those days, Mexico City was in all its glory, and more like a European metropolis.

Naturally, the Saraos, the banquets and the receptions were shaken, but I was particularly interested in the military issue, and, in truth, I was not disappointed in that aspect. The stop on September 16 was impressive: I have never seen greater martiality than that of the Mexican soldier. I, who have seen the English Royal Guard parade, dare to say that the Military College of Mexico has nothing to envy him. In its closed order, French influence emerges at every step. This can be seen, above all, in regimental music. In the

---

to Colombia, on April 9, 1948, to interrupt the conference of the Organization of American States (OAS) that ended with the Bogotazo. Díaz- Versón said that he had the evidence in file A-943 in his office of the Anti- Communist League of Cuba, whose archives were destroyed under the orders of Ernesto "Che" Guevara on January 23, 1959.

[151] Fidel Castro, Enrique Ovares Herrera, Alfredo Guevara Valdés and Rafael del Pino Siero slept at the residence of the Cuban consul Carlos Tabernilla Dolz, the general's brother. The next day, Ambassador Guillermo Belt took them out of the country on a Cuban cargo plane.

first row of their bands, the French place only drums, and infantry horns in the second. This aggregate, called *the click*, remains active almost all the time, producing a background of vibrant notes in the marches that the rest of the band executes. Also, when the main music ceases, the golden thunder of the clarions and the continuous beating of the drummers comes to the fore. This is known as the *reprise des clairons*. In Mexico, this tradition remains to the letter today.

But it is not in vain that the United States is the superpower that everyone is looking to. When I first saw Mexican troops in 1938, the soldiers looked like prints from overseas. The steel helmets and the flight of the cap collected were the exact image of the French *poilu*. The men on horseback could have been dragons of the Second Empire. By 1953, however, khaki and the "made in USA" helmet were already dominant. As for weaponry, it was in full evolution in those days, although the infantry still carried the Mauser system carabiner, and the police the 7 mm Mondragón rifle. Nowadays, all that profile has changed.

In 1954, new invitation, this time to Venezuela. At that time, the president was General [Marcos] Pérez Jiménez, and the oil boom augured a beautiful future for the country. Venezuelan hospitality was regal. As soon as I expressed a wish, a plethora of assistants and officials rushed to satisfy him. I always kept a beautiful memory of that visit. I will be forgiven, however, for what I am going to say, and that is that our Venezuelan brothers did not seem to have any idea of time. Accustomed to the rigid protocol and punctuality of our ceremonial, the carelessness about the time when an act began or ended shocked me somewhat. A military magazine in Havana, for example, broke up at the right time and did not last two hours. The units passed the grandstand without interruption, with only twelve steps between the tail of one column and the head of the next. In Caracas, on the contrary, the parades opened with enormous delay, and sometimes up to five minutes elapsed between the passage of one regiment and the next. Hours and hours passed without the end being seen. The infantry school, like that of almost all Ibero-American nations, was German. The troops passed at the pace of a goose, *in der regiments kolonel* with excellent rhythm. The same can be said of public and private schools. His *gemacht* was enhanced by the grace with which the Caracas teenagers accompanied the rigid Prussian movements.

On armaments, it seemed to me to be very modern, almost all of European origin, although it seemed to me that its acquisition was made without taking into account the needs of the country. For example, huge siege cannons passed by, already discarded by the great powers. What use could they have in Venezuela in modern warfare, where light weaponry is excellence?

I cannot avoid, on the other hand, drawing a parallel between this country and Mexico, because in the Aztec army, under the bright appearance, politics has wreaked havoc. The President's friends were rewarded with the rank of major general (a Mexican officer informed me that there were about 800 generals on the payroll at the time) and the troops' readiness left much to be desired. Captain Cueto, a graduate of the Mexican War College, wrote a confidential report on his return that I had the opportunity to read. As a result, I met with him before the trip. Cueto pointed out the great communist infiltration in this school, through civilian teachers who taught in it. Subsequently, Cueto, who became a lieutenant colonel, was shot by Fidel Castro. In Venezuela, on the contrary, the training of officers and soldiers was carried out at a feverish pace, and the ranking was observed jealously. Both missions were extremely pleasant to me. It was all flattering, with no discordant notes, and with no other responsibility on our part than to make a good impression that would benefit Cuba.

Upon my return, another task of a very different nature awaited me. The United States had invited General Tabernilla on a tour of 21 forts and military installations. His state of health prevented the general from accepting, and the American Chancellery reiterated the invitation, with the request that it be sent to another chief. President Batista thought of me, and I was appointed for the trip. General Tabernilla appointed the two officers who would accompany me: Lieutenant Colonel Catasús[152], of the Air Force, and Lieutenant Colonel [Manuel] Varela Castro, of the Mechanized

---

[152] Felipe Antonio Catasús Pazos (July 6, 1917-January 5, 2003) went into exile on January 1, 1959 and died in West Palm Beach, Fla.

Regiment. Colonel Barquín, at the time Cuba's Military Attaché in Washington, asked for authorization to join the group. When I was consulted, I replied that I was not inconvenient.

A Cuban Air Force plane took us to Washington D.C., where we were received with all honors. There he made his presentation that would be my assistant during my stay in the United States, a tall, redheaded colonel, by surname [J. E.] Treadway. Shortly thereafter, this colonel became United States Military Attaché to Cuba, a position he held until 1958.

We stayed at the Hotel Mayflower and remained in the capital almost three days. I first received a visit from an official of the State Department and then a lunch in Fort McNair, in the same capital. The luncheon was attended by a large number of officers and some civilian staff. Our ambassador, Dr. Campa[153], was among them, as was Dr. Andrés Vargas Gómez[154]. But now I have

---

[153] Miguel Ángel de la Campa y Caraveda (December 8, 1882-August 19, 1965), son of Spaniards, was a diplomat from 1906 to 1958. Doctor of Civil and Public Law. In 1937 he was appointed Undersecretary of State and Secretary of State in 1940 and 1952-1955. Ambassador to Spain, Italy, Mexico, Japan, the UnitedNations and the United States from 1955 to 1958. He died in Miami.

[154] Luis Andrés Vargas Gómez (May 14, 1915-January 13, 2003), one of the many grandchildren of Generalissimo Máximo Gómez Báez. He did not finish high school at the Instituto de Segunda Enseñanza in Havana by getting involved with his brother Pedro in the struggle against Machado as members of the Partido Unión Revolucionaria Comunista. Both were expelled from the party in 1932 with other comrades who criticized the COMINTERN's analysis of the political and social situation in Cuba. On January 3, 1934, he married Helen Whyte, widow of the diplomat Calixto Sánchez García from whose marriage the future worker leader Calixto Sánchez Whyte and his sister Margaret were born. He entered the diplomatic service in 1935 as chancellor in Key West and New Orleans until returning to the Ministry of State in Havana in1938. He received his law degree from the University of Havana in 1942 but never set up a law firm. In 1949 he was special adviser to the Board of Economic Affairs of the Ministry of State when he was assigned to the Cuban delegation to the United Nations in New York. He participated in the GATT Conference in England in 1950-1951 and the following year the Batista regime assigned him to the Economic Section of the Ministry of State. He divorced Helen Whyte in 1955 by having affairs with María Teresa de la Campa, the divorced daughter of his boss, with whom he married in 1960. Together with the former communist José Camejo-Argudin, they were the only members of the Ministry of State who were not purged by the Castro regime for their friendship with Raúl Roa. On March 3,

a doubt. Having lost my file in Cuba, I usually must trust my memory. For example, a major general of the United States presided over the event, and I know he was the commander of Fort McNair, but his name eludes me[155]. Nor am I certain that it was Dr. Vargas Gómez or the First Secretary of the Embassy, Dr. Averhoff[156]. In any case, I derived great satisfaction from seeing my compatriots, and from the great courtesy displayed by our host.

A visit to the Pentagon was a must, but what took me by surprise was knowing that the agenda had been modified, for a six-minute visit to the Joint Chief of Staff, General Matthew Ridgway[157], and that this general had gone to Havana when President Prío took office, being me his dean on that occasion. Ridgway was a hero of World War II. It was he who replaced the famous General [Douglas] MacArthur in Japan, as well as in command of the UN troops in Korea. His task had been ungrateful, as this was the first of the wars waged by the United States with the purpose of not winning

---

1960, he was appointed ambassador to the United Nations in Geneva, but defected the following month and in Miami was director of a clandestine CIA radio station. He infiltrated Cuba with his wife in 1961 and after the failure of the invasion of Playa Girón they obtained asylum at the Embassy of Ecuador. During a night out of the embassy, he was arrested and sentenced to death in Case 318 of May 23, 1962. The intervention of mother, founder of communist organizations, with Fidel Castro, managed to commute his sentence to 30 years in prison. He returned to Miami on December 25, 1982, where he later died.

[155] Colonel George W. Gibbs was the commander of Fort McNair at the time.

[156] Octavio Augusto Averhoff Sarra (September 6, 1911-March 12, 1999), son of the rector of the University of Havana and secretary of Education, Justice, State and Finance of President Machado. He studied law at Tulane University in the early 1930s. Married to Miguelina, daughter of Miguel Ángel de la Campa. He was Minister Counsellor of the Embassy in Washington in 1956. He was naturalized as a U.S. citizen on September 17, 1984. He died in Coral Gables, Florida.

[157] Matthew Ridgway (March 3, 1895-July 26, 1993) his father was an artillery officer growing up in various military bases during his childhood. Graduated from the Military Academy at West Point where he later taught Spanish. During World War II he was commander general of the 82nd Division of Paratroopers with whom he participated in the battles of Sicily, Normandy, and the Bulge. Appointed Major General and head of the United Nations forces during the Korean War replacing General Douglas McArthur. In 1953 he was appointed chief of the U.S. Army General Staff until his retirement on June 30, 1955.

them. This strategy, condemned even in the most elementary military manuals, has been religiously followed by the great country of the north ever since, and led in a straight line to the disaster in Vietnam. MacArthur's protest at Truman's decision to be defensive while the Chinese communists beat up the U.S. soldiers motivated their relay. His replacement, as I said, was Ridgway. This general maintained with dignity the pavilion of his homeland until the end of the contest. If I remember correctly, his wife was Filipino[158]. Beautiful and fragile like almost all his compatriots, he spoke a magnificent Spanish. On that occasion, the general told me that he had learned a lot from her. I remember that, during his stay in Havana, Ridgway always tried to speak in Spanish.

In the Pentagon, when the Chief of the Joint Chiefs of Staff arrived, he shook my hand warmly, exclaiming, "Did you think I had forgotten you?" He then handed me a silver cigarette case, with my name engraved on it. For my part, I offered him a box of cigarettes, from our president. In fact, President Batista had given me only two boxes, destined for the Secretary of Defense and the Assistant Secretary for the Army. They were cedar, precious, and it occurred to me to acquire three more, for unforeseen cases. It was one of these I gave Ridgway. The interview was cordial and full of reminiscences of his stay in Havana.

Before leaving on our tour, which would include 21 forts and military installations, I had to appear before the Inter-American Defense Board. This body is part of the OAS, and as inoperative as this one. However, very distinguished officers have passed through it, and it was an honor for me to visit its headquarters.

The day before the event, Colonel Barquín came to my hotel room. I was to make a speech on the occasion of my appearance. The speech had been prepared in Havana, and now Barquín brought several notes that would modify his text. In reading them, I found that the proposed changes were not at all favorable to President Batista. They were even real attacks on our government.

---

[158] In December 1947, General Ridgway married his third wife, Mary Princess "Penny" Anthony Long (1918-1997), born in Virginia, who was not Filipino. They were married for 46 years until his death.

I didn't like it at all, and I let him know. I think I even told him that, if he was unhappy with our regime, why didn't he quit? On my return I noticed what happened to General Tabernilla. On that occasion, the general did not reply to me, and I do not know what action was taken against the colonel until the following year, when his arrest took place for other reasons.

The United States Army placed a Convair aircraft at our disposal. Prepared for long trips, it had cabins with all the comforts, which allowed us to rest during the flight. In this way, we arrived fresh to the next stage.

We flew south first, west afterwards, north, and finally east, back to the capital. The tour covered twenty states, and we visited such important facilities as Fort Benning [Georgia], Fort Bragg [North Carolina], Fort Knox [Kentucky] and, finally, Fort Belvoir [Virginia]. There were also others no less remarkable. For example, Fort Jackson [South Carolina], the first, was the Recruit Induction Center. We could see there how the new soldiers were sorted, examined, vaccinated, dressed, and finally set up for instruction. There was then compulsory military service, and the injection of young blood was continuous. In order not to tire, I will touch on just a few aspects: I could see, among other things, the atomic cannon, a large-caliber piece capable of launching nuclear projectiles many kilometres away. I witnessed the tests being carried out on the new M-14 rifle, which was intended to replace the *Garand*. By the way, the reign of the M-14 was short-lived. He was displaced by the M-15, which soon gave way to the M-16.

In short, what a demonstration of power! And what a wonder of organization! I returned to Cuba convinced of the invincibility of the United States. If that was the impression they wanted to give me, they did it to the fullest.

Something very flattering for me was the final act in which, already back in Washington, I was awarded the medal of "Honor to Merit"[159]. I guess this decoration was nothing extraordinary and

---

[159] The Legion of Merit medal was awarded by President Dwight Eisenhower "for outstanding meritorious conduct in the performance of outstanding services to the United States government."

was given to many visitors. But it was for me that, by listing the reasons for which I was granted, one of them turned out to be the "efficiency and honesty" demonstrated in the organization of the CAFSA. In fact, efficiency had been the work of many, and honesty was not relevant, but I was left with doubts as to why they mentioned the fact.

Naturally, when we returned to Cuba, we wrote a report with our impressions[160]. I seem to recall that, among the considerations, was that of the antiquity of our armament compared to that of the United States. They were already replacing the *Garand*, and we were still with the old *Springfield*!

I'm not exaggerating. Actually, I had direct instructions from President Batista in that regard. There was the antecedent of an offer made by the US government in the time of General [Ruperto] Cabrera. According to him, our Armed Forces would receive war surpluses from our northern neighbors at a ridiculous price (one dollar per rifle, for example). The Navy and Air Force rushed to accept, but the then-Assistant General of the Army, Soca Llanes, declined the offer. We are not going to analyze now the causes that he had for it; the truth is that the Army continued as before. My mission was to get the old offer afloat. On the occasion of my visit to the Pentagon, I met with the Assistant General, General [Paul Donal] Harkins. He told me that it was not up to him to decide on this matter, but that he would inform the State Department. Five days later, while I was in Fort Bragg, I received the cable that the Department's agreement had been obtained, and that three general officers would immediately leave for Cuba to study our needs. Thus, the Light Battalion was created, with *Garand* rifles and the corresponding support armament.

THE BARQUÍN CASE

In 1956, our Military Attaché in the United States, Colonel Ramón Barquín López, was arrested for conspiracy. He took advantage of

---

[160] The commission headed by Díaz Tamayo returned to Havana on June 5, 1955 after three weeks in the United States.

one of his regular trips to Havana. His immediate agents were Lieutenant Colonel [Manuel] Varela Castro (who had accompanied me on my tour of the American bases the previous year), Commander [Enrique] Borbonet [Gómez], Captain Gabino [Rodríguez] Villaverde, and Second Lieutenant José Fernández Álvarez. The conspirators were recruited exclusively from among the academy officers. The objective, declared by them during the trial, was to return Cuba to constitutional rhythm through the deposition of the President and the subsequent call for elections.

What were his chances of success? In our opinion, very few. Barquín, a staff officer, and outside Cuba for years, was an unknown to the soldiers who, on the other hand, blindly followed Batista. It was only logical that many academics should feel aggrieved by the government born on March 10. Our president carried out the promotions *ad libitum*[161], without worrying in the slightest about the ranks. Recall that this was the main motive of the conspiracies prior to 1933, but to think, as Barquín thought, that with only a group of officers he was going to impose his will on a fanatical troop of the *Indian* was, as the poet sang, the "vague dragonfly of a vague illusion." Moreover, the conspiracy was not so secret that it did not perspire, and the Military Intelligence Service knew more about it than has been admitted. Batista played with Colonel Barquín like the cat with the mouse, although later, in the court-martial, he observed the same clemency as with Fidel Castro. I have come to the conclusion that, having conspired so much in his life, President Batista felt compelled, as a matter of ethics, to be benevolent with those who practiced the same trade.

Barquín was one of the best placed officers of our Army, and undoubtedly, the future general. For the time being, as has been said, he held an enviable position, albeit a low-paying one when compared with other chiefs of this period. Perhaps this was one of the factors of their discontent. Perhaps informal conversations with some American official led him to think that he had the support of the United States for a coup he considered feasible. It is also possible that his contacts with Colonel Varela during our two-week

---

[161] At your pleasure.

tour of the United States led him to a mistaken appreciation of his possibilities. On January 1, 1959, Barquín had his real chance. Ido Batista, failed the general [Eulogio] Cantillo in his management to form a government, Barquín was freed from his confinement and took charge of the command. It was up to their decision that the armed forces in full, together with the Authors and the students, resolutely confronted the Communists, preventing them from coming to power. Far from that, Colonel Barquín spent his time in small personal revenge, in having the Military Intelligence Service arrested in full, as well as all the superior officers. The next day, he sent Castro the news that he could move forward, that he had the right path. On his orders, Lieutenant Colonel Varela handed La Cabaña over to "Che" Guevara, and Commander Borbonet opened the doors of Columbia to Camilo Cienfuegos. After Waterloo, Marshal [Étienne Jacques] MacDonald assumed, by order of Louis XVIII, command of the French Army. MacDonald called all the officers committed to Napoleon and said, "Go abroad or hide, because soon the royal officers will come and I won't be able to do anything for you."

Colonel Barquín, on the other hand, handed over hundreds of security men to the rebels, including Lieutenant [José] Castaño [Quevedo][162] and Commander [Jesús] Sosa Blanco. Castro sent

---

[162] José de Jesús Castaño Quevedo (June 16, 1914-March 6, 1959) was born in the Santa Fe neighborhood of Havana. His father, Paulino Castaño, was a captain of the Army. He enlisted in 1933 and by competitive examinations acquired the rank of corporal and sergeant major, while working as a typist and translator of seven languages he spoke. He was a professor of languages at the Caribbean Military Academy. He obtained the rank of sub-lieutenant and from 1940 to 1952 he joined the Repressive Group of Subversive Activities (GRAS) and the Military Intelligence Service (SIM). In 1950 he heads the Department of Anti-Democratic Activities during the Communist effervescence against the Korean war. He was BRAC's chief of operations. Arrested after Batista's escape, he was accused by Radio and Television artist Alicia Agramonte Marrero of killing a student. A revolutionary court sentenced him to execution on March 4, 1959. According to Phil Agee, the CIA defector, the head of the CIA station in Havana, James A. Noel, sent the journalist Andrew St. George, who had interviewed the rebel chiefs in the Sierra Maestra, to talk to Ernesto «Che» Guevara to save Castaño's life. Guevara replied that Castaño would be executed not for being Batista's henchman but for being a CIA agent. Two days later, Castaño was shot dead in a dungeon in La Cabaña.

Barquín to rest at his home and subsequently removed him from office, appointing him Ambassador Ex-officio in Western Europe, a position he held for several months.

Lieutenant Colonel Varela, a graduate of the 1944-1947 promotion, was second lieutenant on March 10. This blow, in which he took part, brought him to the higher degree he held. Why did he conspire? Because, as the French say, appetite comes with eating. We have already seen in the previous pages a similar case that, unfortunately, it was up to me to denounce.

Commander Borbonet owed it all to Batista. His father, the colonel of the same name and a personal friend of the president, was retired on 10 March. Being already an elder, he was called to service anyway, also receiving a residence in Columbia so that he could live quietly his last days, and all this without obligations of any kind. With Batista's support, his son entered the Cadet School in 1942 for a two-year course. On March 10, Batista gave another proof of friendship, promoting him to commander and appointing him mayor of Cienfuegos. Later, he indulged him in his desire to create a paratrooper company, sending him to Fort Benning for training. Clearly, Colonel Borbonet was oblivious to gratitude. Convicted in the same court-martial as Barquín, he was released with him on 1 January. By order of his boss, he oversaw locking the hundreds of officers and soldiers already mentioned in the Columbia jails. When Camilo Cienfuegos' column arrived, he handed the camp and these men over to the communists. Subsequently, Borbonet joined the Marxist regime and continued in Cuba until his death in recent years[163].

One case that I would venture to describe as pathetic is that of Lieutenant José Fernández Álvarez[164]. Magnificent organizer,

---

[163] Enrique Borbonet Gómez died in an accident in Cuba in October 1979.

[164] José Ramón "El Gallego" Fernández Álvarez (November 4, 1923-) was a native of Santiago de Cuba, where he first studied. He joined the Army on August 30, 1940 and graduated from the Cadet School in 1947. In April 1956 he was sentenced to four years in prison for his participation in the Conspiracy of the Pure. On January 1, 1959, he personally arrested José Castaño Quevedo, who had arrested him in 1956, and General Eulogio Cantillo Porras. Two weeks later, Fidel Castro appointed him director of the School of Cadets. He was then head of

magnificent executive, number one in his class (1945-47), number one in the Artillery School. Graduated with high grades from Fort Sill Artillery School. Efficient and dedicated as an officer . . . However, he never went from second lieutenant.

Why? I'd say by circumstances of character. According to some of his former comrades, with whom I have spoken, Fernandez was extremely unpleasant in his dealings, both with his peers and with his superiors and subordinates. And in Cuba there is no greater crime than being *pesao*. No boss wanted him in his unit and, therefore, no one ever took him into consideration for a promotion. On March 10, he was deprived of promotion by seniority or opposition. Hence his proclivity to conspiracy: it was his only way out. His prison in Isla de Pinos led him to meet other communist inmates, who were impressed by his ability. When Batista fell, these communists recommended him to Raul Castro, and that was his big moment. Today he is a member of the Central Committee of the Party and a leading figure in the Castro regime. Lieutenant Fernandez is an exponent of so many others involved in the Barquín conspiracy. If we knew how to better appreciate their conditions, it would have been perhaps the worst scourge of our enemies.

In his book *The Prince*, Machiavelli states that any conspiracy, however failed, harms the rulers. Barquín did it to us, a lot. All the conspirators were graduate cadets, not only from Cuba, but also from prestigious foreign academies. With them we lost their knowledge and their experience. On the other hand, although some sixty officers were tried or dismissed, the number involved was considerably greater, and many of them were involved in subsequent attempts, because the leniency of the sanctions encouraged others to do the same. It may well be said that, until 1959, there was always some kind of conspiracy.

---

the militia and army battalions that defeated the invasion of Playa Girón in April 1961. Later he held different positions in the Castro regime including deputy minister of the Revolutionary Armed Forces until 1970; Minister of Education (1972-1990); and Vice-President of the Council of Ministers (1978-2012).

CHAPTER VII

THE CIA AND THE BRAC

One day in the last quarter of 1955, I was invited to a lunch at the Presidential Palace by President Fulgencio Batista. There was nothing extraordinary about this, for the President liked to seat the generals at his table, together with government ministers and other personalities. *I felt small among those men of so much power, but since they were all known and there was some friendship between us, I also felt comfortable and honored at the same time, for being sharing with the main personalities of the government of that moment. I also knew that some of those present their preferred to see me dressed in civilian clothes or not to see me in those places. The situation in the Republic was already difficult. Even I, who was the least important in the group, was very anxious to learn about so many things that were already happening all over the country. In saying the above, I am not just referring to what was going to be discussed there, but in general.*

When he took his seat, the Prime Minister did not occupy the head, but the center. From him, to the right and left, the guests of lesser to greater importance were placed, and so all around, so that the highest category came to stay in front of him. It was the case that, for some reason, the least important was a third- rate official, invited for some specific reason and, as I have already said, he stayed with the President. For these people Batista employed a great touch, not without a good mood. He said to their ears, for example: —Did you like the lobster? Why don't you repeat it? The chef we have is a terrible drunk, but he cooks very well.

Returning to the thread of the narrative, I will repeat that there was nothing extraordinary about that invitation, but what really caught my attention was the quantity and quality of the guests. I remember, among others, the Prime Minister, Dr. [Jorge] García Mon-

193

tes[165], the Minister of the Presidency, Dr. [Andrés] Morales del Castillo, the Minister of State, Dr. Carlos Saladrigas[166], and the Minister of the Interior, Dr. Santiago Rey Pernas[167]. Military, General Tabernilla, Brigadier [Rafael] Salas Cañizares, *head of the Havana Police*, and I *then Inspector General of the Army,*

---

[165] Jorge García Montes (October 19, 1897-June 21, 1982) was born in New York when his father was exiled there during the War of Independence. He graduated from the Law School of the University of Havana in 1917. A member of the Liberal Party, he was a representative of the province of Las Villas (1922-1933) and had to go into exile after the fall of the Machado regime. He returned to Cuba three years later after the amnesty and was elected Senator for Las Villas. Appointed Prime Minister (February 24, 1955- March 26, 1957) and Minister of Education (1957-1958). He returned to exile through the Colombian embassy on March 13, 1959 and arrived in Miami at the end of that month. In 1970, with Dr. Antonio Alonso Ávila, he published the book Historia del Partido Comunista de Cuba. He died at Mercy Hospital in Miami.

[166] Carlos Saladrigas Zayas (October 13, 1900-April 15, 1956) was born in Havana. He graduated in Civil Law from the University of Havana in 1922 when his uncle Alfredo Zayas was president. In 1931 he was one of the founders of the revolutionary organization ABC. He participated in the "Mediation Conferences" sponsored by the US ambassador between the opposition and the government of President Gerardo Machado. In 1933 he was appointed Secretary of State and Justice in the Cabinet of provisional President Carlos Manuel de Céspedes; Secretary without Portfolio in February 1934 in the government of President Carlos Mendieta and three months later Secretary of Justice. In 1936 he was appointed Minister of Cuba in England. Prime Minister under Batista from October 1940 to August 1942. He competed as a presidential candidate for the Democratic Socialist Coalition, which included three parties in the 1944 elections won by Dr. Ramón Grau San Martin. He devoted himself to his profession as a lawyer from then until 1952, when Fulgencio Batista entrusted him with the chairmanship of the Consultative Council and later the Ministry of Labour, later becoming Minister of State. He died in Havana after a long illness.

[167] Santiago C. Rey Pernas (April 7, 1908-October 6, 2003), son of a veteran of the War of Independence, was born in Cienfuegos. Graduated from the Law School of the University of Havana. He was delegated to the Constituent Assembly of 1940 the same year he was elected governor of the province of Las Villas. He was senator of Las Villas from 1944 to 1958. Batista appointed him Minister of the Interior on 23 February 1955. On January 1, 1959, his residence on the corner of D and 21st streets in El Vedado was looted when he obtained political asylum at the Chilean Embassy. There he stayed 73 days before going to Santiago de Chile and moving to Mexico City. He settled in Miami in July 1961, where he later died.

Founding President of the Armed Forces Loan, and Insurance Bank, President of the Military and Naval Circle (under construction), President of the Cuban Polo Federation, and President of the Equestrian Federation of Cuba.

As is always the case in these cases, the conversation fell on irrelevant issues, but as the different dishes were being served, it focused on the need to effectively deal with communist activity. As the President informed us, the United States government had asked us to create a 'Repressive Bureau of Communist Activities'. This would be an autonomous body, and its mission would be to record and classify the Cuban communists. It was in the interest of the State Department that the president of the BRAC should be a general of the Army. The reason for the lunch was to discuss which of us was best suited for the position.

The enumeration began: General Tal: Impossible! It is indispensable where it is now. General Which: Don't even think about it! His character does not conform to that kind of work. And so on to mention them all, except me. And it occurred to me to exclaim: — Gentlemen, please! You didn't leave a puppet with a head. The only one they haven't named is me!

—Well, you're yourself, kid! "You are the man!" said the President, gleefully pointing at me. Not a word! You're appointed!

Those present applauded, accompanying their applause with a "Bravo!" When leaving, Dr. Saladrigas called me aside and, smiling, said in a low voice: —General, the president has taken the piss from you. We knew from the beginning that you were the candidate. To your satisfaction, let me tell you that it was the State Department that unofficially suggested it to you. Looks like he's got some really good friends over there.

Those words have always been present to me. I never knew to what fact to attribute the deference of the United States government to me. And it was not the last time, as we will see later. But, well, it's all in the realm of conjecture.

We left for Washington on an Air Force plane, just as we had done less than a year before. I was accompanied by the retired commander of the Secret Police, [Enrique] Fernández Parajón[168], and the first lieutenant Castaño, later in the military prisons of La Cabaña, where he was shot personally by «Che» Guevara.

At Washington Airport we were greeted by a CIA colonel, who took us to a hotel in the capital. Every day, in the early hours, he would pick us up a car, which would take us to the headquarters of this secret service. It was located in the outskirts, hidden behind massive vegetation. It is impossible to imagine the size of the building, nor the variety of offices and equipment it contained. Day after day, for ten hours, we received intensive instruction, with short breaks and some time for lunch and lunch. So it was for a month, less Saturdays, and Sundays. The instruction, very varied, consisted of films, lectures, demonstrations, and classes, all directed by seven instructors who took turns in explaining the different subjects. These instructors still accompanied us during lunch hours, and at the table they continued to ask us questions or clarify dark points.

The course covered the history of communism from the Industrial Revolution to the present day. We studied their tactics and the use of doctrine by Russia to extend its empire. We were treated about communism in Cuba, with a psychological study of its leaders, of its immediate ends. Day after day, the diabolical conspiracy developed before our eyes worldwide, to overthrow the institutions of the West and seize power in our countries. I was struck by the part devoted to the 'useful fools', as they are often called today, or 'travelling companions', as the Communists themselves call them. They are these people who are not communists and do not even sympathize with communism, but for one reason or another they play into their hands.

I had read something about the subject, but that month of study in the capital of the United States turned out to be a real revolution. For me it was access to a new world. Many of the things that happened in Cuba and that previously went unnoticed to me, I contemplated from then on with a meridian clarity. What I can't ex-

---

[168] Enrique Fernández Parajón went into exile on January 1, 1959 on the same plane with Fulgencio Batista.

plain is how, with such complete knowledge of the global complex and, even more, of Russia's intentions on Cuba, the CIA allowed the famous fourth floor of the State Department[169] to support Castro and facilitate his coming to power. And above all, that Cuba be left to its own devices, as was subsequently done[170].

Before turning to the subject of graduation, I would like to mention the attentions that our Embassy in Washington had with us. Our then ambassador, Dr. Álvarez de la Campa, has already passed away. Of the other officials, a few I have seen again in exile. But how vivid are the impressions of those four weeks left in me! On Sundays, after six days of constant application, the Embassy opened its doors to us. We enjoyed there the magnificent yantar, the cultured conversation of its inhabitants, as well as the inspiring presence of their wives and children. Though almost thirty years have passed, may my gratitude go to all of them.

Upon graduation, we were greeted by the director of the CIA, Mr. Allen Dulles. I must admit that the interview was the worthy culmination of our studies. It's two years since I read a story about this character in the *Miami Herald*. If the memory is not unfaithful to me, Mr. Dulles would have declared before a committee in the Senate to ignore the fact that Castro's movement was communist. I do not know what reason he would have for making this statement, but if the news is true, Mr. Dulles laughed in the very beards of the august congress. I can say that, in those days, the CIA's attention to the events in Cuba was intense, and its knowledge of our situation meticulous.

Our interview with the director of the Central Intelligence Agency lasted about 20 minutes. After asking ourselves if we had enjoyed

---

[169] The fourth floor of the State Department was where American foreign policy was formulated.

[170] Cuba was abandoned to Soviet orbit when President John Kennedy, to resolve the Missile Crisis quickly in October 1962, allowed the United States, in exchange for the Russians removing 42 nuclear rockets from the island, to remove 104 nuclear missiles from England, Italy and Turkey; promised never to invade Cuba; forbade exiled Cubans from attacking Cuba; and allowed a Soviet combat brigade to remain on the island indefinitely in violation of the Monroe Doctrine.

the course, and if we were satisfied, he immediately entered the matter. His project, which we Cubans later called the "Bureau for the Repression of Communist Activities" (BRAC), was much broader than I initially thought it would be. It would consist of thoroughly investigating, and filing, both communists and those who showed leftist ideas. Our cooperation was essential to achieve absolute control over the members of the party, as well as over the penetration of its apparatus in Cuba. Then, Mr. Dulles explained to us that our country, due to its geographical position, was the number one objective of communism in America, and that the United States could not allow Cuba to fall into the hands of Moscow. He instructed me to convey to the Havana government that they would provide the necessary funds for the BRAC to become an effective agency. He added that we would be a pilot institution and that, if successful, many other countries in Spanish America would soon establish other BRAC, using Cuba as a model.

I returned to Havana in amazement at how much I saw and heard. Also, my vanity grew pointless. Choosing me for that task was a backing, both for my President and for the United States. I felt like the central character of a silent, but no less powerful, organization that would help protect Cuba and the West from exotic doctrines.

Rocked by those dreams, I returned to Havana, and immediately went to meet with President Batista. I explained to him in great detail the outcome of my mission, and emphasized the danger Cuba was in, and the powerful help we could expect from the United States. *I tried to convince the president to make a law or laws that would force the communists to identify themselves, to know about their movements and activities, but the president did not agree because he thought it unnecessary. I was just a junior. He was the one who had to answer my propositions. I did my best because I was convinced we were already in the Kremlin's peephole.*

As usual, Batista listened to me attentively, without saying a word until I finished. He did not interrupt me once, nor did he show signs of impatience, but when I had finished, he took the floor, and it was like a bucket of cold water to me. Here is, more or less, the opinion of the President:

—It's okay about the BRAC. We will proceed to create it immediately, but no American money. You don't realize that this gift is an indignity to us. The BRAC will run on Cuban funds, and we'll do what we can[171].

That meant complete frustration. The giant future was dying in the cradle. Liberated to our own means, we could do little. Our President underestimated the Communists! That was a conclusion that I came to, above all, having still fresh the indoctrination that I had just received. Perhaps he was right in the inconvenience of receiving foreign funds because, in the end, it is the one who pays who commands, and the differences in criteria could have contributed to friction, but thus, practically without budget, the BRAC became, from the beginning, a squalid and quasi-symbolic body. And from my resignation, which occurred twelve months later, he ended up becoming a mere auxiliary of the Military Intelligence Service. The BRAC should have been an autonomous, silent institution, detecting any vestige of communism, wherever it may be. The information collected would eventually be passed on to the security forces, who would act with knowledge of the facts.

Stop it. Instead of millions, I had a budget of $210,000 for the first six months. Although empowered to recruit the necessary staff, the limited means forced me to resort to elements from the agencies that I had previously controlled. That is, CASFA and the Military and Naval Circle. Also, many military and police officers offered their services to me in their spare hours. Dr. Salvador Díaz-Versón, a convinced anti-communist and a great connoisseur of the subject, provided us with his incredibly rich archives, which included documents of the greatest importance. As time went on, I became convinced that this archive was one of the things the backyard communists feared the most. In many cases, they were newspaper clippings from the 1930s and early 1940s. In them, Blas Roca Calderío, Lazaro Peña, Juan Marinello, etc., competed

---

[171] The BRAC was created by Presidential Decree No. 1307 on May 4, 1955. The organization was initially chaired by Minister of the Interior Santiago Rey Pernas. Martín Díaz Tamayo was appointed its Vice PresidentDirector General by decree on June 4, 1955, just as Lieutenant Colonel José J. Figarola Infante was appointed administrative secretary of the BRAC.

in licking the boots of Colonel Batista, whom they called *Messenger of Prosperity* and *True Father of the Cuban People*. I remember a great headline in the newspaper Hoy, where the comrades cried out in chorus: "We demanded for Colonel Batista the torpedoes of a general!"

MY TRANSFER TO ORIENTE

It should be noted that my differences with General Tabernilla, which at no time were cordial, had been accentuated for some time. Maybe one of the ingredients was my withdrawn character. On the occasion to which I shall refer, however, a comment made by me in the privacy of my office triggered the incident. The comrade in arms before whom I made the comment repeated it to the general, and the latter went indignantly to the Palace to complain to the President. Batista made me call, very sorry, and after going round and round the matter, he proposed the passage to Oriente for a season. I think his intention was to separate us until the mood cooled, but seeing what things are, I, usually so quiet, reacted vividly.

Almost desperately I told President Batista: The Army is heading for a hopeless cliff. Bounce all the generals, starting with me, and anyone who gets in the way of Cuba's cause. Make a new staff and start over. That night he had a Council of Ministers. We had started talking at 7:00 P.M. It was a date to ask me to be head of the Orient. The council called him and he waited until 9:00 PM that we didn't say goodbye. But at the indicated time I said to him: When the Armed Forces collapse, not one institution of the Republic will remain standing; nor will you, Mr. President, pointing my right index finger at you. It was a problem with General Tabernilla Dolz, motivated by the visit of the new English Ambassador[172], who began his diplomatic work in Cuba. It was a simple and un-

---

[172] Díaz Tamayo is confused with the date of the event, as British Ambassador Alfred Stanley Fordham (September 2, 1907-April 6, 1981) was assigned to Havana on October 18, 1956. Fordham approved the sale of British tanks and aircraft to the Batista government in 1958 and two years later became Ambassador to Colombia.

important thing, but since I was the one who commented on it, it formed a tremendous mess. I gained the relief of the General Inspectorate, the presidency of the Armed Forces bank that had organized and led it myself with a group of distinguished officials; the leadership of the BRAC; the presidency of the Military and Naval Circle; the presidency of the Equestrian Federation; the leadership of the Polo Federation and the comfort of being close to my family in Havana.

I know that when I don't like a thing that brings responsibilities and serious things for what I stand for, I'm a bit of a mess. I didn't ask for anything, but for things to be done well. Naturally, I did not accept the President, with all the respect imposed by his high office, to go and occupy that magnificent post. I begged him to retire, to get sick or whatever he had to do with me, but to give that unfair taste to someone who was right, no. And I didn't, and nothing happened. Later I went to Oriente, but in another way. I went because I believed that what was needed in Oriente was conduct, not a master of the province.

Returning to the case of the English Ambassador, it was a problem of confusion with Lieutenant Colonel [Gustavo] Cowley [Galicians]. I felt that an army officer like him, especially, could not confuse a question of trust with an object of cheap gossip. General Tabernilla was not offended, I simply explained to the colonel what I saw, that I did not consider it correct, simply. Colonel Cowley was to me a man of confidence. I never believed in him or anyone else. He was promoted later, as was natural when that behavior has atmosphere. But I can't help but understand how harmful those kinds of people are. May God have him in glory, like many others who proceeded wrongly yesterday. With all that, I'm glad I helped him twice.

I thanked the President for his intention to use me where it was needed most, but in this case I knew what the real cause of the transfer was. I explained to him the reason for my comment that, on the other hand, he should not have left my office. I also explained how upset I felt about a series of circumstances that I saw were not happening. I added that, if those circumstances were not remedied, the Army would crumble from pure demoralization. Having reached this point, I asked for my retirement.

As usual, Batista listened to me without interrupting me. Impassive face and with eyes fixed on me. At the end of my shoot, he took the floor to answer me:

—Have you gone mad? How can I withdraw you? You're obfuscated! You don't know what you're talking about. It's okay. He's still at your post. Go home now and freshen up, but from now on, try to get along with "Old Pancho."

Among the many things I must thank President Batista for, is how tolerant he was with me that day. The resolutions I put forward, although expressed in a respectful tone, were still too harsh and direct to be told to a president. This condescension was not a sign of weakness in Batista. The president felt so confident of his authority, he could afford to handle me like he did.

On the other hand, nothing was so afraid of General Tabernilla as the replacement of Brigadier del Río Chaviano, let alone for me. This was his brother-in-law and his trusted man. My presence in Oriente would change things a little in Regiment 1. It is quite possible that knowing that the punishment of General Díaz Tamayo would consist precisely in my transfer to Oriente, I preferred to leave things like this, and this was terminated.

I continued to organize the BRAC, but not for long. After two months, the President summoned me again. This time he informed me that it had become imperative to remove Brigadier del Río Chaviano from Oriente, *which he continued to do of his own over there*[173], and that I, precisely I, should take the command there, that I would officially receive the orders through General Tabernilla. Thus, when the general communicated the President's order to me, I was ready to carry it out[174].

---

[173] José López Vilaboy, in Motives and Guilty of the Destruction of Cuba (Publisher of Books Puerto Rico, 1973), page 323, pointed out that Alberto del Río Chaviano was removed from the Eastern Command "because he was incapable, drunk, abusive and disloyal."

[174] «Movement in the High Offices of the F. Armadas», *Diario de la Marina*, April 28, 1956, 1.

I have asked myself several times what Batista meant when he told me that I, myself, should take the lead in Oriente. The President was extremely cunning. Perhaps he wanted to make it clear that he had not forgotten my behavior of weeks ago, but I know that, when I was in Santiago de Cuba, I was trying to reconcile a series of circumstances that placed the Army in an unfavorable light[175].

I took the plane and left for my destination. Everything was done with such haste, that I didn't even hand over the BRAC's command. Later I learned that Colonel Aquilino Guerra [González] had been appointed in my place[176]. Neither was Brigadier del Río Chaviano in Santiago to greet me. His removal was sudden and sharp. I suppose in all armies these things happen late in the evening.

When I went to Oriente with the mission of taking over that military command, a personal attack had been carried out against me. This news forced me not to take my family with me until 10 days later. We were only two assistants, two drivers and two enlisted people who were at my service because of the moment we were living. I always have faith in our God. Well, nothing happened.

As soon as I had the command in safe hands, I brought my wife, mother-in-law and children. They occupied the Chief's house, intended for the Chief of the Regiment, which was located almost outside the military compound, opposite the post through which the attackers entered on July 26, 1953.

---

[175] Díaz Tamayo assumed command of Regiment No. 1 on May 3, 1956.

[176] Colonel Aquilino Guerra González was appointed Vice-Director of the BRAC on April 30, 1956 and was replaced five months later by Colonel Leopoldo Pérez Coujil. In the summer of 1957, the position of Deputy Director was replaced by that of Director General of Investigations of the BRAC, which was taken over by Lieutenant Colonel Mariano Faget Díaz. First Lieutenant José de Jesús Castaño Quevedo assumed the department called the Central Agency of Operations with branches in each Army regiment and in each Naval Post of the Navy and in the Propaganda and Materials Section. The Section was advised by journalists Edmund Chester and Salvador Díaz-Versón, and historian Herminio Portell Vilá.

A few days I had been in my new command, when upon entering my home for lunch, Rosaura, my wife, came out to meet me and said: —You have a visitor.

He was an invalid American, sitting in a wheelchair. He would be about 45 years old, tall, with blond straw hair. I was identified as Mr. [Lyman B.] Kirkpatrick[177], CIA supervisor for Latin America. I invited him to lunch and, while he was preparing lunch, we went to the bar. Once alone, he snapped at me: — General, we want to know what happened to him. I came here specifically to find out.

I laughed and replied: —Ah! You don't know that? Well, me neither!

He didn't insist. We went slowly to the dining room and, after lunch, I drove him to the airport, for his return to Havana. I never heard from him again.

My task in Oriente was not so difficult, nor was it necessary to make major changes. It was enough that I established my usual line of conduct. As soon as I knew the rules of the game, Eastern society opened its doors to me. As for the Army, it was the first time that I was back in command of troops since my retirement, back in 1951. To my satisfaction, I found a Rural Guard still fit

---

[177] Lyman B. Kirkpatrick, Jr. (July 15, 1915-March 3, 1995), born in Rochester, New York, graduated from Princeton University in 1938. During World War II he was an Army intelligence officer in London. In 1947 he joined the CIA where he was executive assistant to director Allen Dulles when he was afflicted with polio in 1952. He was crippled and used a wheelchair for the rest of his life. In 1953 he was appointed inspector general of the agency until 1961. He drafted the confidential report on the failure of the Bay of Pigs invasion, exonerating President Kennedy and holding Dulles responsible for the disaster. The report served to fire Dulles, who, being replaced by John McCone, thwarted Kirkpatrick's cravings for the position. In April 1962 he was created a special administrative position as executive director until he resigned from the agency in 1965 to be a professor of political science at Brown University. In his memoirs, The Real CIA (1968), described Díaz Tamayo as "a tough but correct army officer." He indicates that after the general left the BRAC, "there was evidence that the BRAC could be very enthusiastic in some of his interrogations. We thought that much more could be done in the recruitment and training of its investigators and surveillance personnel and there was a desperate need for the consolidation of the files of all the investigative agencies, of which there were many. " He retired from Brown in 1982 and died at his Virginia residence.

and, under proper command, responding with discipline and pride to his uniform. Weapons, on the other hand, are very old-fashioned. The cavalry, disappeared as a unit of line, was found only in the squadrons, although, unfortunately, in an inadequate number. It now seems appropriate to me to drop a few words on the progress of the Army from 1952 onwards.

In several pages of this book, I have spoken about the evolution of our Armed Forces: First, the Rural Guard, totally on horseback. Later, under José Miguel Gómez, the Permanent Army appears. Following 4 September, the only substantial change in the organization resulted in the replacement of the Cavalry Thirds (which were one per regiment) by infantry battalions. Only the Third of Columbia survived. Then, except for the creation of some schools, such as the Superior General of War and the General of Classes, plus the acquisition of medium and light tanks and two 25 mm anti-aircraft battalions, there are no major alterations.

The senior command was exercised by a Major General Chief of Staff, and the Chief of the Armed Forces was the President of the Republic. The Navy had its own chief, who in the early days was a Ship Captain. Later, during the Second World War, the Navy received new units, its troops increased and the Chief successively became a commodore, a rear admiral and, finally, an admiral. The Police, included in the Armed Forces from 1933, was usually commanded by a colonel or a general of the Army, although there were some chiefs from the corps itself.

Although there were three brigade generals in the respective positions of Adjutant General, Headquarters-Master General and Inspector General, he was the first of these, that is, the Adjutant General, the most important character. This was reasonable, because being the Executive Officer, command was exercised through him. All the details of command and organization depended on this chief.

We have already seen how, after temporarily occupying this position in the early morning of March 10, I was relieved by General [Eulogio] Cantillo. Was the designation of this one a success? I think so. It will be remembered how in Kuquine I thought it was him and not General Tabernilla the Chief of Staff. In his role as

Assistant General he was efficient, capable and a magnificent planner, but when in 1957 he was removed from his natural environment by sending him to the area of operations, the results were unsatisfactory, because Cantillo's experience in commanding troops was almost nil. Also, the gift of command is born with the individual, it is not acquired, and this general almost lacked it. He was a bureau man, an operations man, a map man. Many great generals have had this limitation but, aware of it, they exercised their influence, sometimes decisive, through men often inferior to them, but who, due to their type of personality, dragged their troops into superhuman efforts.

Another of Cantillo's limitations was his excessive adherence to American military doctrine. Graduated from several schools in the United States, he followed everything that came from that country as an article of faith, to the letter, and without considering our idiosyncrasy. Having suppressed the cavalry, he did the same. Instead of horses he sent jeeps to the Rural Guard, at the rate of one jeep per post. Naturally, the jeeps did not arrive at the posts and sheds. In any case, the tours had to be made, so that the rural guards, lacking in rides, borrowed the poor peasants' Jamaicans. This undermined the prestige of the Rural Guard in the men of the countryside, for whom the famous couples, mounted on huge percherones, had come to constitute a myth. Another thing: the jeep was so comfortable and tempting to the heads of unit, that many intended it for their personal use. During my command in Oriente I could see that many couples, lacking vehicles in which to move, reported as realities journeys that they had not done.

My stay in Oriente province lasted eleven months. And how many reminiscences it brought me! Being second lieutenant, back in 1936, he had come in disgrace to this regiment. Also on that occasion I had been there for eleven months, which I enjoyed very much, despite feeling the Sword of Damocles on me. In addition, it was in Santiago de Cuba that, despite my rank, I served as Squadron Leader. My first independent command!

I can't say that in 1957 it was all a bed of roses. The armed opposition to the regime of 10 March was beginning to materialize, but I believe I have the right to affirm that with my actions, I contributed to calm the moods and neutralize the enmity of many in favor of President Batista.

An honor conferred on me was the award of a medal of recognition by unanimous agreement of the mayors of the province. The governor of Oriente, Mr. [Luis] Casero[178], sent me the resolution, although, after thanking him, I felt obliged not to accept without the authorization of the President, authorization that never arrived.

About Mr. Casero, although of Authentic extraction and very far from sympathizing with the government, he had the courtesy to declare, in the television program Ante la Prensa, that with six provincial military chiefs like me, there would not be the slightest problem in Cuba. Although I think the praise is exaggerated, I thanked him very much and I continue to thank him.

The third reason for satisfaction was the support given to me by the living classes of Santiago de Cuba on the events of 30 November. Representatives of the various social classes, industry, commerce, banking, etc., came spontaneously to the Moncada Barracks, where they had words of praise for me.

... And one day Fidel Castro landed. My behavior in those days was what I considered appropriate with the means at hand. However, it has been criticized by some of my comrades in arms.

Castro's disembarkation took place in the early hours of December 2. The General Staff knew about this adventure. He knew the name of the ship, the number of men on board, where it was headed, and how to intercept it. Nothing was done and, what is worse, nothing was communicated to me until 3 p.m. on that day, despite

---

[178] Luis Felipe Casero Guillén (November 22, 1902-August 15, 1998) Born in El Cristo, Oriente, he was never governor. Elected mayor of Santiago de Cuba from 1944 until April 1951, when he was appointed Minister of Public Works in the government of Carlos Prío (1948-52). Candidate for Vice-President for the Authentic Party in the frustrated 1952 elections. Falsely implicated in the attack on the Moncada barracks on 26 July 1953, he was tried and acquitted. He was in the insurance business. He collected funds for Carlos Prío's clandestine Authentic Organization, so he had to go into exile in Jamaica and returned to Cuba in January 1959. He returned to exile in Miami with his family in 1971, where he later died.

having taken land in territory under my jurisdiction. The Chief of Squadron [12 of the Rural Guard] of Manzanillo, Captain Charity [B.] Fernandez, in whose territory the disembarkation took place, and placed in that position by General Tabernilla, communicated the fact directly to the General Staff, without informing me as well. With this, I remained for several hours in the greatest ignorance. Nor, neither Caridad nor his brother-in-law, the second lieutenant [Achilles] Chinea[179], made the least effort to contact the expeditionaries. What a performance so different from that of the Holguin Squadron Leader in 1931, when upon hearing of the landing in Gibara, he marched with his forces on the enemy without waiting for reinforcements or orders! The performance of Caridad Fernández will remain for another to judge. Fidel Castro paid him the favor by shooting him in [February 1959]. Chinea enjoyed Castro's friendship for a while, but at last he had to go into exile. That's how the devil pays those who serve him well!

But I'm getting ahead of things. On the evening of November 29, the head of the Regimental Intelligence Service, Commander Ar-

---

[179] Aquiles Chinea Álvarez (May 12, 1926-December 19, 2005) born in Manacas, Las Villas. He was chief of the post of Niquero of the 12th Squadron of the Rural Guard, when there he had a dispute with Lieutenant Colonel José M. Salas Cañizares and seriously wounded him by throwing his Jeep to kill him. He was imprisoned in Isla de Pinos and when he left on January 1, 1959, he was appointed by Colonel Ramón Barquín as head of the San Antonio de los Baños air base. Nine days later, while in the Rebel General Staff Building at Columbia Camp, a 45-caliber bullet was fired at his chest trying to commit suicide by embarrassing himself that the Revolutionary Directory had taken the weapons in his custody from the base. To Fidel Castro, asking him why he took the shot, he said: "I believe in you Fidel; I believe in revolution, but I could not bear so much weight." He served as a witness against former Corporal Ezequiel Pérez Villalobos before a revolutionary court on March 5, 1959. Two months later he testified against Captain Gabriel Ulloa Franqui, who was sentenced to 15 years in prison. Chinea was granted asylum at the Brazilian Embassy on 25 March 1960. He traveled to Brazil and from there he went to Miami on July 6, 1960, where he obtained political asylum. On November 1, 1966, he moved to Los Angeles, California, where he naturalized as a U.S. citizen on November 20, 1970, and changed his name to Arch Christy. He died in Las Vegas, Nevada.

cadio Casillas Lumpuy[180], informed me that something would happen in Santiago de Cuba in the early hours of the morning.

As a matter of urgency, I summoned the following leaders at midnight on the same day:

- Commodore [Mario] Rubio Baró[181], Chief of the Eastern Naval District.
- Lieutenant Colonel Álvaro Miranda, Chief of the National Police.
- The aforementioned Captain Casillas, Chief of the Regimental Intelligence Service.
- First Lieutenant [Antonio] Gutierrez [Valdés][182], Chief of the Microwave.
- To the heads of units at Moncada Barracks.

---

[180] Lieutenant Colonel Arcadio R. Casillas Lumpuy (1919-1959) on January 1, 1959 was invited by the military chief of Guantánamo Square, Commander Roberto Franco Lliteras, seconded by Captain Raúl Vila and Lieutenant Joaquín Zumbado Armenteros, among others, to attend a conciliatory interview with the guerrilla leaders to ensure the surrender of their forces without reprisals or revenge. His colleagues prepared a tricky trap for him and he was arrested when he arrived at the meeting place. He was quickly sentenced to death along with other military personnel by an improvised Revolutionary Court. When they were taken to the firing squad on a pickup truck, Casillas lunged at a custodian and snatched the rifle from him. From the balcony of the town hall, rebel guards machine-gunned the vehicle, killing the prisoners and some rebel guards. His brother Joaquín Casillas Lumpuy had died the same way the previous day in Santa Clara, while struggling with the guards who drove him in a truck to the wall.

[181] Mario Felipe Rubio Baró (September 20, 1914-September 11, 1993), a native of Jovellanos, Matanzas, was a frigate captain and assistant to the chief of staff of the Navy on August 5, 1953 when he was appointed chief of the Eastern Naval District. In 1957 he was Commodore and Director of the Cuban Naval Academy. He was imprisoned in El Morro de la Habana in January 1959 with 130 officers and enlisted in the Navy. He was tried by a revolutionary court and sentenced to 12 years' imprisonment in May 1959, and all his property was seized. He went into exile in Miami on August 16, 1970 and naturalized as a U.S. citizen on May 22, 1976. He died in Miami.

[182] Antonio Gutiérrez Valdés was shot by the rebels with more than a hundred other Batistians without trial at the Loma de San Juan on January 11, 1959.

After transmitting to them the information received by Captain Casillas, I gave them orders to quarter the personnel and take any measures they deemed appropriate to ensure the security of the forces under their command.

I had no jurisdiction over the Navy, but Commodore Rubio Baró took note of the deal, and agreed with me as to the gravity of the moment, taking identical measures.

I sent a code to all squadrons and units under my command, instructing them to take precautions in their respective commands, as well as alerting the civil authorities. *At one time, all troops were ordered to be quartered, which displeased some high commanders.*

It dawned on November 30, and at last the expected occurred: a diversionary action aimed at covering the landing of Fidel Castro, which took place two days later. The instruments were always useful fools, especially young students[183]. It consisted of sporadic shootings in different parts of Santiago de Cuba. The main attack was carried out against the Police Headquarters. It wasn't strong enough to take it, but they did succeed in setting it on fire. Unfortunately, something like this happened, because a branch of the University of Oriente, I think the School of Plastic Arts, gave the back of the headquarters building. The Communists entered the School, and from there they launched flammable materials. The Headquarters was a wooden house of the nineteenth century, and it burned like gunpowder. They were sent a reinforcement of 25 soldiers and an officer, thus averting the danger. Three Communists[184] and three soldiers of our own were killed. The rioters

---

[183] Fidel Castro tried to emulate José Martí's Fernandina Plan on February 24, 1895, with the uprising of his followers in all the provinces. José Antonio Echeverría, leader of the Revolutionary Directory (DR), previously agreed with Castro in Mexico that the students would begin the insurrection across the island on November 30, 1956, when the Granma expeditionary yacht was expected to disembark. At the last moment, Echevarría abandoned the plan and the only one who fulfilled it was Frank País, who was not from the DR, with his people in Santiago de Cuba. The Granma, overloaded with 82 men, weapons and additional gasoline, took two days longer than estimated.

[184] The rebels killed were Tony Alomá, 29, a Public Works employee; Otto Parellada, 28, a lineman; and José "Pepito" Tey, 23, president of the Oriental

also occupied the Institute of Second Education and the Normal School, although they did not approach the Moncada Barracks. Then they disappeared, leaving the three dead already mentioned and some weapons. We were also informed that another attack was being prepared against the Maritime Police Headquarters. Preventively, I sent them an officer and 25 soldiers and so, if they really tried to attack, this attack was avoided. That was all. *The Moncada barracks and its military hospital remained intact.*

On page 47 of his book Response, former President Batista writes that the disturbances in Santiago lasted three days, and that it was necessary to send a battalion under the orders of Lieutenant Colonel [Pedro] Barrera to restore normalcy. And all this because "I lacked the conditions to face the situation."

With all the respect I have for my former boss, who, on the other hand, is no longer among us, I do not find it wrong to have quartered the troops, both to protect the soldiers and prevent them from being killed in the streets, and to have a maneuvering mass. It's such an elementary measure, I don't know why some bosses criticized me. As for the riots, they were already over on the night of the 30th[185]. Colonel Barrera was sent to me without me asking, and I attribute it to General Tabernilla's unwillingness toward me, who wished me to be relieved of command, and returned to appoint for him his brother-in-law, Brigadier del Río Chaviano[186].

Brigadier del Río Chaviano was married to the sister of the great lady Esther Palmero, wife of the Gen. Francisco Tabernilla and Dolz. That was a big problem for me because the brigadier was

---

University Student Federation. Tey and his men attacked the police station from the front, while Parellada and his followers attacked from the back.

[185] Santiago de Cuba was pacified in three days with a death toll of a dozen on both sides and a deaf civilian who did not hear an order to stop.

[186] Colonel Pedro Barrera Pérez wrote: "During my performance in the Sierra I had felt the enormous distance that existed between the Chief of Staff General Tabernilla and the Chief of the Maceo Regiment in Oriente, General Martín Díaz Tamayo, because General Tabernilla put whatever obstacles were in his power to make Diaz Tamayo fail and convince the president of the need to send Colonel Río Chaviano back to Oriente." "Why the Army Didn't Defeat Castro," *Free Bohemia*, August 20, 1961.

for the boss more than his brother-in-law, he was a son. That displeased the General-in-Chief greatly, for I was not a saint of his devotion. Why wasn't I? Well, for a lot of things that didn't match the boss's. I didn't know how to say yes when a no came to mind, after knowing that the right thing was the opposite of yes. Or because I was catching up to all the things that were convenient to the Armed Forces institution, and even beyond these. We could quote many things, but I have never lived from the unpleasant things.

I interpreted the unexpected arrival of the Barrier Battalion as a violation of ethics, and of respect for my hierarchy. To even think that Brigadier del Río Chaviano could send Regiment 1 back was childish. It was one more of the blind sticks that had been given for some time, but for the moment I also considered it a personal insult to send a battalion, with orders to act independently, and all that in my own command, in my own territory. He also stationed separately, in the Provincial Government Palace, and not in an Army barracks. Barrera had enough tact to present himself to me immediately, and to maintain daily contact with me, but that did not diminish the magnitude of the grievance because, following the instructions he received, he acted with complete independence, reporting only to the General Staff . . .And all this in a territory of my jurisdiction.

I remember that as soon as the first planes with the companies of Barrera began to arrive, I phoned General Tabernilla, and asked him for an explanation of that. He told me he didn't know, that that was an order from the President. I begged him then to let me talk to him. I finally managed to communicate, and the President spoke to me with great cordiality, asking me about my wife, the children, etc. As soon as I could I said these words:

—Mr. President, I hope my replacement is already on the way.

—Your relay? But why are you taking over?

"Because this duality of command that you have created is intolerable to me, without taking me into consideration at all." Under these conditions, I cannot and should not continue here.

Far from getting angry, contradicting me or nodding with me, Batista laughed, made me see how necessary I was in Oriente, and ended up saying to me:

Don't be like that. I sent you to Barrera to support you. He's there to help you, he'll be here for a few days, and he'll be back. What you tell me about duality of command is clearly a misinterpretation. You are indispensable in Oriente, etc.

The truth is, I softened up. I should have insisted on the relay and I didn't. The cordiality and affectionate way the President spoke to me acted in the usual manner. Also, I did not want to create new problems, and I ended up accepting the situation, as long as Barrera was only there for a few days.

To end on November 30, at three o'clock in the afternoon of that day, the only shots felt in the province of Oriente were those caused by the *Thompson machine guns* of a small armed group led by Dr. Laureano Ibarra[187]. This gentleman had had business with my predecessor, Brigadier del Río Chaviano, and held the position of Administrator of the Customs of Santiago *by the work and grace of the head of the regiment that we relieved in April 1956 that made him possess many undue benefits that I will not mention for professional ethics. That's a long and sad story for the heroic province.* Ibarra had been authorized to hold several men in arms, and this was one of the problems I had to face during my stay in Oriente. Otherwise, and of course, arrests and investigations were carried out in the days that followed, but I did not believe in the obligation to order the death of anyone. If it is estimated that "he had no conditions," then what am I going to do to him?

The question of Castro's disembarkation and his subsequent internment in the Sierra, where he became strong, and from where he left to become the owner of Cuba, is an issue open to controversy. It seems inconceivable that such a thing could happen. On more than one occasion I have stated that Batista used Castro to frighten the non-combatant opposition, and that the latter, given its

---

[187] Laureano Ibarra Pérez was a lawyer and was a second-education teacher and elected representative in the November 1958 elections. His residence was looted on January 1, 1959.

choice between two evils, threw itself into the arms of the government. I won't comment, at least on these lines, but it's only fair that I break a spear in defense of the Armed Forces.

My humble opinion is that Castro was something like a small animal that we had hidden in one of our hands so as not to let it grow and squeeze it at any given time until it perishes. This had or should have happened when the government was in favor and everything was fine. But the little animal continued to grow and grow until it became so strong and great, that that hand that should have prevented its growth and disrupted it in time, could not do it, because its hand became weak and the little animal became a giant satanic, helped by unconsciousness, ignorance and hatred.

The poor soldiers are disoriented with the things they see in the Sierra Maestra and outside. The bosses don't stimulate them from here. They are only required to do so, but it does not seem that there is a firm intention to put an end to those weeds that perhaps many good mothers conceived. Unfortunately, it was like this, in less time than I thought. I wanted to tell the president once, but with the experience of many others, it would have been an explosion that hardly anyone would have believed. I was only guided by the parts of operations, the help that individuals in power gave and international propaganda. It was also necessary to add the refusal of the Americans Roy A. Rubottom, Jr.[188] and William Wieland, the lack of cooperation of the peasantry and the people in general and the abuse to which the Armed Forces were all subjected, without obtaining real successes with our magnificent soldiers, sailors and airmen, at the right time and in the right place. The police also played a very important role in the cities. Then

---

[188] Roy Richard Rubottom, Jr. (February 13, 1912-December 6, 2010) was born in Brownwood, Texas, and studied at the University of Texas until enrolling in the Navy in 1941 as a lieutenant and finishing five years later with the rank of commander. He began his diplomatic service in 1947 and in September 1956 was appointed Undersecretary of State for Inter-American Affairs. Influenced by his assistant William Wieland, he insisted until 1960 that Fidel Castro was not a communist. He then changed his mind and favored the CIA's attempts to assassinate Fidel Castro and Rafael Trujillo. He was ambassador to Argentina 1960-1961 and administrator at several universities until his retirement in 1973. He died in Austin, Texas.

what was needed, from top to bottom, was the desire to win and the lack of preparation in guerrilla warfare.

In his own defense, President Batista states that many of his subordinates did not act as they should, or betrayed him. That is, it places responsibility in others, and never on their person. What he or others said about me is of no concern to me, but I cannot tolerate our flags fading. For better or worse, the President had absolute power in his hands. That power was not delegated to anyone. Military operations in Oriente were led by him, and not a single unit moved without his consent. As a soldier, General Batista's incompetence was notorious, but nonetheless, he repeatedly disavowed the operations plans suggested to him by the General Staff, to impose his own ideas. If that is added to the constant subordination of the tactical to the political, I think that everything is more than explained. Poor army! Poor soldiers, with their blind faith in the *Indian*. Like Napoleon's *grognards*, our men also growled, but never to accuse the President. Others were the incompetent ones. Others the corrupt. Never Batista! Medel tells me that in prison, the former soldiers, now imprisoned as war criminals, talked about Batista having to leave because he had been betrayed, but that he would return. Of course I'd come back! He would come to the front of 30,000 men, and then true justice would be done!

Poor soldiers: simple, faithful, naive. Those sacrificed of all times and in all countries by unscrupulous politicians. See the victorious wars waged by the United States since 1945. More than fifty thousand young Americans died in Vietnam for the sake of a policy that went from the stupid to the perfidious. And what about the Vietnamese soldiers who believed in the Great Democracy, who ultimately abandoned them to their fate?

On December 2, at 3 pm, I was notified *from Havana* of the disembarkation of Fidel Castro, *which occurred at about 6:00 AM*. It was Sunday, and we were meeting at that time in my office the Officer of the Day, my assistant, Captain [Gabriel] Ulloa Franqui, and me. The communication was made by General Tabernilla himself, who ordered me, not to appear at the scene, nor asked me what I had done, but to send an officer and 25 soldiers to reinforce the squadron of Manzanillo, there was Caridad Fernández. I showed him that the detachment would have to go by land, because it did not have air transport. He then told me to take the first plane of the Cuban Aviation Company that arrived.

I proceeded to carry out the order, appointing to command the aforementioned Assistant Captain Ulloa Franqui. Shortly after meeting at the airport, a twin engine arrived, from which the passengers were disembarked to accommodate the soldiers and, within a few minutes, these arrived in Manzanillo. The next day I was asked to send another officer and 25 more soldiers, and the appointment fell on the second lieutenant Gilberto Costa Cairo. I also learned of the arrival in operations of a battalion commanded by Commander Juan González González.

If things had happened as they were supposed to militarily be, that the head of the Regiment No. 1 I would have been ordered to disembark immediately or as soon as possible and, at least, they would have consulted me, with all the right that a regimental chief had by regulation, I should have known what was happening, but only God knows what that and many other days, there happened. I know that I will take to the grave that great doubt of what happened that memorable day, why I was not warned in time nor did they want me to intervene in such a matter, that with only two squadrons of the Rural Guard, it would have been resolved. But, let's look back and see how much blood, how many tears and how many lives have been lost by mistake, by revenge or by betrayal.

The expeditionaries fell one by one into our hands, but we missed the opportunity to capture Castro. Why? Because far from intercepting them, they were pushed into the Sierra. And why did you act that way? Why wasn't what was due done? We had every chance. Everyone! And they didn't take advantage. Former President Batista tells us on page 291 of his book *Response*: "Fidel Castro's group could easily and quickly be annihilated. However, humanitarian reasons, democratic scruples and the clamor of a part of public opinion prevented it." Oh my! What humanitarian reasons, what democratic scruples and what public opinion are you talking about? He encompassed all three factors. Here, as in the Moncada, Batista personally prevented Fidel Castro from being eliminated once and for all. At least this statement, as well as what it adds later, on page

292, that it was by order of the President that the persecution was suspended, has the virtue of saving the responsibility of the chiefs who commanded there, because at all times the strategy, and even many tactical aspects, were dictated from Havana.

Sometime later, speaking with Mr. Fabio Freyre, General Administrator or co-owner of the Central Media Luna, near the place of landing, he told me that on the day of the events he had learned first-hand that about one hundred armed men dressed in olive green had landed in Punta Colorada (Belic), where there was only a two-man station. That on his behalf, the Deputy Administrator of the Central appeared at the post of the Rural Guard of Niquero, and told the Chief of Post, second lieutenant Achilles Chinea, what was happening. That the disembarked were vomiting and could not even walk, and that there was a doctor attending them *very hurried, but it was not known why*. Mr. Freyre continued to tell me that Lieutenant Chinea did not leave for the scene until two hours later. The lieutenant's obligation was to immediately notify his superior, the *Squadron Leader in Manzanillo and the Chief of Regiment No. 1, which I never knew I would*, and then march toward the enemy and make contact.

On page 49 of the same book Response reads: "General Díaz Tamayo, head of the military territory, and Colonel Barrera, head of the operations, contributed to the strengthening of the belief in the General Staff that the struggle had ceased on the part of the group that disembarked on December 2."

I never had anything to do with the Sierra Maestra. That was taboo for me. Reasons: intrigues against all those who disagreed on many things, which need not be mentioned. Or did I drop out of my Army degree for fun?

Perhaps Barrera Pérez said so, as he informed Dr. Márquez-Sterling, and he records it in his story, but I never spoke of that possibility. How could I do that without having data in my possession? I did go to the Sierra Maestra, but to bring cigarettes, money and other necessities to the troops who had fought there. Nothing else. All that was headed from the Palace.

But anyway. After the initial actions everything seemed to quiet down. Lieutenant Colonel Barrera returned with his battalion to

Havana and I, for my part, after a reasonable period of time, renewed my request for relief. It took several months, but it finally arrived. A final word on Oriente. I had a turbulent time, and sometimes I had to proceed with some energy, but at no time did I stop receiving the greatest proofs of affection from the Santiago. I left great friends among all social classes, and many of them testified to me that friendship in difficult times.

My new destination was the Military District of La Cabaña, that is, the Artillery Regiment, *in the first days of April 1957. I flew back to Havana with my family.* I relieved Brigadier [Julio] Sánchez Gómez[189], who passed to Regiment 5 of the Rural Guard.

General Tabernilla had been Chief of La Cabaña for many years, and he had special regard for him. It is still curious that the President appointed me, first to relieve Brigadier del Río Chaviano from Oriente, this general's brother-in-law and trusted man, and later, to send this property to Tabernilla. In a way, that contributed to widening the differences between the two of us. Did the President wish to neutralize Tabernilla's influence in both commands? President Batista had a very special sense of humor, and his intentions were inscrutable.

General Tabernilla was jeopardizing operations in Oriente for hearing and defending del Río Chaviano, who had so much influence that President Batista ordered to divide the territory of Oriente between General Cantillo and the General del Río Chaviano, instead of calling it to the military disciplinary order.

I wasn't as attached to La Cabaña as I was to Columbia, but nevertheless, I loved my new command. First, it was an area full of history. This fortress dates to the 18th century, and the decision to build it was a direct consequence of the seizure of Havana by the English in 1762. The first works began in 1763, and were completed in 1774. The Cabaña is the most complete example of the Vauban system in America, that is, the fortification in counterdependence. The field marshal Don Silvestre de Abarca directed the works. Invisible from the sea, its walls dominate by land the bay and the city

---

[189] Brigadier Julio Sánchez Gómez was sentenced by a revolutionary court to 25 years in prison on June 2, 1959 for complicity in Batista's coup d'état.

of Havana. La Cabaña is also located on a higher level than Morro. That is why in the sixteenth century, when the military engineer Battista Antonelli arrived in Havana to build the Morro, he reported: "It will be useless to build the castle, if La Cabaña is not fortified. Whoever dominates that hill will be the owner of Havana."

My command in this great fortress lasted less than a year, and I don't remember there being any noteworthy episode there. Brigadier Sánchez Gómez had done a beautiful job of organizing, and the staff seconded me beautifully. Also, as the problems in Oriente increased and the insurrection took shape, some of the personnel moved into the area of operations. It was my job to train them as best I could before leaving, and to care for their relatives in Havana. I also resumed my duties as Chairman of the Military and Naval Circle, and waited for developments.

From La Cabaña I went to the General Staff as Assistant General, as Director of Intelligence (G-2) and as Director of Operations[190] (not knowing what the superiors were doing with the operations). The recommendations of the operations officers were of no value unless they coincided with the Joint Chiefs of Staff and the Presidential Palace.

Our army was a poor army, but it really had a great preparation, except for guerrilla warfare. I didn't have it because our superiors didn't want to send at least two companies to Fort Gulick, Panama. I remember that Colonel [Clark] Lynn[191], the head of the American Army mission, granted me, with the permission of the American Army, the dispatch of two infantry companies to the place if our superiority approved. When we had everything ready

---

[190] He was appointed Director of Operations on January 25, 1958 during the reorganization of the Army.

[191] Clark Lynn, Jr. (December 4, 1912-March 19, 1999) was born in Washington, D.C. and graduated from the Military Academy at West Point in 1934. During World War II he was a liaison officer for a division of the Chinese Army. In 1951 he was assigned to the Military Advisory and Assistance Group in Turkey. In 1957 he was assigned to the post in Cuba, where he remained until March 1959. He was then sent to the Caribbean Command in the Panama Canal area until 1961. He retired in 1964 as Inspector General of the Artillery and Rocketry Center in Fort Sill, Oklahoma.

it was elevated to the consideration of the supreme chief, General Batista, and the answer was, no. I think he was ill-advised. That happened as in February or March 1958. There was plenty of time. I don't know who interrupted this.

Speaking again of the Directorate of Operations, I wish to state that my only function was to receive the parties, to list the dead on both sides and to inform my superiors. When it came to relating the dead on both sides, there were discrepancies in the high command, that is, there was no agreement on the real numbers and what should be put. Realizing that I was not good at reporting, although if I was telling the truth, I delicately preferred that the operations part be done by my superiors instead of the report that I had to sign. I took that chance, but I didn't want to lie. Our men realized it and so did our enemies. No, that wasn't right.

On Sunday evenings the President invited us to eat at the Palace or at the residence in Columbia. There was good food, boxing, and basket. At about 3:00 AM the following Monday, the parts of the Sierra Maestra arrived. The strong expressions of the President and the other guests were noticeable. The information was unfortunately not favorable, after reading them. I'm talking about mid-1958 and later. Despite everything, the President maintained the calm of his investiture.

One of those mornings, almost dawning, the already extinct Doctor Jorge García Montes, Premier of the Government at that moment, making a separate question to me: General, when are you going to end the little game to the soldiers that exists in the Sierra Maestra? Doctor, what you ask me brings them to you. [The following handwritten page is missing here.]

The things that happened within the Army had to be lived to believe them. The irresponsible way in which the military chain of command was broken by sending a junior officer [Colonel Barrera] by surprise to send another superior officer within the command assigned by national laws has no name. Such cases can only be seen when the supreme leaders have no academic basis, when an Army is governed as a political party without leaders or because there is fear of something that is not externalized.

AMENDMENTS

It would now be useful to talk about the changes that had taken place during the 1950s in the structure of the army.

During the French Revolution, the Minister of War, Lazaro Carnot, set up a governing body that would allow him to control from Paris the functioning of the different armies of France. This was laying the foundations for what was then the General Staff.

Taking advantage of the lesson, the Prussians organized the Generalstab and, later, the Oberkommando der Wehrmacht (Supreme General Staff of the Armed Forces).

This Joint Chiefs of Staff, placing all armed forces under one will, eliminated old rivalries and made modern military operations possible. By World War II, the United States had also adopted the system, and we took it from them.

Towards 1956 General Tabernilla passed from Chief of the Army to Chief of the Joint Chiefs of Staff, being replaced by Major General [Pedro] Rodríguez Ávila[192]. Both the latter and Tabernilla were promoted to lieutenants general.

As for the other branches of the General Staff,

- The former Personnel Department became the G-1.
- The Intelligence Service became the G-2.
- The former General Aid became the G-3.

---

[192] Colonel Pedro Barrera Pérez wrote that "It is convenient to explain that the creation of the Joint Chiefs of Staff caused, from its origin, serious friction among the high leaders of the Armed Corps. General Martín Díaz Tamayo had been in charge of the Army for years, but he was eliminated by General Tabernilla, who questioned his loyalty; General Eulogio Cantillo, who, because he was not one of the most capable generals, should have had that command, was also unknown to the Joint Chief of Staff, who had already reserved that position for his unconditional collaborator, General Pedro Rodríguez Ávila, whom all the officers considered inept for such a high investiture, but had the merit of having been used by General Tabernilla to destroy the reputation of General Jorge García Tuñón, from the very beginning of the military coup of March 10, 1952. " "Why the Army Didn't Defeat Castro," *Free Bohemia*, September 3, 1961.

- The Headquarters-Master General became the G-4.
- Inspection became the G-5.

In all cases, the heads of these departments were major generals. The 'G', by which the sections are called, comes from the German 'Grosse' (large). It was on the occasion of this restructuring of the General Staff that several brigade generals were promoted to major generals, including myself, but this did not mean in practice any change in procedures. The authority continued to be concentrated on President Batista, and the Navy and Police chiefs continued to address him directly, not through the Joint Chiefs of Staff. General Tabernilla continued to directly command the Army, while the Chief of General Staff, Lieutenant General Rodríguez Ávila, had virtually no command. These were the conditions that prevailed when I became a G-3, that is, what had previously been an Assistant General. And with this my cycle was completed because, as you will remember, this was the first position assigned to me on March 10, 1952.

It was from this position that I was able to have a complete picture of our situation because, although it was not my responsibility to make the important decisions, it was inevitable that my Department, when implementing the directives of the President, would have first-hand information. What in its beginnings I had to live in Oriente, I could now contemplate in perspective, and as part of a whole. The failure to drown the communist outbreak in its beginnings, the failure to destroy Fidel Castro when it was possible to do so, now came to our faces, because the Marxist international conspiracy was already at stake. The journalist Herbert Matthews[193] went up to the Sierra without hindering us, with all guar-

---

[193] Herbert Lionel Matthews (January 10, 1900-July 30, 1977) was born in New York to a wealthy Jewish family. Upon graduating from Columbia University in 1926 he began as a reporter for the *New York Times*. He was a correspondent for the Italian invasion of Abyssinia and favored the Republicans in their reports on the Spanish Civil War. He left his wife and children abandoned in New York for a decade while covering European conflicts and World War II. A heart attack forced him to return to New York in 1949 where he was created a special position as a reporter-editorialist in the New York Times. He was the first journalist to interview Fidel Castro in the Sierra Maestra, writing three articles with 6,790 words, published on February 24, 25 and 26, 1957. His propaganda reports over

antees, to dump in the American press his interview in which he idealized the new Robin Hood[194].

And why had Mr. Matthews gone up to the Sierra? What was this foreigner doing in our homeland, dictating who Cain was and who Abel was? He was nothing less than an old-fashioned philo-communist, a veteran of the Spanish Civil War, where he had served as a correspondent in the international brigades. Now, paid for by one of those 'liberal' newspapers in the United States, the *New York Times*, was his instrument to contribute to the fall of our President.

To what extent was the policy pursued by this President responsible for the events? The Kuquine agreements were very different from what was subsequently done. Batista would be at the head of the government only for a while, long enough to get the country on track and call for new elections. Both President Prío and many other authentic ones, and the United States government itself, were alarmed at the possible triumph of the Orthodox, infiltrated to the core by the Communists. The coup d'état cut the Gordian knot and the Cubans, with this experience, perhaps learned to be somewhat more restrained in the future. Subsequently, subsequent elections with Batista as candidate were out of the question. Batista, with his magnetism, with his ascendancy over the troops, would remain as a possibility for the future, but not as an immediate aspirant in

---

the next two years glorified Fidel Castro and the rebels and influenced the U.S. government to put an arms embargo on Cuba and force Batista out of power. In 1959, he described Castro as "the greatest hero in the history of Cuba," slowing down José Martí. It was self-titled "The Man Who Invented Fidel Castro." In contrast, Castro complained of being "tired of that old man who thinks he's my father and is always giving me advice." The New York Times banned him from reporting on Cuba after he insisted on July 16, 1959 that Fidel Castro was anti-communist and that the Cuban people did not want elections. He retired in 1967 and died bitter and frustrated in Adelaide, Australia. In 1997, the Castro dynasty erected a monument where the interview took place in 1957.

[194] Díaz Tamayo told the press that Matthews' visit to Fidel Castro was "an imaginary interview" because it was impossible for anyone to cross the lines of troops surrounding the sector in which Castro operated. The general said: "This interview was prefabricated for the purpose of helping the psychological warfare that is taking place in Cuba." R. Hart Phillips, "Cubans Debating Rebel Interview," *The New York Times*, March 1, 1957, page 8.

an election that, necessarily, would have to be fraudulent. I would not have understood these things if he had not explained them to me before March 10. But none of this was like this. Once in the chair, his mastery of circumstances was too complete. Nothing limited him, and he could not resist the temptation to continue in the presidency. The power is intoxicating, I recognize it. I enjoyed it and I know what it means. There's the nub of the question!

There is another facet in Batista that is too well known, but that is not inappropriate to mention. In his heart, the President was a convinced Democrat. Democrat who, not being able to come to power democratically, used other means to do so. Once at the top, he tried to behave democratically, and to be recognized as such. It restored freedom of the press and constitutional guarantees. And it is well known that the opposition press will always whip the president of any republic, even if it is the reincarnation of Christ. How could he think that, with the ease of doing so, that press would not attack him? So, after all, it was in the precision of suppressing that freedom. He did not decide for absolute democracy or total dictatorship, because to establish that total democracy he would have had to leave the presidency and, as for being an absolute dictator of body and soul, he lacked a vocation for it. For all this, his policy was erratic and indecisive. He was not bloody, but at no price was he willing to give up what was so dear to him, and for that he had to kill. Step by step, public opinion, which if not favorable at any time, had been at least indifferent, became decidedly hostile to him. But public opinion alone does not overthrow an authoritarian government: it is the external factor, in this case the United States, that carries it out. Because now these come into play.

It was always incomprehensible to Cubans, and I myself came to understand it in exile, that figures of renown within this country, that most of the press, that legislators, that radio and television, observe conduct that is harmful to the interests of their homeland. What do they do out of ignorance? Because of hormone problems? Because of emotional conflicts? Out of conviction? Never mind! In other countries, and they would not have to be totalitarian, they would be tried for treason and treated as traitors. However, the laws of the Great Democracy protect them and even punish those who denounce them. As far as Cuba is concerned, and no matter how badly we were doing it, all that press to which I am referring, congressmen and even the State Department happily proceeded to destroy Batista, their sincere friend, and to replace him with Fidel Castro, a Communist and bitter enemy of the United States.

We have already said many times that President Batista was never popular, but for a people disappointed, back from the authentic myth, that it was he or another who governed their destinies left him little less than indifferent. The great merchants, industrialists and banks did not see him with bad eyes, since their respect for property and their wise economic policy were, before them, their best credentials, but when they saw that the American government was moving away from him, they thought: "A dead King, King put." And if the neighbors of the North supported the new Robin Hood, it was only fair that they supported it as well. None of this holds Batista responsible but let us also record the blindness and irresponsibility of many.

Another ominous symptom was the discomfort in the upper echelons of the Armed Forces. When the disaster struck, some bosses began to pass their money abroad and to prepare their escape. There were those who spoke to the enemy to buy his security. From my belvedere in the old General Auxiliary, I watched the drama unfold daily. Parts of the desertions, the casualties suffered, the fires came to me. All that could be avoided and, until the last minute, the situation was remedied. And this opportunity presented itself with the elections. If they were won by the opposition candidate, Dr. Marquez-Sterling, the masses would have abandoned their fighting attitude and left Castro alone with his small group of communists. I firmly believed that this was the plan, and several times I commented on it within my family. What a surprise to see that the winner was the government candidate, Dr. Rivero Agüero!

I remember how almost on the eve of the election, we were summoned to the General Staff conference hall in Columbia, instructing us to make the election completely free. However, right there, on the sidelines, someone told me that the already prepared ballot papers were sent in bags to the eastern provinces, with the government candidate as the winner.

I still believe that it was in the President's mind to hand over the presidency to Marquez-Sterling. What made it change at the last minute? Or is it true that General Batista never intended to abandon effective power, and that upon taking office Dr. Rivero Agüero would become the head of the Joint Chiefs of Staff? Despite seeing him relatively often, I never caught the slightest hint of him one way or the other. Nor do I believe he entrusted anyone with his true purposes.

And in that sounded the aldabonazo, *l'hôte inconnu* who came to decide the matter. It was the American ambassador[195] who, on instructions from his foreign ministry, informed the president that his government had stopped supporting him. I mean, he had to go. This interview has been reflected, in great detail, in the book *El Cuarto Piso*, later written by said ambassador.

---

[195] Earl Edward Tailer Smith (July 8, 1903-February 15, 1991) was a native of Newport, Rhode Island, and a graduate of Yale University. He was a financier and investment broker, a member of the New York Stock Exchange. During World War II he was a lieutenant colonel in the Army and the Air Force Intelligence Service. Director of finance for the Republican Party in Florida and four times delegate to the Republican National Convention. President Dwight Eisenhower appointed him ambassador to Cuba in June 1957 and resigned on 20 January 1959. He had never been a diplomat and did not speak Spanish. President John Kennedy offered him the post of ambassador to Switzerland in 1961 but rejected him. In 1962 he published *El Cuarto Piso* where he blamed the US State Department for the bad decisions that helped bring communism to power in Cuba. He was mayor of Palm Beach, Florida, during 1971-1977, and in June 1982 President Ronald Reagan appointed him to the Presidential Commission of Broadcasting to Cuba to carry out Radio Martí. He died in Palm Beach.

CHAPTER VIII

THE DRUNKEN CONSPIRACY

Since the "Barquín" conspiracy, many others had occurred, and some ill-intentioned people mixed my name with several. When someone once told Napoleon that, being the owner of half of Europe, he could already live in peace, he replied: —They will never leave us alone, we have too many things.

I never had much, and I also refrained from sinking my hands into the river of gold that flowed around me. But I think that's exactly what bothered more than one. Also, seeing that nothing could be done to remedy the situation, I isolated myself even more. Without being me Napoleon, they didn't leave me alone either. When the President, half serious, half joking, alluded to the fact that my name appeared in lists and confidences, I replied: —You see, Mr. President, that is what I told you before: you must withdraw me. Better for everybody.

So things went on until one good day a new conspiracy was discovered. He was called "one of the drunks," because the officers involved were meeting at a bar in a Havana club. Among the conspirators was a first lieutenant, *my private secretary of correspondence. That officer never dared to tell me anything about it. Neither could I notice since I only saw him once a day to talk about my daily correspondence and that was it. I had absolute confidence in him for being a serious man, capable and loyal to the Army.* So, because my secretary was involved, so was I. Perhaps because the President was fed up with my tensions with the Chief of the Joint Chiefs of Staff, he decided to cut to the chase. Through the Chief of the Army, General Rodríguez Ávila, I was informed that the presence of my secretary in an attempt had given me something to talk about, and that the President believed that I should leave for a while. That I was given the choice between the Cuban Embassies in Washington or in Paris, to go to them as a Military Attaché. Here is what I replied to the proposal: "Tell the President that, if I am a traitor, I will remain the same in France as in the United States. And nothing less than a traitor in uniform. I don't accept that traitor rating from anyone. *That I have not conspired against anyone and that I do want to be withdrawn from the Army so that the problems with my person end.* I do not want to go anywhere: the solution is to retire and, waiting for that retreat, I will go right now to my house and there I will wait for the decision that my superiors make, but here I will not return." *Having said that, I took the attention position*, greeted the general and took the elevator back to my home. There, I considered myself under voluntary house arrest. *I didn't say a word to anyone.*

Maybe that wasn't right. Although I squared off and greeted him before retiring, I actually left my old friend and hierarchical superior, General Rodríguez Ávila, with the word in his mouth. He could have had me arrested right there, but he didn't. I guess he felt uncomfortable because he knew where the shots came from. I also imagine that there were calls, conversations and deliberations about what to do with me. Apparently, the solution of retiring due to illness was adopted and so it was published, but I, unaware that the note had already been given to the press, had the idea of going to the Spanish Casino. Once there, my friends tricked me into playing squash, and I took part in three games. *It was like 12: 00 noon on Sunday. It was a tremendous sun. Looks like there were hounds in the area and they put the high command on alert. Surely, they were men of the great policeman Irenaldo Garcia, who had reached the delicate position of head of the SIM, as if that had been done for anyone.* Then I went home and went to bed early, because the exercise had tired me.

The fact that the "sick" enjoyed such good health produced hilarity and even a photograph in the press. At 3:30 in the morning, a commander and a first lieutenant came looking for me. The major general was arrested and taken to the SIM card without further ado. Apparently, the arrest warrant against me never occurred, but a comment from the President in the presence of the head of the

SIM, Lieutenant Colonel [Irenaldo Remigio] García Báez[196], was interpreted by him as such.

The SIM chief required my urgent presence. The officers who went to drive me to the SIM acted with all kinds of looks, and one of them, who now lives in Miami, was always saddened, and for me, what a humiliation! After that and so many more things that I believe countless out of shame for the honorable Cuban army, although it hurts many, I did not expect more. That night I felt like the most unhappy man in the world.

It wasn't until seven o'clock in the afternoon that I was brought into the presence of the SIM chief. Since the previous morning I had spent it in a small room, with a table and a chair for only furniture. How I scrambled at that time! How quickly I perceived then how everything was coming downhill, how the country was falling apart around us! To what extent was I responsible for the debacle? History would say its last word. And then, how would it sound in the ears of the citizens that a major general, one of the true authors of March 10 had been imprisoned for conspiracy? What to expect then from those who did not feel tied to the government? How the opposition would enjoy all that!

When I finally saw myself in the presence of Lieutenant Colonel García Báez, he asked me to sit in front of him in his office. In reality there was no accusation against me, and everything became general: that I had been seen with So-and-so, that if I knew Zutano, but nothing else. I ended up saying to him: —Look, Irenaldo, this thing that is happening to me, this thing that you are doing with me, can also happen to your father (Brigadier Pilar García) or others at any time. This is slowly collapsing. As I see it, terrible events will soon occur in Cuba. I want you to tell the president that by having me arrested, he's making a character out of me. You are mistaken in thinking that I could conspire. I would never think of hurting the army or the government. What I want is to be calm. Leave me alone and you'll have nothing to fear from me.

---

[196] Irenaldo Remigio García Báez (March 17, 1924-November 29, 2006) was born in Matanzas and was the son of Brigadier General Pilar García.

In fact, I was slowly released and returned home. I was confined for 17 hours *without my family knowing what was going on with me.*

And what had happened? As I said before, my departure from Squash at the Spanish Casino must have been a source of irritation. I was later told that, during the meal at the Palace on the day of the famous game, the President commented: —Martin is looking for us to have him arrested.

From these words, García Báez, who was attending the meal, drew the conclusion that Batista wanted me imprisoned and ordered me arrested. That's why I was arrested in the early hours of Saturday through Sunday. The fact that I was not released until Sunday afternoon means that the President did not find out until that time that I was in the SIM, and immediately ordered that I be released. This is an example of cheap servility.

Then came the negotiations for my retirement. Commander [Alberto] Boix Comas[197] oversaw mediating between the General Staff and me, and the final formula was the retirement due to illness, which I have already mentioned. Indeed, from the appearance of the decree I remained calm in my house, but is the word "quiet"? Day by day I saw how a bodyless ghost, as was the Sierra Maestra, collapsed, not a dictator, but an entire political-economic system. *It was a few days of anguish for me because of the affection I felt for our Institution, which was already in precarious for all the things that came together at once.*

My departure from the Army surprised many people, civilians and soldiers, because they knew that something serious was happening when we made that serious determination. As we saw later, only twenty-seven days later what we all know was formed. That made me feel even sadder because I didn't think the mess was going to happen that same month. We were all surprised by the attitude taken by President Batista. The other bosses had nothing to do, but follow the chief.

---

[197] Alberto Boix Comas, spokesman for the Army, former priest, and former professor at the Los Escolapios school in Guanabacoa.

I think Batista failed March 10 almost at birth. How different it is when one pleads, before making a fact, to the arrogance that unfolds after the fact is made. Batista wanted to do so many juggling games with Cuba, with Fidel and politics, that the trick went wrong. So bad, that he sank his friends, he sank and his name, and sank for a hundred years or more to one of the most beautiful and advanced republics of the globe. His blindness, his Machiavellian tricks and maneuvers plunged him into the depths of the darkest abyss known to man. Who can deny this?

Several works I have consulted in these days to give consistency to what I am writing at the moment. *En el Cuarto Piso*, of Mr. Earl Smith, penultimate ambassador of the United States, in the *Historia de Cuba*, of Dr. Márquez-Sterling and *La Daga en el Corazón*, of Dr. Mario Lazo[198], the course of the events. Another

---

[198] Mario Roberto Lazo y Guiral (March 21, 1895-March 25, 1976) was born in the Guatemalan embassy in Washington, D.C., where his father Antonio Lazo Arriaga (1857–1938) was Guatemalan minister to the United States and his mother María Lorenza Guiral y Domínguez (1863–1897)was the daughter of the Marquise de MontRoig of Madrid. He naturalized as a U.S. citizen in February 1917. He enlisted in the New York National Guard on June 29, 1916 and with his brother Antonio (1887-1956) were assigned in Cavalry Squadron A to patrol the Mexican border in Texas for six months. Graduated in Law from Cornell University on February 14, 1917, where he was a member of the Quill and Dagger Society. Commissar-in-Chief of the U.S. Army on November 26, 1917. He was Deputy Chief of Staff, Harbor Boarding Headquarters, Hoboken, NJ, until August 1918. He was later a commanding officer of the Division 16 Headquarters Company in Camp Kearny, California, until his discharge on December 31, 1918. From there he traveled to Japan, China and Italy for six months. Upon returning to New York, he worked in a bank and was a lawyer at the Masten&Nichols law firm from January 1921 to October 1925, when he began studying Civil Law at the University of Havana. On December 30, 1925, he married Gertrude Minshall Hopper (1900-1958) at the Church of the Transfiguration in New York and they had three children. After graduating on June 29, 1928, he swore in Cuban citizenship and established the law firm Mario Lazo &Jorge E. Cubas. The firm represented the U.S. government and large corporations, such as the United Fruit Company, Freeport Sulphur and Cuba Sugar, and U.S. banks, as well as Cuban entrepreneurs. On February 17, 1936, Time magazine described him as "Attorney No. 1 on the island." After his divorce from Gertrude, he married the widow Carmen de la Guardia y Calvo, at St. Augustine's Church in Marianao, on September 2, 1954. His cousin Carlos Marquez-Sterlingy Guiral attended the wedding. In early 1959, he traveled to Washington, and in the company of the new Cuban ambassador, they asked Lyman B. Kirkpatrick, inspector

book that I have read with great interest is *Motivos y Culpables*, by Mr. [José] López Vilaboy[199]. The author makes numerous historical mistakes, especially in dealing with our war of independence, but it is nevertheless worth studying. I cannot explain why Mr. López Vilaboy had such a violent attack on Batista, from whom he received nothing but benefits. Apart from accusing him of being a thief, selfish, incapacitated, etc., what really makes him stand out, perhaps unintentionally, are the President's most favorable features, namely his goodness and his good sense of friendship.

We know the work of Mr. Vilaboy at the head of different government companies, mainly in the Cuban Aviation Company. I think he did an excellent job, which he does not miss the opportunity to say himself in the book, but how can he become a modest journalist and a millionaire if not for the protection of President Batista?

We see the President sponsoring him again and again in his endeavors as an entrepreneur. He holds it against clicks as powerful as the Tabernilla. He cleared his path of obstacles and obtained for him credits of millions. And soon we see the editor of a newspaper of little circulation in a position to absorb, from his peculiar, up to 20% of the shares of a large company.

In his viciousness, he goes so far as to say that the President thought only of money, and that in all business he had to be given a share. It occurs to me to ask: in the many deals that Mr. López Vilaboy did to the underworld of El Indio, did he have to contribute to fill his coffers? If the answer is yes, he becomes an accom-

---

general of the CIA, that the U.S. government recognize the revolutionary government as the only method of restoring order. He was arrested on April 17, 1961, at the beginning of the Bay of Pigs invasion and upon his release he obtained asylum at the Italian Embassy in Havana. He took refuge in the United States and in 1968 published *Daga en el Corazón*, blaming President Kennedy for the defeat of Bahía de Cochinos and the surrender of Cuba to the Soviet Union. In 1974 he established the Watergate Defense Fund to assist his friends E. Howard Hunt and Bernard Barker, accused in the case. During a trip from Miami to his home in Norfolk, Connecticut, he died of a heart attack halfway through Richmond, Virginia.

[199] José Ramón López Vilaboy (March 7, 1907-March 2, 1989) editor of the newspaper Mañana. In 1953, it acquired 22% of Cubana de Aviación's shares.

plice of a malpractice. If it is negative, then it turns out that Batista was not as voracious as he says.

Mr. López Vilaboy also confesses that the worker leader Calixto Sánchez[200], guilty of anti-government activities, Batista sets him free and lets him leave the country at his request. A few months later, this same gentleman disembarks at the head of an armed expedition.

In other passages, Mr. López Vilaboy directs his shots against the then First Lady, Mrs. Martha Fernández. He assumes it even influencing Batista to the point of making it vary in his decisions. I believe in this being able to give an informed opinion.

Circumstances influenced the President, but never the people, much less his wife.

On page 256 of her book, the following passage appears, as evidence of Mrs. Martha Fernandez's meddling in her husband's affairs.

> One day, having lunch at his house in Kuquine (he, Martha and I), General E. Cantillo arrived, who shared the table and we dedicated ourselves to examining the general things of Cuban politics of those times, but in the end we talked to him, Martha and myself alone, and among the things we commented was the good result that had given the newspaper *Mañana* a plan of gifts of houses and other articles, which had allowed us to make more than 60,000 subscriptions. Martha, excited about the information, said, "Kuqui (so she said to General Batista) why don't you put up a newspaper like Vilaboy with a gift scheme to make money?" That is of no importance, but it is symptomatic of Doña Martha's ambition, which had too much influence on Batista's new life.

---

[200] Calixto Sánchez Whyte (February 3, 1924-May 28, 1957), born in Glasgow, Scotland, was a Canadian Army veteran during World War II. In 1949 he was elected secretary general of the National Air Federation and member of the Executive Committee of the Confederation of Cuban Workers (CTC). Upon disembarking with the Corinthian expedition, Calixto Sánchez Whyte and 15 expeditionaries of the Authentic Organization surrendered to the army after being besieged and promised that he would respect their lives. However, Batista ordered that they be executed on 28 May 1957 in retaliation for Fidel Castro's guerrilla attack on the Uvero barracks on the same day, where 11 soldiers were killed and 19 wounded.

I knew Mrs. Martha well, and the words put in her mouth are typical of her. Her purpose, however, was always to flatter the visitor, setting an example for her husband to follow. Too well she knew that the President did not have to put in a little newspaper to get a few pesos.

Returning to the course of the narrative, I found myself in my house, almost always in my small library-office, alone with my books, a priest friend came to my house. I received it and it turned out that I had a letter from Fidel Castro, asking me to meet him in the Sierra. ~~I didn't even want to touch the letter and said to the priest~~[201]:

"Father, please keep that letter and return it to the one who wrote it." Tell Mr. Castro that my differences with the government in no way imply that I am with a movement that I know to be communist. And let me give you this advice: just say Mass and do not be complicit in what is coming over Cuba.

This priest was Spanish. His name was Friar Balbino, of the Discalced Carmelites. At the end of January 1959, he came back to my house and said:

—You were right, Fidel Castro is a communist.

I must come back to the issue that during my seven years as a general, I kept some isolation from my bosses and my classmates. I must not blame anyone for them: only in my way of being. Perhaps, if there were more communication between them and me, there would be less misunderstanding. I was more explicit with the President, as long as he consulted me. In those cases, he listened to me with great attention, although reserving, of course, the final decisions.

In my junior grades I had good friends with whom I departed and joked, but both as Inspector General or as Chief of the military districts of Oriente and La Cabaña, and finally, as Assistant General (G-3), only with my family and with some intimate opened me to confidence.

---

[201] It seems that he doubted whether to include the following anecdote since he scored NO in the margin.

Once withdrawn, I was able to release a little of what I call my inhibitions. Naturally, I stopped attending the Military Circle, but I was welcomed to other clubs, especially the Spanish Casino. I also spent more time with my family. My mother, for example, had come to live with me. The days when she rebuked me for having enlisted in the army of the nation were long gone. Rosaura, my wife, as well as my mother-in-law, always made her feel at home. God bless you! Their years of deprivation were at last compensated for! I had the satisfaction of seeing that nothing was missing from him while he was at our house.

As for what was happening around me, it can best be seen in the books I recently mentioned. How, from my home, I watched day by day the agony of the regime! And it is nothing new to say that President Batista was one of the great responsible, but when I am told that the Army was sold, that the soldiers did not want to fight, I come up with this other approach: Isn't it remarkable that these soldiers were quite resistant to the combined effort of Russia, the United States and Castro? And what about those owners of estates, ~~Orientals, Camagüeyans,~~ ~~Villagers~~, who went to the communist armed bands and said to them: -There is a detachment protecting my property. You can kill them without difficulty, because there are only five of them, and when I arrive you will think that you have nothing to fear from me and you will open the door for me.

Poor soldiers! How could they not be demoralized? But see the behavior of those who had to die in front of the wall. And what about the Fourth Floor officials of the State Department? Ambassador Earl Smith has already taken it upon himself to put them in their place. Some of them have already passed away, but I am not generous enough to wish them eternal peace. May the souls of our shot men torment you, both in your last moments and in the afterlife!

DEBACLE

There is no point in adding new words to everything that has already been said and written about 1 January. Only these impressions: I remember that the populace kept a lot from throwing themselves into the street until, around noon, it became clear that the public force would not react, by the work and grace of the new headquarters. A reorganization against the famous revolution should have been thought of. But it is necessary to admit that he was less bloody than at the fall of Machado. While members of the Armed Forces were fighting for the homeland, most of the population buried the Republic more and more. As for me, I was already retired and was not bothered at all. However, a few days after the Communists arrived in Havana, a group of bearded men appeared in my house. They came from a Dr. Armando Fleites, who nowadays practices as a doctor here in Miami, and at gunpoint they took my private car. I was not at home, and on my return, I found my poor wife and my mother-in-law very agitated. The days passed, and a friend of ours, Mrs. Martha Montenegro, came to the house and informed us that they had seen the car parked in front of the Hotel Capri, and since my wife had a spare set of keys, she and Martha went to the hotel and returned with the car. For the second time the "boys" of Fleites returned, this time in number of more than ten armed men, and for the second time they took the car.

Two days later my mother-in-law received a gentleman, who told her that he was the father of Armando Fleites. Very attentive and chivalrous, he came to apologize for the conduct of his son, whom he did not hesitate to describe as bold. Years later, Mrs. [Martha] Montenegro, whose husband had a gas station at the time, was there when Dr. Armando Fleites stopped for gas. Martha recognized him and, without entrusting herself to God or the Devil, she stepped in and put this lord in gold and blue. Martha told me that the man did not respond, but with his head down he finished filling the tank and left without saying a word.

There existed in the legal body of our Army an Auditing Commander by the surname Nin. He was retired, but Castro had called him to service. One day Nin telephoned me and informed me that Case No. 4 had just begun for the events of March 10, 1952. He added that because of the workload he had, he begged me to write him a report myself with the discharges he deemed appropriate for my defense. I replied that that took time, because I needed to refresh my memory and look for data that I didn't have at hand right now. Things stayed that way, but this put me on notice that sooner or later I was going to have difficulties.

Almost immediately came from the United States the major general (retired) Ralph Truman[202], cousin brother of President Truman. Our friendship had begun years ago, when this chief, a veteran of the Cuban-Hispanic-American war, had come to Cuba on a semi-official mission. This general wanted to explore the possibilities of cooperation of the two governments, to establish historical-military parks in the theater of operations of that contest. On that occasion I oversaw attending to him.

Also, desiring to visit Daiquirí and San Juan, places where he fought, I sent him on an Army plane with the then Captain Medel, co-author of this book.

General Truman continued to reciprocate with me, and in 1958, he invited Medel and me to a convention of veterans from his former division, 35th Infantry[203]. On that occasion, President Batista sent him as a present a nice box of cigars that I delivered to him in Topeka, Kansas.

A curious fact: years later Mrs. Oliva Truman, the general's wife, told me that there was a frank enmity between Eisenhower and the Trumens[204], and that when Eisenhower came to the presidency he demobilized and disbanded the 35th Division to mortify them. This unit had always included the military branch of the Truman family. With Eisenhower[205] dead and the Democrats back in power, this veteran division of so many wars[206] was once again reconstituted.

---

[202] Ralph Emerson Truman (May 10, 1880-April 30, 1962) was born in Kansas City, Missouri. He was a veteran of the Cuban-Hispanic-American War, the Philippine, General Pershing's Expedition to Mexico, the World War I Meuse Argonne Offensive, and as major general led the 35th Infantry Division during 1940-1941. He visited Havana in October 1955, April 1957 and February 1958.

[203] He arrived in Key West on a flight of Aerovías Q on September 17, 1958, en route to Topeka, Kansas.

[204] On the sidelines: I am not authorized to say this} because of political differences that apparently existed between Generals Ike and Truman [205] Dwight D. Eisenhower (October 14, 1890-March 28, 1969)

[205] Dwight D. Eisenhower (October 14, 1890 – March 28, 1969)

[206] On the sidelines: Reorganized. We will talk about this, because I must not correct my teacher, neither playing.

Well, at the beginning of 1959 [Ralph] Truman arrived in Havana[207]. The old soldier urged me to go to the United States. General, —he told me— go immediately to the United States.

You're at tremendous risk. Trust me. I know what I'm telling you. You will come to my house until you can get on your way.

The truth is that I did not act as hastily as I should, and that was about to cost me dearly. I did not disregard General Truman's advice, but I felt that I had nothing to reproach myself for and let the days pass despite this being the second warning I received.

The third came to me peremptorily. The agency that replaced the Military Intelligence Service (SIM) was the DIER. One day in late March[208], a call was received. It was someone whom I had done I do not remember what service, and who was now militant in the ranks of the DIER. The message was: "The head of the DIER has been ordered to arrest General Díaz Tamayo and General García Tuñón. He is now taking a nap, but as soon as he gets up, he will go to prison."

I immediately called another friend of mine, Mr. Eloy Garcia, telling him what was happening to me and that I needed to talk to him. Eloy replied, "I'll be right there."

When we met, he took me to his son Joaquin's house, who had just married and lived with his wife in a nice apartment. The son answered affirmatively to the father's request: "I want you to keep Díaz Tamayo here until I can find him a better hiding place."

~~I suggested to Mr. Garcia that he~~[209] contact Brother Balbino, who twice visited my house, the first to bring me Castro's letter, and the second to apologize for not having understood in time that Castro was a communist. On this second occasion, he offered himself for

---

[207] On the sidelines: On the same day, January 1, 1959, at 9: 00 a.m., he called me long distance from Missouri.

[208] Memory error since he went into exile in the middle of the month. "Yesterday, another twenty-three Cubans went into political exile," *Diario de la Marina*, March 17, 1959, p. 9-B.

[209] On the sidelines: I was the one who made the contact. There is no explanation for the fact.

whatever good he could do for me. Now I remembered, and Mr. Eloy Garcia went to see him. Brother Balbino had me take him to his parish in Miramar, which was near my house. There I felt calm for the first time, in the peace of the Lord, because nothing gives a greater feeling of peace and tranquility than the interior of a temple.

He didn't stay quiet for long, Brother Balbino. I had another friend, Mr. Danilo Mesa[210], who at that time held the position of Undersecretary of the so-called Ministry of Recovery of Embezzled Goods. I told the priest that Mr. Mesa was trustworthy, and there we both went that same afternoon.

Danilo Mesa received us immediately, and immediately called a man who at that time was acting as a link between Castro's civil group and the Communist Armed Bands (FAR) This man was called Duarte, and they called him "El Indio" Duarte.

It could be said that Duarte's answer was as follows: —I imagined that you would call me to interest you in your friend Díaz Tamayo. I want you to know that either he's in jail, or he'll be arrested any minute, because those are Raul's orders.

And poor Danilo, with the best of intentions, said to me: — General, hide out for two or three days, that I will fix the matter for you.

---

[210] Danilo Federico Mesa Díaz (September 16, 1917-March 19, 1990) was born in Marianao and owned the hi-fi sound equipment store "California Alta Fidelidad" in La Rampa. He was a fundraiser for the July 26 Movement and public contact for the underground boss in Havana. On November 25, 1956, he received a wire in Havana with the signal of the disembarkation of the Granma expedition. Arrested in December 1958 and beaten at the Tenth Station of Colonel Conrado Carratalá in El Cerro. He was released from prison after four days by Colonel José Martínez Suárez, territorial inspector of the Fifth Military District, whose daughter was married to Mesa's brother-in-law. He went into exile in the last week of December 1958 and on his return to Havana in January 1959 he released Colonel Martínez from prison. He arrived in exile in Gainsville, Fla., on October 12, 1961, where he worked in a bookstore and his wife Rosa was a librarian at the University of Florida. He became a naturalized American citizen on 5 May 1976 in Gainesville and died there.

The poor believed that he was still in the time of the fierce baptism, in which personal management was enough to free a man from prison and even from death.

Brother Balbino then called the ambassador of Spain, Marqués de Vellisca. Mr. Lojendio[211], that was his surname, told the good priest that he was sick at the time and that he, for his part, could not give me asylum, because Spain did not have a treaty with Cuba in that sense, but that he would call him the next day, in which he would have the problem solved by another Embassy. And that's exactly what happened. The next day the Spanish ambassador informed us that he had dealt with the Chilean ambassador, and that he had agreed to asylum, but that unfortunately he had so many asylum seekers that he could not admit one more. Fortunately, the ambassador of Ecuador, Mr. Chiriboga[212], had shown himself propitious, and it would be he who would shelter me.

So, the next day I went to the address he gave me. It was an apartment building, and, on the first floor, the first secretary of the Embassy of Ecuador was waiting for me with his wife. When she saw me, she grabbed my arm and, followed by her husband, we went down to the embassy car. In it we returned to the Embassy of Ecuador, where I finally found haven. I had left behind my companion and mother-in-law who, having nothing to fear, would meet me in the United States.

For a month and a half, I would have to live at the Embassy headquarters, along with three other asylum seekers. I remember their names: Dr. [Manuel] Ampudia[213], who was Minister of Health in the government of President Batista and today, unfortunately,

---

[211] Juan Pablo de Lojendio e Irure (May 17, 1906-December 13, 1973) was Consul of Spain in Santiago de Chile in 1932 and after several other diplomatic posts, ambassador in Havana from 1952 to 1960, when he was expelled after an argument with Fidel Castro in the CMQ television studio.

[212] Virgilio Chiriboga (1898-February 1, 1980)

[213] Manuel Ampudia González (March 11, 1898-March 1, 1972) was president and director of the National Tuberculosis Council. He resigned as professor of the Faculty of Medicine of the University of Havana on January 28, 1959. He arrived in Miami on May 17, 1959. He died in Midland, Texas, when he slipped out of a chair, hit his head against the wall, and fractured his first cervical bone.

died. Also Mr. Evaristo Marina[214], Director today of the Aerospace College in Miami. Finally, Mr. Camilo Padreda[215]. He and I played *canasta* some nights, and within the circumstances we spent very pleasant evenings, because on the other hand we did nothing but eat and sleep, and as entertainment we read or contemplated the events on television.

Bernard Shaw said that humor alone saves a human being from ridicule, because man is truly a wretched being. I am convinced that irrational animals are happier than us. Only instinct and memory work for them. For them there is only the present moment. Once they fill the need that that moment requires, they go to bed quietly, without thinking about where the next meal will come from. The cattle, when they go to the slaughterhouse, quietly await their turn to be sacrificed, ruminating with their eyes narrowed with pure peace of spirit. But the human being agonizes day by day. Intelligence and reasoning, whatever their positive aspects, torment him with doubts, uncertainties, passions, premonitions. And fear, fear, fear everywhere.

That was never more obvious than in 1959, when the Communists came to power, because it is true that many people felt sympathy for Castro, and it is only fair that they expressed their joy by all available means, but it is no less true that from the beginning the ruthless and implacable character of the Revolution was seen. The bankers, owners of industries and businesses, directors of private schools, homeowners, clearly saw what was coming at them, and amid their terror rivaled in flattering Castro, in the hope of melting him.

The following case is told to me: The owner of one of the main industries invited Castro to go fishing. A magnificent yacht took them to the place where the fish abounded, and it is said that

---

[214] Evaristo Luis Marina (December 1, 1930-June 20, 2009) born in Caibarien, Las Villas. Founder and director of the Miami Aerospace Academy from 1969 to 1989 when the school closed after several scandals.

[215] Camilo Amancio Padreda Vázquez (August 25, 1932--), a native of Havana, left Ecuador for the Dominican Republic in May 1959 and subsequently received political asylum in San Juan, Puerto Rico, on August 17, 1959. Arrived in Miami on November 29, 1960 and naturalized as a U.S. citizen on June 9, 1966.

some divers hooked on the hook of the communist leader large snappers, which he drew amid applause and screams of admiration. There was also splendid food and, of course, lovely girls. Returning to the dock and escorting the visitor to the set of the staircase to say goodbye, he said to him, "No, sir, it is you who are leaving: this yacht now belongs to the Revolution." And when the industrialist, without knowing what to say or what to do, he went to take his car, a bearded man said to him: "This car was bought with money that you stole from the town and now it is ours. Go on foot."

To what extent this account is true, I cannot guarantee it, but I do know what similar things happened frequently in those days. When the "government" declared that the merchants had defrauded the tax authorities for years, and that an investigation would now be made into the taxes that had not been paid, the merchants declared that it was true that they had stopped paying them, but that they had done so out of patriotism, because the previous governments, since the "pseudo" republic was inaugurated in 1902, had been corrupt and immoral, and most of their officials a band of thieves. Now, thanks to the Revolution, the word "honesty" regained its meaning, and they, who were only waiting for that Revolution, would voluntarily surrender the withheld taxes. Indeed, the accountants made their harvest in those days, putting the accounts in order. The communist regime received millions and millions delivered by the merchants, and then took away their businesses.

The president of the Cuban ranchers declared that he would contribute to the Agrarian Reform with 3,000 heifers loaded. Castro took the heifers, thanked him, and then took the rest of his cattle from the ranchers.

A truly popular measure was the Urban Reform. The tenants were told of the various rented houses, as well as the apartment houses, that they did not have to pay any more rent, and that the house was theirs. If they weren't so frightened, the landlords would have put the scream in the sky. Of course, the tenants did not have the slightest scruple in appropriating what was not theirs and that, in time, communism would take away from them as well.

When the judgment of the commander [Jesus] Sosa Blanco, the Sports Palace was filled with people who shouted and asked for a wall for that brave officer. On the day of his execution, invitations were distributed to radio and television artists, and very few stopped attending the execution.

There were thousands of shootings, after trials in which there was not the slightest guarantee for the accused, and all were applauded by loud crowds. Crowds applauded with equal enthusiasm the executions of the Mambises, who cheered the Spanish governors and, shortly after, the very general Máximo Gómez as he entered Havana.

Let it not be said that Cubans are not brave. Proof of this has been given throughout history, fighting with the pirates during the sixteenth and seventeenth centuries, against the English in 1762, in which they overcame the poor regulars of Spain, invaded their organisms by tropical cachexias. Subsequently, I believe that our wars of independence proved this well. But the human being is the human being, and nature always returns by its means.

Note that I am not talking about the low people, who have nothing, or the mere populace, who have no flag and who only expect the opportunities to take advantage of them. Nor do I speak of the resentful, who lovingly cherish their hatred of Humanity. I refer to people who are outdated, normal, in a medium or high position. They are those who study, work and produce for the country, but who, when danger brushes them with their cold finger, it makes them lower their heads and reach the greatest abjections.

Since the advent of the Republic, the humble little soldier, with his khaki uniform and rifle, had guaranteed their property, safety, enjoyment of their property, but by 1959 the little soldier had disappeared, and instead the dirty and smelly bearded man appeared. The average citizen, giving a tooth with a tooth of pure panic, smiled cowardly and, as a defense, stuck to the doors of his home posters of "Fidel: this is your house," or "Thank you, Fidel." That there were exceptions to all this? Of course, there always are! The *Diario de la Marina*, for example, went down with flags in the wind. There were some press that, in a more discreet way, made their observations, and journalists who did not miss the opportunity to publish articles where the opposition was already emerging. But how few, how few were there...

Returning to reality, time was passing. Apart from reading, I didn't do anything but eat and sleep. Also, as I said before, Padreda and I used to throw our little basketball game.

And the day of our departure arrived. The ambassador drove us to the airport, and we entered it up to the runway. We had to wait in the back, on a little road, and when we were warned, we got in the car to the same plane. The usual ones, and to whom I have referred before, were already on the terrace shouting horrors at us. Many are now in Miami, purified by the waters of the Jordan that seems to be the Strait of Florida.

As I later learned, the press still dared to publish: "The Diaz are flying away." I was most grateful to the Ambassador for his many attentions to me. He also gave me a letter for a brother, manager of a bank in Quito, who was very useful to me, as will be seen.

When we landed in Guayaquil, the press was waiting for us, and interrogated us. I was parked in my statements, perhaps because of my usual reservation. Unfortunately, one of the journalists interpreted me as having behaved "arrogantly" and referred to me as the "arrogant general."

Three days we were in Guayaquil. From there we pass to Quito, capital of the nation. At the end of them, my companions left by plane, but it occurred to me to make the journey by rail, to obtain a broader vision of the country.

The experience couldn't have been more original. It was a narrow-track railway, uphill all the time and bordering mountains. Sometimes the slope was so steep that the train had to stop, go back through a diversion to an opposite slope, and then go full steam ahead to, with the impulse, save the rebel slope.

This happened several times. When we reached a certain place, we saw that there had been a landslide on the side of the mountain. The slippage had dragged the line, and with it to a very modern train, newly acquired in England. There, in the background, you could see the wagons peeled off. But the road had already been repaired and we were able to continue. I have the impression that this happened with a certain frequency, because the rescue groups were already organized and acted very quickly.

The contrast between Guayaquil and Quito cannot be greater. The first, located at sea level, and crossed by the Guaya River, is humid and hot. Many of its buildings are of the familiar Spanish colonial style. I remember that many products from the interior come from the river, especially the bananas, which are beautiful. The clusters float downstream until they reach the landings, where they are chosen and taken ashore.

And finally, we arrived in Quito, Padredas, who had accompanied me on my adventure, and me.

The capital is located 3,000 meters above sea level. The climate is delicious: dry and temperate. The people were very kind. The truth is that I could not complain about the attentions I received. I also perceived a certain partiality in favor of Castro, but I was there enough to see that the constant shootings were changing public opinion.

In Cuba, I hadn't bothered to get money out of the country. I never thought I would have to leave, and since my accounts were very clear, I felt able to face any investigation into my assets. That is, the house in which I lived, my wife's inheritance, and ____ pesos in the bank, of which they were also ____ from Rosaura, and ____ from my savings.

I must confess my naivety, but one day the Vice President of the Industrial Agricultural Bank, which was where I had my account, called me to insinuate: —General, why don't you spend some money abroad? You never know when you might need it.

I did not give importance to what I was saying, and he, for his part, asked me for authorization to spend 6,000 pesos in the United States. I replied authorizing it. And those 6,000 pesos were the ones that saved me who knows how many needs, because thanks to them I lived passively in Quito and, later, in the United States.

I now turn to Mr. Chiriboga, the Ambassador's brother in Havana. His position in Ecuadorian banking allowed him to be very useful to me. Besides, I was his guest on more than one occasion, and his attentions to me had no limit.

In the United States, General Ralph Truman did not remain inactive for a moment. After my departure, he returned to Cuba to take care of my wife and children, as well as Commander Claudio Medel and his family. The latter got $2,000 out of the country, and he got us all a quick visa to the United States[216].

A brushstroke on this hospitable country. Like almost all our capitals, it has its old, delightfully colonial part, full of reminiscences of conquerors and great patriots. Abundant is the Indian, always dignified, and gloomy. There is a tribe[217], I don't remember what it's called, that still mourns for Atahualpa. They are not seen in Quito, but in provinces. They go through the streets and from time to time, they stand in front of some white man and spit at him: You are to blame for the death of the Inca.

I couldn't help but inquire about the military. Also the Prussian school, although already affected by American influence. There was some concern about Peru, which for years has shown great aggressiveness towards them, infinitely weaker. They told me that part of the border in Ecuador and Peru was the Zarumilla River, but that during the 40s the river, by one of those tectonic overturns of the Andes, changed course, leaving now to the south a large territory of Ecuador. The Peruvians did not waste time and occupied the lands left by the Zarumilla. To the protests of the Ecuadorians, they replied that it was established that the course of the river was the border, and that they were not to blame for the fact that that border had changed. Moral: that the big fish always eats the boy.

The days passed quickly if one considers the demonstrations of friendship and hospitality received from Ecuadorians. But also the anxiety for the future, my separation from loved ones, the situation in Cuba, all this detracted from my spirit. And when news reached us of the shooting of so many men, many of whom served at my command. How sad!

---

[216] Claudio Medel did not leave Cuba in 1959. He immediately joined the Rebel Army with his rank of captain. He was arrested in August 1959 for participating in the Trinity conspiracy and sentenced to imprisonment.

[217] The Cañaris.

As for my entry into the United States, I had no doubt. I knew that I had quite a few relations in the government and, above all, General Truman, who always honored his surname. Because in fact, at four months, my path had been laid out and I took the plane to Miami[218].

---

[218] He received his American visa on May 27, 1959 and two weeks later arrived in Miami on June 8.

PHOTOS

The Díaz Tamayo family with the matriarch Paulina Tamayo de Díaz seated.
From left to right: Salvador, Ramón, Marcela, Clemente, Isabel,
Luis and Martín.

At Columbia camp on March 10, 1952. Four of the coup leaders. From left to right: Luis Robaina, Díaz Tamayo, FranciscoTabernilla Dolz, and Eulogio Cantillo Porras.

Military stop at Paseo Martí in Havana, May 20, 1952.

Inspected the Pinar del Río barracks with Colonel José Fernández Rey in 1952.

Muster at Columbia camp was one of his usual occupations.

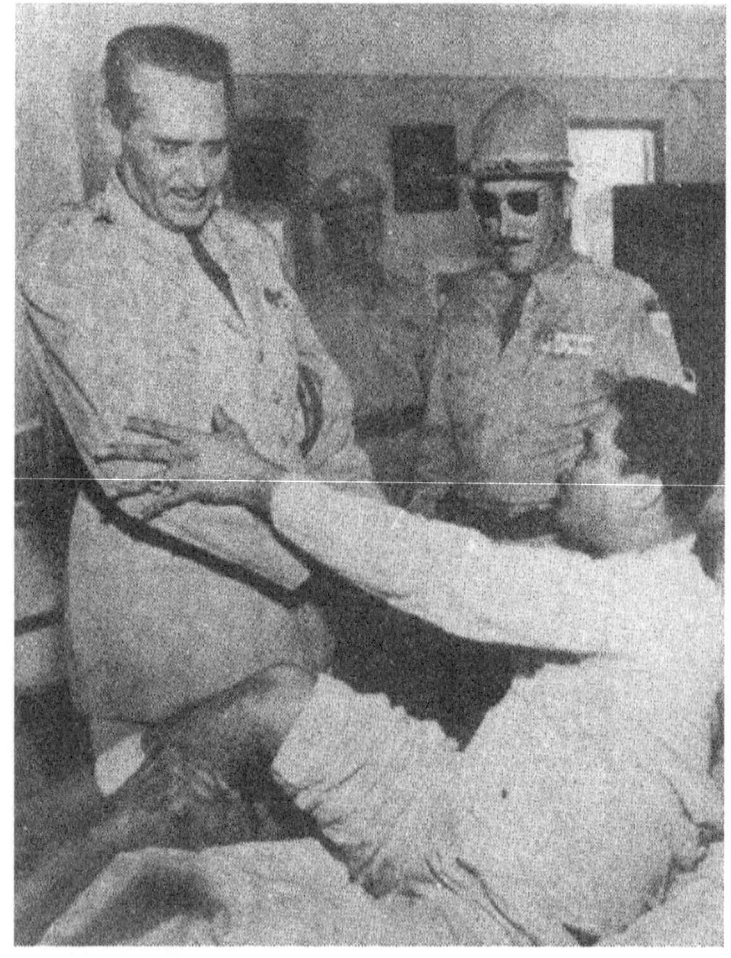

In the military hospital visiting the wounded from the attack on the Moncada barracks in Santiago de Cuba led by Fidel Castro on July 26, 1953. He is accompanied by the head of Regiment No. 1, Colonel Alberto del Río Chaviano.

Decorating the 19 coffins in the Moncada barracks of soldiersand policemen killed during the assault of July 26, 1953.

He was trained by the CIA in May 1955 to organize the Bureau for the Repression of Communist Activities (BRAC).

During a visit to the Inter-American Defense Board in Washington, he was accompanied by Colonel Ramón Barquín López (second from the left) and Lieutenant Colonels Manuel Varela Castro and Felipe Catasús Pazos.

Press conference on 3 December 1956, as head of Regiment No. 1 in the Moncada barracks, announced the suppression of the rebel uprising in Santiago de Cuba, resulting in 11 dead and more than 30 wounded.

Dr. Arnold V. Arms gave him the key to the city of Kansas City, Missouri, in September 1958. He is accompanied by Commander Claudio Medel.

With General Ralph E. Truman in Topeka, Kansas, in September 1958.

With his family in exile in Hialeah in 1972. From left to right: Martin, his wife Lourdes Alemán Freyre, the general, and Roraima. Sitting: Rosaura Menéndez with Martín Juan Díaz Alemán, and Aurora Hernández de Tejada.

In Miami he led the grouping of the Professional Armed Forces of Cuba in Exile.

The Revolution of 1933, the 1952 Coup d'état, and the Repression of Communism

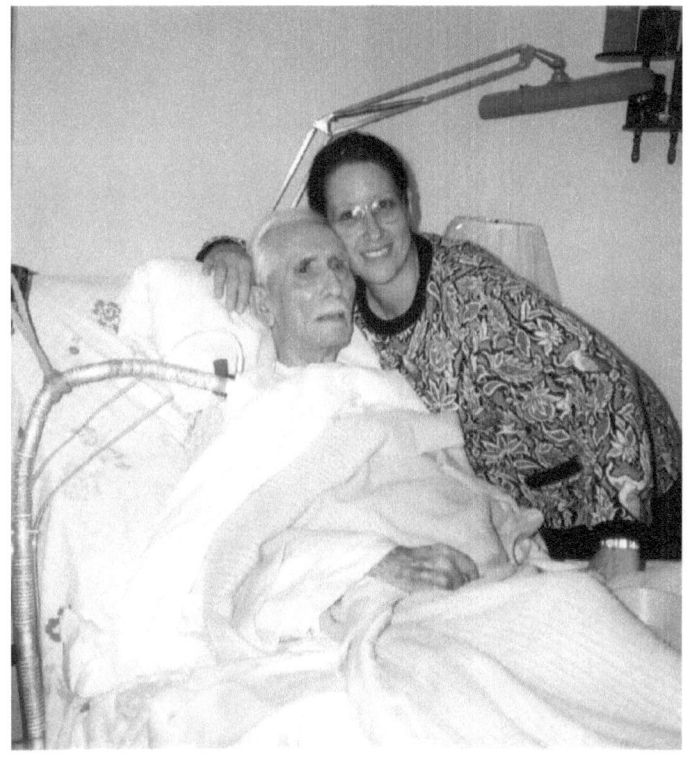

The last photo of the general, afflicted by Lou Gehrig's sclerosis, with his daughter Roraima in 1995.

ONOMASTIC INDEX

A

Abarca, Silvestre de, 218
ABC, 11, 64, 70, 76-77, 109, 131, 194
ABC Radical, 75
Abril Rivas, Julio, 110
Acción Revolucionaria Guiteras (ARG), 110
Adam Silva, Ricardo, 59, 63-64, 66-67, 75
Advisory Council, 122, 161
Agee, Phil, 190
Agnew, Spiro, 61
Agramonte Marrero, Alicia, 190
Agramonte, Matanzas, 143
Agrarian Reform, 242
Agricultural and Industrial Bank, 26
Aguilar, Commander, 146
Aguilera, Francisco Vicente, 69
Alabama, 55
Alba Luque, María Soledad "Marisol", 17
Alegría de Pío, 16, 143
Alemán Casharo, José Manuel, 105, 109
Alemán Freyre, Lourdes, 261
Alemán Urquía, José Braulio, 109
Alerta, newspaper, 124
Alfonso Pozo, Miguel "Clavelito", 157
Allied Omnibus Cooperative, 13, 139
Alliegro Milá, Anselmo, 161
Alomá, Tony, 210
Alonso Ávila, Antonio, 194
Alonso Pujol, Guillermo, 28
Alquízar, Havana, 56
Álvarez Barrios, Sócrates, 150
Álvarez de la Noval, Miguel, 92, 151
Álvarez Margolles, Francisco, 147
Álvarez, Alberto, 105
Ampudia, Manuel, 26, 240
Angulo, Andrés, 59
Antonelli, Battista, 218
Aponte Hernández, Carlos, 105
Arbenz, Jacobo, 23, 28
Argentina, 62, 214
Armed Forces Loan, and Insurance Bank, 195
Arms embargo, 18, 222
Army Headquarters-Master General, 79, 118
Army Museum, 58
Arroyo Arenas, 12, 43, 122
Arteaga del Tercio, Liutenant, 52
Arteaga Law, 40
Artemisa, 39, 40-41, 52, 139
Artigas Rabelo, Ricardo Anacleto, 17
Artigas, Ricardo, 17
Artillery School, 94, 95, 192
Association of Lottery Sellers, 17
Asunción, Paraguay, 28
Audiencia de Santa Clara, 83

265

Autobuses Modernos, 23
Averhoff Sarra, Octavio Augusto, 185
Aviation Officers Club, 118

B

Bacardi, 24
Banes, Oriente, 97
Baquero Díaz, Gastón, 161
Barcelona, 83
Barker, Bernard, 232
Barnet, José Agripino, 83
Barquín, Ramón, 9, 18, 22-23, 27, 129, 160, 164, 184, 186, 188-192, 208, 227
Barrera Pérez, Pedro, 9, 16, 138-139, 152, 211- 213, 217, 220-221
Bashirov, Gumer W., 180
Batista, Alejandro, 93
Batista, Fulgencio, 9- 21, 23-25, 28, 30, 43, 50, 52, 56, 59, 64, 65-75, 79, 81-83, 85-86, 88-89, 93-94, 97-100, 103-104, 106-109, 113-114, 121-122, 125-155, 157, 159-164, 166, 170-173, 176, 179-80, 183-184, 186, 188-194, 196, 198, 200, 202, 206, 211- 216, 218-219, 222-225, 230-233, 235, 237, 240
Bauta, **43**
Bay of Pigs, 28, 145, 204, 232
Bayamo, Oriente, 97, 133, 139, 179
Bayer and López Joffre, Antonio, 122
Belén School, 105, 132, 180
Benedi Beruff, Claudio, 161
Benítez Valdés, Manuel, 27, 52
Bertini Alessandri, Laura, 62

Besada Valdés, Carlos Miguel, 143
Bilbao, Spain, 121
Bilbatúa, Antonio, 121
Bisset Coll, Ángel, 30, 91, 92
Blanco Cañizares, Manuel, 27
Blanco Montalván, Antonio, 95
Blanco Rico, Antonio, 22, 130
Blanco, Rufino, 52
Bogotá, Colombia, 17, 180
Bogotazo, 17, 180-181
Bohemia, 16, 25, 76, 106, 121, 156, 211, 221
Boix Comas, Alberto, 230
Bolivia, 101, 156
Borbonet, Enrique, 18, 24, 27, 189, 190-191
Bosch, José "Pepín", 24, 27
BRAC, 13-14, 25, 162, 190, 193, 195, 198-199, 201-204, 256
Brazil, 10, 17, 23, 83, 163, 208
Brigade, 2506, 28, 117, 145, 151
Brother Balbino, 238-239, 240
Bureau of Investigations, 9, 17, 50, 92

C

Cabo de San Antonio, 35, 114
Cabrera Bosque, Mario, 116, 148, 152
Cabrera Rodríguez, Ruperto, 116, 139, 141, 147
Caffery, Jefferson, 81
Caimito del Guayabal, 43
California, 95, 231, 239
Camacho Aguilera, Julio, 20, 23
Camagüey, 63, 67, 90-92, 116, 145
Camejo-Argudin, José, 184

Campa, María Teresa de la, 184
Campa, Miguel Ángel de la, 184-185
Campos Marquetti, Generoso, 161
Campos Pontigo, Narciso, 178
Canada, 11, 101
Cantillo, Carlos, 134, 147, 148
Cantillo, Eulogio, 13, 18, 25, 134, 147, 191, 221, 250
Cantón, Luis, 101
Capitol, 156, 165
Caracas, 139, 182
Caramés, José, 156
Carbó, Sergio, 15, 70-73
Caribbean Military Academy, 190
Carnot, Lazaro, 220
Carrasco Artiles, Nelson, 159
Carratalá, Conrado, 239
Cartaya Gómez, Nicolás, 28
Casa Minerva, 19
Casablanca, Cuba, 132
Casanova, José Manuel, 105
Casero, Luis Felipe, 207
CASFA (Armed Forces savings and Insurance Fund), 161, 176-177, 199
Casillas Lumpuy, Arcadio R., 208
Casillas Lumpuy, Joaquín, 209
Castaño Quevedo, José, 14, 25, 190-191, 203
Castaño, Paulino, 190
Castellanos Rivero, Nicolás Dionisio, 112
Castillo de Atarés, 76, 79-80, 90, 92-94, 118, 151, 169
Castillo de la Fuerza, 58, 67
Castillo del Príncipe, 124
Castillo Márquez, Rafael del, 58

Castro, Fidel, 9, 15-18, 21, 23-25, 27, 92, 110-111, 138, 155-157, 163, 171, 178, 180-181, 183, 185, 189, 191, 207-208, 210, 214-216, 222-224, 233-234, 240, 254
Castro, Raúl, 178
Catasús Pazos, Felipe Antonio, 183
Cayo Confites, 111
Central Andorra, 39
Central Park of Havana, 107, 165
Céspedes y Quesada, Carlos Manuel de, 59, 62, 70, 72, 83, 105, 194
Chandler College, 87
Chester, Edmund, 12, 138, 203
Chibás Rivas, Eduardo, 105-106, 111-112, 156
Chibás Rivas, Raúl, 24
Chicho Pan de Gloria, 156
Chile, 11, 99, 100, 101, 138, 194, 240
Chinea Álvarez, Aquiles, 143, 208, 217
Chiriboga, Virgilio, 240, 245
CIA, 14, 18, 20, 23, 25, 27-28, 145, 162, 185, 190, 193, 196-197, 204, 214, 232, 256
Cienfuegos, 58, 83, 160, 191, 194
Cienfuegos, Camilo, 190-191
Civic Military Institute, 83
Civic Military Junta, 21
Civic Rural Schools, 83
Clavelito, 156, 157
CMQ television, 240
Cobas Reyes, Mario, 161
Cojímar, 95
Cold War, 14
Colón Cemetery, 17

Columbia Camp, 10, 12, 20, 43, 57, 76, 116, 137, 143, 162, 208
Communist Party of Cuba, 56, 87, 104
Communist Party of Mexico, 87
Consolación, 36
Conspiracy of the Cigars, 129, 135, 160
Constituent Assembly of 1940, 194
Constituent Assembly of the Yaya, 62
Constitution of 1901, 73
Constitution of 1940, 161, 166
Conte Agüero, Luis, 156, 172
Cordillera de los Órganos, 35
Córdoba Gómez, José, 49, 50
Corzo Izaguirre, José Raúl, 27, 151
Cossío del Pino, Alejo, 122
Costa Rica, 31, 111, 140
Court of Accounts of the Nation, 177
Court of Auditors, 177
Cova, Antonio Rafael de la, 15, 31, 179
Cova, Carlina de la, 31
Cremata Valdés, Radio, 122, 161
Crittenden, John Jordan, 92
CTC (Confederation of Cuban Workers), 161, 233
Cuba Aeropostal, 19
Cuba Sugar, 231
Cuban Academy of History, 69
Cuban Anticommunist Board, 27
Cuban Aviation Company, 215, 232
Cuban Electricity Company, 17
Cuban National Aviation Curtiss, 23
Cuban Naval Academy, 209
Cuban Polo Federation, 13, 195, 201
Cuervo Navarro, Pelayo, 134
Cuervo Rubio, Gustavo, 18
Cyclone of '26, 48

D

Dallas, Texas, 180
Daytona Beach, 19, 23, 127
Delgado, Erasmo, 52, 56, 58
Department of Anti-Democratic Activities, 190
Diario de la Marina, 9, 26, 124, 132, 157, 202, 238, 243
Diario Nacional, 156
Díaz Balboa, Balbino Emilio, **156**
Díaz Landa, Pedro, 177
Díaz Menéndez de Kanar, Roraima, 7, 30, 31, 173, 261, 263
Díaz Menéndez, Martín, 30
Díaz Ordóñez, Salvador, 95
Díaz Tamayo, Clemente, 20-22, 30, 249
Díaz Tamayo, Elena, 30
Díaz Tamayo, Isabel, 30
Díaz Tamayo, Julio, 30
Díaz Tamayo, Luis, 30
Díaz Tamayo, Marcela, 30
Díaz Tamayo, Martín, 9, 18, 28, 34, 124, 199, 211, 221, 249
Díaz Tamayo, Ramón, 30
Díaz Tamayo, Salvador, 30
Díaz, Andrés, 37
Díaz, Flores, 40

Díaz-Versón, Salvador, 180, 199, 203
Dina, Evelio, 67
Directorate of Operations G-1 of the Army General Staff, 135
Dolores School, 105
Dominican Republic, 24, 50, 111, 116, 142, 157, 163, 166, 180, 241
Dragon Barracks, 76
Driggs Acosta, Fernando, 91, 95
Drunken Conspiracy, 22
DRUNKEN CONSPIRACY, 227
Duarte Oropesa, José, 11, 124
Dueñas Robert, Víctor, 139
Dulles, Allen, 197, 198, 204

E

Ecuador, 26, 101, 185, 240, 241, 246
Eisenhower, Dwight, 23, 187, 226, 237
ElCristo, Oriente, 207
El Cuarto Piso, 226
El Día, 70
El Fígaro, 70
El Morro, 114, 209
El Pañolón, 39, 40
El Salvador, 81
England, 29, 175, 184, 194, 197, 244
Enlistment Club, 10, 64, 66-67, 78
Equestrian Federation of Cuba, 13, 195, 201
Esténger Neuling, Rafael, 161
Estévez Maymir, José A., 24
Estrada Palma, Tomás, 10, 36, 111

F

Faget, Mariano, 110, 203
Fajardo, Ángel C., 101
Fajardo, Captain, 91
Falla Bonet, Eutimio, 105
Fe Pérez, Ernesto de la, 24
Federation of University Students, 87
Fernández Álvarez, José, 189, 191
Fernández Miranda, Martha, 14, 127, 173, 233
Fernández Miranda, Roberto, 9, 126, 137, 138
Fernández Parajón, Enrique, 14, 196
Fernández Rey, José, 145, 252
Fernández Wong, José *El Chino*, 20
Fernandina Plan, 210
Ferrara, Orestes, 55, 61, 155
Ferrer Guerra, José D., 28
Figarola Infante, Tulio, 28, 101
Fleites Díaz, Armando, 25, 236
Flor, Ricardo de la, 22
Focsa building, 151
Forest, Mario E., 76, 119
Fort Benning, Georgia, 187, 191
Fort Bragg, North Carolina, 187-188
Fort Jackson, South Carolina, 187
Fort Knox, Kentucky, 187
Fort McNair, 184, 185
Franca Álvarez de la Campa, Porfirio, 71
France, 53, 62, 80, 108, 154, 221, 228
Franco Lliteras, Roberto, 208
Fraternity Park, 11, 87, 165

Freeman, Charles Seymour, 74
French Foreign Legion, 51
French Revolution, 85, 220
Freyre, Fabio, 27, 216
Friar Balbino, 23, 234

G

Galbond, Oliver G., 27
Garcerán de Vall y Souza, Julio, 29
García Báez, Irenaldo, 23, 229, 230
García Bárcena, Rafael, 119, 162
García Espinosa, Conrado, 138
García García, Pilar D., 99, 229
García Menocal, Mario, 10
García Montes, Jorge, 27, 194, 220
García Tuñón, Jorge, 17, 28, 138, 144, 154, 221, 238
Garcia, Eloy, 238, 239
Gastón, Melchor, 27
General Staff, 12, 17, 21, 24, 57, 58-59, 62-64, 67-68, 83, 85, 92, 96, 100, 121, 123, 126, 134, 142-144, 146-149, 152, 154, 160-161, 171, 185, 207-208, 212, 215, 217, 219, 221, 225, 230
Germany, 62, 83, 106
Gibara, Oriente, 71-72, 208
Gibbs, George W., 185
Gleichauf, Justin F., 28
Godínez, Elisa, 127
Godoy Loret de Mola, Gastón, 161
Goicouría barracks, 99, 130
Gómez Arias, Miguel Mariano, 83, 99

Gómez Báez, Máximo, 66, 69, 78, 117-118, 184, 243
Gómez Sicre, Clemente Ricardo, 129
Gómez, José Miguel, 10, 40, 83, 205
González Alfonso, Ángel, 123
González, Juan, 16, 216
Grand Masonic Lodge, 10, 64
Granma, 15-16, 143, 210, 239
Grau San Martín, Ramón, 10, 50, 52, 69, 70, 73, 75, 82, 86, 91, 99, 105-107, 110-115, 122, 127, 132, 134, 137, 139, 155, 157, 194
Guanajay, Pinar del Río, 43
Guane, Pinar del Río, 134
Guardia y Calvo, Carmen de la, 231
Guas Inclán, Rafael, 9
Guatemala, 23, 28, 110, 151, 163
Guayaquil, Ecuador, 26, 244-245
Güemes y Horcasitas, Juan Francisco de, 95
Guerrero, Xavier, 87
Guevara Valdés, Alfredo, 181
Guevara, Ernesto "Che", 25, 142, 156, 181, 190, 196
Guiral y Domínguez, María Lorenza, 231
Guiteras Holmes, Antonio, 82, 104, 105, 106
Gutiérrez Fernández, Félix, 22
Gutiérrez Valdés, Antonio, 209
Gutiérrez, Jorge, 28

H

Haitian Embassy, 130
Harkins, Paul Donal, 188
Harvard University, 55

Havana, 10-11, 16-17, 21, 23, 26, 30, 35, 40-41, 48, 50, 52, 55-56, 59-62, 67, 70, 73-74, 76, 78, 81, 83, 85, 89-90, 95, 97, 99, 101, 105, 107, 110-112, 114, 121-123, 127-128, 132, 135, 137-139, 145, 150-151, 156-157, 163, 166, 176, 182, 184-186, 188, 190, 194, 198, 200-201, 204, 215-219, 227, 232, 236-237, 238-241, 243, 245, 251

Havana Audience, 58

Havana Bar Association, 9, 18

Havana Post, 17

Havana Yacht Club, 174

Headquarters-Master General, 117, 137, 221

Hernández Hernández, Manuel, 159

Hernández de Tejada, Aurora, 26, 126, 261

Hernández Hernández, Hernando, 25, 139

Hernández, Blas, 21

Hernández, Manuel, 101

Hernández, Mario, 21

Herrera, Alberto, 60, 62, 81

Herrera, Colin, 44, 102

Hialeah, 29, 261

Higher School of War, 11, 76, 170

Holguín, Oriente, 145, 166

Honduras, 110

Horta Suárez, Elías, 118

Hotel Almendares, 77

Hotel Capri, 25, 236

Hotel Nacional, 53, 59, 66, 73-74

Hotel Presidente, 74

Hotel Waldorf Astoria, 127

Hugo, Victor, 41, 44

Hunt, E. Howard, 28, 145, 232

I

Ibarra Pérez, Laureano, 213

Iglesias, María Consuelo, 92

Imías, Oriente, 96

India, 156, 175

Indonesia, 156

Infantry Battalion, 41, 43, 45, 59, 63, 86, 146

Infantry Division, 14, 133, 138, 149, 237

Infiesta, Ramón, 119

Institute of Havana, 62

Institute of Pinar del Río, 50, 92

Inter-American Defense Board, 145, 186

Isla de Pinos, 45-46, 48, 160, 176, 192, 208

Italy, 29, 62, 184, 197, 231

Izquierdo Rodríguez, Isidro C., 178

J

Jackson Memorial Hospital, 139

Jackson, Andrew, 158

Jacksonville, Florida, 99

Jamaica, 207

Japan, 83, 156, 184, 185, 231

Joint Chiefs of Staff, 20, 22, 133, 170, 186, 219, 221-222, 226-227

Jovellanos, Matanzas, 63, 209

July 26 Movement, 20-21, 23, 26, 239

K

Kansas City, Missouri, 237, 259

Karnley, Patrick I., 27

Kasalta restaurant, 60

Kennedy, John F., 28-29, 158, 197, 204, 226, 232
Key West, 26, 184, 237
King, Joseph Caldwell, 27
Kirkpatrick, Lyman B., 204, 231
KOMINTERN, 56
Korea, 11, 14, 124, 149, 185
Korte, Werner, 31
Kramer, Augustine, 79
Kremlin, 198
Kuquine, 12, 126-128, 130-132, 138, 146, 149, 153-154, 173, 205, 223, 233

L

La Cabaña, 13, 16, 24-25, 59, 75, 78, 95, 106, 123-124, 131, 138, 142, 149, 154, 176, 190, 196, 218-219, 234
La Daga en el Corazón, 231
La Esperanza, sanatorium, 56
La Historia Me Absolverá, 25
La Libertad, newspaper, 70
La Prensa, 70
La Semana, newspaper, 70, 72
Laredo Brú, Federico, 83
Larrubia Paneque, Manuel, 139-140, 148, 152
Las Villas, 24, 50, 83, 99, 130, 140, 143, 145, 149, 194, 208, 241
Lazo Arriaga, Antonio, 231
Lazo Cuba, Carlos, 9
Legion of the Caribbean, 111
Leguina Martínez, Laura, 22
Lenin, Vladimir I., 155
León Calás, Manuel, 76, 119
León García, Rubén de, 28
León y León, Vicente F., 151

Leonard, Ciro, 76, 79-80, 92
Lesnick Menéndez, Max, 156
Life magazine, 157
Llanillo, Eugenio, 50
Llerena, Mario, 163
Lojendio e Irure, Juan Pablo de, 240
Loma de San Juan, 209
London, 62, 204
López Jorge, Rogelio, 102
López Vilaboy, José, 202, 232, 233
López, Clemente, 43
Los Angeles, California, 110, 149, 208
Louis XVIII, 190
Lugo Abreu, José Antonio, 140
Lynn, Clark, 19, 219

M

MacArthur, Douglas, 185, 186
MacDonald, Étienne Jacques, 190
Machado, Gerardo, 10, 45-46, 53-65, 67, 71-72, 81, 83, 85, 87, 90, 98, 100, 103, 105, 108-109, 124, 134, 139, 184-185, 194, 236
Madariaga Aróstegui, Juan Ignacio de, 114
Madison Square Garden, 101
Madrid, 29, 231
Maduro, Bobby, 109
Magoon, Charles E., 36
Magruder, Charles B., 14
Maisí, Oriente, 96
Maltiempo, battle, 167
Man, Marcelo, 104, 106
Mañach, Jorge, 27

Managua Camp, 114, 138
Managua, Nicaragua, 28
Mañana, newspaper, 156, 232, 233
Manzanillo, Oriente, 97, 207, 215, 216, 217
Marianao, 21, 43, 60, 87, 110, 137, 231, 239
Marina, Evaristo Luis, 26, 241
Marinello, Juan, 199
Márquez Cárdenas, Gustavo, 140
Márquez-Sterling, Carlos, 20, 70, 109, 121, 172, 217, 231
Martí Pérz, José, 210, 222
Martin Elena, Eduardo Ernesto, 102, 145, 146
Martínez Mora, Daniel G., 28
Martínez Sáenz, Joaquín, 156
Martínez Suárez, José, 239
Martínez Villena, Rubén, 56
Masferrer, Rolando, 122
Mason, Alfredo, 38, 53
Masten&Nichols, 231
Matanzas, 20, 76, 91, 99, 104, 112, 117, 129, 139, 142, 209, 229
Matos Rodríguez, Urbano, 123, 140, 141, 142
Matthews, Herbert, 222, 223
McCone, John, 204
McPortland, Nicanor, 86
Medel Fuentes, Claudio, 29-31, 33, 63, 80, 118, 246
Mejides, Andy, 29
Meléndez, Enrique, 52
Mella, Julio Antonio, 11, 86-87
Méndez Peñate, Rodolfo, 87
Mendieta Montefur, Carlos, 82-83, 166, 194

Menéndez Hernández de Tejada, Rosaura, 25
Menéndez Hernández de Tejada, Rosaura, 7, 30, 77, 132, 245
Menéndez y Hernández de Tejada, Rosaura, 132
Menéndez, José E., 22
Menocal, Raúl, 27
Mercy Hospital, Miami, 194
Mesa Díaz, Danilo Federico, 239
Mexico, 11, 13, 17, 50, 62, 87, 92, 101, 110, 127, 133-134, 157, 160, 163, 181, 183, 184, 194, 210, 237
Miami, 17, 19-20, 23-24, 26-29, 31, 50, 52, 71, 92, 109, 112, 116-117, 122, 124-125, 129, 131-135, 137-139, 142-143, 145-146, 150-151, 156, 158, 166, 172, 180, 184-185, 194, 197, 207-209, 229, 232, 236, 240, 241, 244, 247
Miami Beach, 23, 29
Miami Herald, 157
Military & Commercial Aircrafts, Engines & Accessories, Inc., 29
Military Academy, 76, 92, 115
Military and Naval Circle, 13, 161, 175, 195, 199, 201, 219
Military Aviation, 76
Military Intelligence Service (SIM), 129, 134, 149, 189-190, 199, 238
Ministry of Defense, 13, 134, 148, 164
Ministry of Education, 109
Minshall Hopper, Gertrude, 231
Miramar Yacht Club, 77
Miranda, Álvaro, 209
Miró Cardona, José, 18
Missile Crisis, 29, 197

Modotti, Tina, 87
Moncada Barracks, 15-16, 21, 25, 96, 121, 124, 138, 156, 163, 178-179, 180, 207, 209-211, 216, 254-255, 258
Monroe Doctrine, 29, 197
Monte de Barreto, 78
Montenegro, Guillermo Arturo, 17
Montenegro, Manuel Ralph, 17
Montenegro, Martha, 236
Montes, Armando, 63
Montes, Armandp, 70
Montmartre, cabaret, 22
Montreal Pact, 156
Mora, Menelao, 156
Morales del Castillo, Andrés Domingo, 166, 194
Morales Patino, Luis, 28
Moreno Romani, Juan A., 91
Morín Dopico, Antonio Jesús, 110
Morro Castle Supply Co., 17
Moscow, 56, 86, 87, 157, 198
Mujal Barniol, Eusebio, 161

N

Napoleon, 85, 190, 215, 227
National Guard, 27, 29, 231
National Lottery, 17
National Police, 17, 30, 50, 52, 99, 117, 122, 130, 156, 209
National Sports Directorate, 83
Navy, 28, 71-72, 74, 78, 87, 90, 94, 105, 111, 132, 150, 166, 177, 188, 203, 205, 209, 214, 222
Negret, Julián, 150, 151
New Orleans, 184

New York, 17, 55, 62, 101, 127, 139, 184, 194, 204, 222-223, 226, 231
New York Times, 222-223
Newport, Rhode Island, 226
Nin, Commander, 236
Niquero, Oriente, 16, 208, 217
Nixon, Richard, 61
Noel, James A., 190
Normal School, 210
Norway, 157

O

O'Bourke, Lieutenant, 66
Officers' Club, 59, 119, 146, 161, 163
Operation 40, 27
Orfila, Marianao, 110
Organization of American States (OAS), 181, 186
Oriente, 11, 62, 97, 100, 105, 139, 166, 172, 177-178, 200-204, 206-207, 210-213, 215, 217-219, 222, 234
Ovares Herrera, Enrique, 181

P

Padreda Vázquez, Camilo, 241, 244
Padrón Pérez, Gerardo, 100-101
País, Frank, 16, 210
Palma Soriano, Oriente, 166
Palmero, Esther, 211
Palmira, Santa Clara, 151
Pan American Airlines, 23
Panama Canal, 36, 100, 219
Pardo Llada, José, 156
Parellada, Otto, 210

Paris, 62, 83, 138, 221, 227
Paseo del Prado, 107, 165
Pawley, William Douglas, 23, 27
Payret Theater, 87
Pedraza, José Eleuterio, 10, 27, 50-51, 64-65, 68, 78, 88, 97, 103
Peña, Lázaro, 199
Pentagon, 27, 185, 186, 188
Pentarquia, 71, 73
Pentón, Evelio, 26
People's Revolutionary Movement (MRP), 28, 160
Perdomo, Lt. Cor., 56, 64, 67
Pérez Alfonso, Cecilio, 101
Pérez Benitoa, Manuel, 174
Pérez Coujil, Leopoldo, 203
Pérez Hernández, Faustino, 26
Pérez Jiménez, Marcos, 182
Pérez Mejides, Pedro E., 106
Pérez Serantes, Enrique, 178-179
Pérez Villalobos, Ezequiel, 208
Pérez, Clemente, 44
Peru, 23, 101, 172, 246
Piad, Carlos, 18
Piedra Negueruela, Orlando, 9
Pinar del Río, 10, 35-36, 39, 50-52, 91, 95, 104, 117, 124, 133, 166, 172, 252
Pineda, Antonio, 67
Pino Cruz, Laureano, 21- 22
Pino Siero, Rafael del, 181
Platt Amendment, 13, 55, 74, 103
Playa Girón, 117, 151, 185, 191
Poli, Marta, 22
Portela Möller, Guillermo, 71
Portell Vilá, Herminio, 11, 119, 124, 203

Portugal, 166
Post 4, 43, 163
Pote Bridge, 60
Prensa Libre, 15, 71, 73
Presidential Palace, 72, 76, 137, 150-151, 193, 219
Presidio Modelo, 45, 48
Prío Socarrás, Carlos, 11, 17, 105, 111, 124, 157, 158
Prío Socarrás, Francisco, 105
Professional Armed Forces of Cuba in Exile, 29
Professional School of Journalism " Manuel Márquez-Sterling", 71
Public Spa La Concha, 174
Puerto Rico, 92, 160, 202
Punta Brava, 43
Punta Colorada (Belic), Oriente, 217

Q

Queens, N.Y., 99
Querejeta Valdés, Gregorio, 77
Quesada, Héctor de, 63
Quill and Dagger Society, 231
Quintana, Jorge, 121
Quito, 18, 244-246

R

Radio CadenaHabana, 122
Radio Martí, 226
Rancho Boyeros, 93, 126
Ranchuelo, Las Villas, 157
Ravelo, Demetrio, 66
Ray Rivero, Manuel, 28
Reagan, Ronald, 226
Rebel Army, 21, 31, 92, 246
Regalado Santana, José, 27

Regiment No. 1, 15-16, 124, 161, 178, 203, 216-217, 254, 258
Regiment No. 10, 124
Regiment No. 2, 91
Regiment No. 3, 99
Regiment No. 4, 99, 104, 117, 145
Regiment No. 5 of the Rural Guard, 99
Regiment No. 6, 144
Regiment No. 7, 117
Regiment No. 8, "Riús Rivera, 145
Reichhardt, Bernard E., 28
Remedios, Las Villas, 83, 143
Repressive Group of Subversive Activities (GRAS), 190
Revolutionary Democratic Front (FDR), 145
Revolutionary Directory, 208
Revolutionary Directory (DR), 210
Revolutionary Insurrectionary Union (UIR), 110
Revolutionary Nationalist Movement (MNR), 162-163
Revolutionary Socialist Movement (MSR), 122
Rey Pernas, Santiago, 105, 194, 199
Reyes Delgado, Gustavo de los, 176
Reyes, Eduardo, 143
Ridgway, Matthew, 185, 186
Río Chaviano, Alberto del, 15, 24, 180, 202-203, 211-213, 218, 254
Rio de Janeiro, 17
river Canímar, 106
Rivero Agüero, Andrés, 20, 172, 225-226
Rivero Collado, Carlos, 172

Roa, Raúl, 184
Robaina Piedra, Luis, 137, 177
Robaina, Luis, 25, 137-138, 153, 250
Roca Calderío, Blas, 199
Rodríguez Ávila, Pedro, 24, 142, 144, 154, 221-222, 227-228
Rodríguez Calderón, José, 24, 132, 150, 153
Rodríguez Couzeiro, Francisco, 27
Rodríguez de la Vega, Adolfo, 21
Rodríguez Hernández, José, 27
Rodríguez Sáenz, Captain, 100
Rodríguez San Pedro, José, 22
Rodríguez Villaverde, Gabino, 189
Rodríguez, Diego, 96
Rodríguez, Oscar, 143
Rodríguez, Pablo, 63-66, 69-70, 73
Rodríguez, Policarpo Luis, 141-142
Rojas González, Juan, 143, 154
Roosevelt, Franklin, 14, 55, 103
Rosell Leyva, Florentino, 9, 24
Royal Winter Fair, 101
Rubio Baró, Mario, 209
Rubio Baró, Mario, 209
Rubottom, Jr., Roy Richard, 18, 214
Ruiz Cortines, Adolfo, 181
Rural Civic Schools, 20
Rural Guard, 16, 36, 41, 90, 99, 104, 111, 134, 139, 140, 143, 159, 180, 204-208, 216-218
Rural Schools, 10

S

Sagua la Chica, Las Villas, 180
Sagua la Grande, Las Villas, 156
Saladrigas Zayas, Carlos, 161, 194, 195
Salas Cañizares, Rafael, 130
Salas Cañizares, José M., 208
Salas Cañizares, Rafael Ángel, 130-131, 140, 150, 194
Salcedo, Commander, 91, 93
San Ambrosio Barracks, 76, 80, 118
San Antonio de los Baños, 208
San Juan, Puerto Rico, 241
San Salvador, 17
Sanatorio de Topes de Collantes, 98
Sánchez Arango, Aureliano, 106, 138
Sánchez García, Calixto, 184
Sánchez Gómez, Julio, 25, 218, 219
Sánchez Mosquera, Francisco Ángel, 27
Sánchez Whyte, Calixto, 184, 233
Sánchez, Regal, 42
Sanguily Echarte, Julio, 56, 59, 62-63, 66, 73
Sanguily Garrite, Julio, 59
Santiago de Cuba, 16, 21, 23, 25, 96-97, 105, 124, 132-133, 139, 145, 166, 170, 172, 178, 180, 191, 203, 206-208, 210-211, 254, 258
Santo Domingo, República Dominicana, 63, 111, 116, 132, 149
School of Cadets, 114, 133, 139, 151, 160, 191
School of Classes, 49

School of Officers, 11, 121, 138
School of recruits, 13, 48, 86
School of Recruits, 46, 91
Second National Front of the Escambray, 25
Secret Police, 14, 58, 196
Secretary of State, 60, 62, 184, 194
Secretary of War and Navy, 60
September 4 Revolution, 10, 59, 132, 135
Shout of Yara, 69
Siboney, Oriente, 180
Sierra Maestra, 21, 24, 149, 155-156, 190, 214, 217, 220, 222, 230
Signal Corps, 130, 143, 151
Smith, Earl E. T., 24, 226, 231, 235
Soca Llanes, Otalio, 117, 141, 144-145, 147, 188
Sogo, Dámaso, 135, 140
Soler, Aurora, 110
Solferino, battle, 167
Solís de León, Sigfrido, 97
Sosa Blanco, Jesús, 190, 243
Sosa Chabau, Eugenio de, 126
Sosa de Quesada, Arístides V., 18, 20, 177
Sosa, Alberto, 27
Soviet Union, 29, 70, 232
Spain, 24, 87, 92, 95, 121, 127, 145, 184, 240, 243
Spanish Casino, 174, 228, 230, 235
Spanish Civil War, 222-223
Spanish Cuban-American War, 95
St. Augustine's Church, Marianao, 231

277

St. George, Andrew, 25, 190
Stanley Fordham, Alfred, 200
State Department, 14, 17, 23, 55, 104, 138, 163, 184, 188, 195, 197, 224, 226, 235
Stewart, C. Allan, 18
Strand Bar, 122
Suárez Núñez, José, 9
SugarCoordination Act, 83
Supreme Court, 29, 83, 105, 166

T

Tabernilla Dolz, Carlos, 181
Tabernilla Dolz, Francisco, 9, 13, 15, 22, 24-25, 138-139, 163, 180, 200, 250
Tabernilla Palmero, Carlos "Winsy", 24
Tabernilla Palmero, Francisco "Silito", 9, 20, 137-138
Tabernilla Palmero, Marcelo, 22
Tacón y Rosique, Miguel, 87
Taft, William, 36
Tampa, Florida, 17, 28
Ten Years' War, 69
Tey, José "Pepito", 210
Tiempo en Cuba, newspaper, 122
Time, magazine,157, 231
Torres Menier, Mario, 56, 66-67
Treadway, J. E., 184
Triana Tarrau, José, 159
Trinck, Georgina, 20
Trinity Conspiracy, 176
Tropicana cabaret, 21
Trujillo, Rafael, 24, 91, 140, 214
Truman, Harry, 31, 116
Truman, Oliva, 237
Truman, Ralph, 31, 237, 246

Tulane University, 81, 185
Turkey, 29, 197, 219

U

Ugalde Carrillo, Manuel, 124, 149
Ulloa, Gabriel, 143, 208
Unión Radio, 156
United Fruit Company, 100, 231
United Nations, 14, 184, 185
United States, 11, 13, 17-18, 27, 29, 53, 55, 58, 61, 63, 74-75, 81-82, 87, 91, 100-101, 103, 106, 108, 116, 127, 133, 135, 149, 154, 156, 158, 161, 182-185, 187-189, 195-198, 206, 215, 221, 223-224, 228, 231, 235, 237-238, 240, 245-247
United States Department of State, 19
University of Havana, 55, 62, 83, 87, 92, 104-105, 108, 110, 119, 122, 156, 162, 166, 172, 184-185, 194, 231, 240
University Student Board of 1930, 162
University Student Directory, 105
UPI, 157
Urban Reform, 242
Uría López, Quirino, 117, 141, 144, 147
Urrutia Lleó, Manuel, 18, 156
USS Maine, 156
USS Manchuria, 74
USS Maui, 74
USS Orizaba, 74
Uvero, barracks, 233

V

Valdés Miranda, Bruno, 110
Varela Canosa, Joaquín, 28

Varela Castro, Manuel, 142, 183, 189
Vargas Gómez, Luis Andrés, 184
Varona, Manuel Antonio de, 18, 27-28, 145
Vasconcelos Maragliano, Ramón, 161
Velazco, Raúl, 18
Velázquez Perera, José H., 118, 147
Venegas, Captain, 123
Venezuela, 13, 62, 151, 163, 176, 182-183
Ventura Novo, Esteban, 9
Verdecia, corporal, 77
Viamonte Jardines, José, 22
Vidali, Vittorio, 87
Vietnam, 186, 215
Villanova University, 17
Villaverde, Cirilo, 42

W

War College, 86, 118, 121, 154, 159, 160, 162, 183
War Council, 135
War Department, 19, 36
War of 1895, 59
Washington D.C., 14, 18, 19, 24, 28, 36, 55, 62, 81, 103, 104, 138, 145, 160, 184-185, 187, 195-, 219, 227, 231
Watergate Defense Fund, 232
Waterloo, 190
Welles, Sumner, 17, 55-56, 62, 74-75, 81, 108
West Palm Beach, Florida, 127, 133, 137, 183
West Point Military Academy, 14, 92, 121, 132, 185, 219
Whyte, Helen, 184
Wieland, William Arthur, 17
World War I, 37, 53, 74, 237
World War II, 14, 23, 28, 74, 103, 109-110, 120, 124, 185, 204-205, 219, 221-222, 226, 233

Y

Yale University, 226
Yánez Pelletier, Jesús, 78
Yeste, Lieutenant, 91
Young Cuba, 105

Z

Zayas, Alfredo, 70, 194
Zumbado Armenteros, Joaquín, 208

ww.ingramcontent.com/pod-product-compliance
ing Source LLC
burg PA
080526
0011B/176